D044647

Sixteen Trends

Their Profound Impact on Our Future

Implications for Students, Education, Communities, and the Whole of Society

By Gary Marx

Because research and information make the difference.

ERS

Educational Research Service
1001 North Fairfax Street, Suite 500 • Alexandria, VA 22314-1587
Phone: 703-243-2100 • Toll Free: 800-791-9308
Fax: 703-243-1985 • Toll Free: 800-791-9309
Email: ers@ers.org • Web site: www.ers.org

Published by Educational Research Service

Educational Research Service (ERS):

ERS is the nonprofit organization serving the research and information needs of the nation's preK-12 education leaders and the public. Founded by the national school management associations, ERS provides quality, objective research and information that enable education leaders to make the most effective school decisions in both day-to-day operations and long-range planning.

Refer to the end of this book for information on the benefits of an annual ERS subscription, and for an order form listing resources that complement this book. Or visit us online at www.ers.org for an overview of available resources.

ERS e-Knowledge Portal:
http://portal.ers.org

ERS Founding Organizations:

American Association of School Administrators
American Association of School Personnel Administrators
Association of School Business Officials International
National Association of Elementary School Principals
National Association of Secondary School Principals
National School Public Relations Association

ERS Executive Staff:

Katherine A. Behrens, Acting President and Chief Operating Officer
Kathleen McLane, Chief Knowledge Officer

Library of Congress Cataloging-in-Publication Data:
Marx, Gary.
Sixteen trends, their profound impact on our future : implications for students,
        education, communities, countries, and the whole of society / by Gary Marx.
                p. cm.
Includes bibliographical references and index.
ISBN 1-931762-48-1
1. Education—Forecasting. 2. Educational planning. 3. Social prediction. 4.
        Forecasting. I. Title.
LB41.5.M265 2006
370.9'05—dc22
2006002687

Ordering Information: Additional copies of this publication may be purchased at the base price of $30.00; ERS School District Subscriber price: $15.00; ERS Individual Subscriber price: $22.50. Quantity discounts available. Add the greater of $4.50 or 10% of total purchase price for postage and handling. Phone orders accepted with Visa, MasterCard, or American Express. Stock No. 0630. ISBN 1-931762-48-1.

Note: The views expressed in this publication do not necessarily reflect the opinions or positions of members of the Creating a Future Council of Advisors, Educational Research Service, or ERS founding organizations.

Contents

Foreword

In 2000, Educational Research Service teamed with futurist Gary Marx to produce the book *Ten Trends . . . Educating Children for a Profoundly Different Future.* That publication has drawn significant attention to the urgency of considering the implications of trends in shaping the futures of educational systems and other institutions. Since then, demand continued to grow for the next generation of the resource valued by thousands of educators as well as leaders in business, government, and the community at large. That is why the Marx-ERS team has reunited to produce this expanded and complex new book.

Sixteen Trends . . . Their Profound Impact on Our Future is by no means the final word on trends affecting our society. It focuses on just a few of the hundreds of trends that will likely have a profound impact on our institutions and on each of our lives. As we think about the future, this book is not intended to end the conversation but rather to start it. A smaller book, *An Overview of Sixteen Trends,* is also available to carry basic information about trends and their implications to expanded numbers of people.

Each of the chapters in this book focuses on one major trend, first summarizing the trend and then outlining the trend's implications for society and education. Each chapter concludes with a listing of questions and activities to stimulate further thought, discussion, and action. These questions and activities are believed to be especially useful to current and future educational leaders, system study groups, and planning teams. Each chapter also includes a listing of suggested resources for additional reading and consideration.

This book is intended to provoke the thinking of anyone in society, from individual voters to policy makers, who stands in a position to shape the future of our schools and education systems, businesses, communities, and even the whole of our society. It is meant to stimulate planning, breakthrough thinking, risk taking, and thoughtful action. Ideas for using the publication are provided in the Introduction chapter under the heading "How can I use this publication?" Additional ideas are offered in the final chapter of the book.

However you use them, we hope the points made within these pages will ignite interest that challenges the status quo and encourages imagination.

Katherine A. Behrens
Acting President and Chief Operating Officer
Educational Research Service

Introduction
The Sixteen Trends

We have a choice. We can simply defend what we have
... or we can create what we need.

"A funny thing happened on the way to accomplishing our plan. The world changed."

Sound familiar? That's why strategic plans, no matter how sophisticated, need to become living strategies or strategic visions.

Defending the status quo has never been very exciting anyway. The excitement comes when we decide to create the future we need, not simply defend what we have. Unless we stay ahead of the curve, we'll fall behind. There is no more status quo. Change is inevitable; progress is optional.

Linear goals are not enough. Looking at tomorrow and seeing it only as a little bit more or a little bit less of today just won't cut it as we move into the future. Surrounded by a world filled with discontinuities, we desperately need to set at least a few audacious goals, the kind that took us to the moon, reduced computers from a dozen racks of equipment to a single handheld device . . . and envisioned educational opportunity for all.

Much of what happens as we break ground on the future will come at us out of the blue. We are in a constant, unrelenting, and exciting race to lay the groundwork for an even brighter future for our children and ourselves. That's why we need to stay in touch with a fast-changing society. In essence, all of us need to be environmentalists, adapting the organization to the needs of the environment at the same time we're adapting the environment to the needs of the organization.

■ Scanning the Environment

All organizations, especially education systems, are *of* this world, not separate from it. To earn their legitimacy, they need to be connected with the communities, countries, and world they serve. Unless they are constantly scanning the environment, educators will soon find themselves isolated . . . and out of touch.

Getting a bead on political, economic, social, technological, environmental, educational, and other forces that are sweeping across the landscape is essential. Understanding these forces is the key to unlocking rigidity and reshaping our schools, colleges, and other institutions for the future.

How can we maintain a 24/7 connection with the environment? One way is to constantly identify local, statewide/provincial, national, and international issues and sort them according to their probability and potential impact. If an issue is high in probability and high in possible impact, we'd better figure out how to manage it, or it will manage us.

There are other ways to scan. Engaging the wisdom of staff, community, and other constituents, we can pinpoint gaps between where we are today and where we'd like to be tomorrow. We can develop statements describing an organization that is capable of adjusting to a fast-changing world and then use the descriptions as part of a scale to rate our flexibility—our ability to innovate.

Frequently, in looking to the future, organizations are eager to explore strengths, weaknesses, opportunities, and threats. We can also involve diverse groups of people in envisioning the characteristics of the organization we want to become, in weighing our assumptions, and in exploring possible scenarios that describe alternative futures. Bottom line: One of the most far-reaching and effective ways of staying in touch with the environment is to identify and consider the possible implications of trends.

A free and open discussion of these societal forces is a first step in tapping the ingenuity of people around us. While we're listening, we might come across fresh ideas. We'll also be able to identify possible wildcards and reveal both intended and unintended consequences of our actions. Understanding trends is so very important to the process of creating a future that we have devoted this entire book to them.

What are trends?

Howard Chase, the father of issue management, described trends as "detectable changes which precede issues."[1] *Webster's Dictionary* has another take. This venerable definer of words refers to them as "a line of general direction or movement, a prevailing tendency or inclination."[2]

■ Massive Trends . . .

Seismic Shifts that Are Shaping the Future

As we scan the environment, nothing stands out more than massive, unrelenting trends. Like the movement of tectonic plates beneath the surface of the earth, they are a signal of seismic shifts.

This book focuses on 16 of those landscape-shaping trends. Each has implications for schools, school systems, colleges, universities, and other institutions, including communities, nations, and the world. Studying and considering the implications of these and other trends enables us to, among other things:

- Get connected to forces affecting the whole of society.

- Keep our organization fresh, energized, and open to new ideas.

- Encourage creativity and imagination.

- Give us the tools to identify problems or crises far enough in advance that they don't become catastrophes.

- Offer an opportunity for us to stay in tune with possible tipping points.[3]

- Identify opportunities we otherwise might not have considered.

- Provide us with an indication that far-reaching trends go beyond today's issues, such as class size, standards, accountability, and testing, but also may have a direct impact on all of them.

- Overcome the isolation of our disciplines, disagreements, and other differences to find the connective tissue that unifies us.[4]

- Help us and those we serve forecast possible futures and even become trendsetters.

- Turn our institution into an even more indispensable, relevant force.

We're about to bring the curtain up on Sixteen Trends. Consider them just the tip of an iceberg; the list is by no means complete. There are many other trends that will have an impact on education and society. Our hope is that this list and the commentary in the chapters that follow stimulate an even more expansive discussion and get us on a superhighway toward creating an even brighter future.

■ Connected Leadership . . .

We're all in this together!

Anyone involved in education is, or should be, a leader, by virtue of the crucial role he or she plays in society.

Connected leadership has replaced isolation. Just as we ask students to learn across disciplines, we also need to *lead* across disciplines. That means, if we're specialists, we should try to be the very best specialists we can become. As desperately as we need depth, it is not a substitute for breadth. Context is crucial. Everything we do affects everything else. The program that guarantees unprecedented benefits for some might bring devastating side effects for others.[5] The expansive needs of our community and the world should guide us as we strive to serve.

How can we connect people? How can we bring them together in common purpose? How can we tap the diversity and richness of thinking in an organization? How can we create a rallying point and ultimately a sense of ownership for what we want to accomplish? How can we stir a sense that "We're all in this together"?

The answer is not that complicated. We simply need to acknowledge the political, economic, social, technological, environmental, demographic, and other forces that are affecting the whole of society. Then, we need to ask key questions, such as:

• What are the implications of these trends for our educational system?

• What are the implications of these trends for what students need to know and be able to do—their academic knowledge, skills, behaviors, and attitudes?

In the process, we might ask some additional questions, such as:

• Do we have a short-range view or a long-range perspective?

Figure I.1
Sixteen Trends . . . that Will Profoundly Impact Education and the Whole of Society

■ **For the first time in history, the old will outnumber the young.**

Younger → Older

(Worldwide: Developed Nations — Younger → Older; Underdeveloped Nations — Older → Younger)

■ **Majorities will become minorities, creating ongoing challenges for social cohesion.**

Majority/Minority → Minority/Minority

(Worldwide: Diversity = Division ←→ Diversity = Enrichment)

■ **Social and intellectual capital will become economic drivers, intensifying competition for well-educated people.**

Industrial Age → Global Knowledge/Information Age

■ **Technology will increase the speed of communication and the pace of advancement or decline.**

Macro → Micro → Nano → Subatomic

■ **The Millennial Generation will insist on solutions to accumulated problems and injustices, while an emerging Generation E will call for equilibrium.**

GIs, Silents, Boomers, Xers → Millennials, Generation E

■ **Standards and high-stakes tests will fuel a demand for personalization in an education system increasingly committed to lifelong human development.**

Standardization → Personalization

■ **Release of human ingenuity will become a primary responsibility of education and society.**

Information Acquisition → Knowledge Creation and Breakthrough Thinking

■ **Continuous improvement will replace quick fixes and defense of the status quo.**

Quick Fixes/Status Quo → *Continuous Improvement*

■ **Scientific discoveries and societal realities will force widespread ethical choices.**

Pragmatic/Expedient → *Ethical*

■ **Common opportunities and threats will intensify a worldwide demand for planetary security.**

Personal Security/Self Interest ←→ *Planetary Security*

(Common Threats ←→ *Common Opportunities)*

■ **Polarization and narrowness will bend toward reasoned discussion, evidence, and consideration of varying points of view.**

Narrowness ←→ *Open-Mindedness*

■ **International learning, including diplomatic skills, will become basic, as nations vie for understanding and respect in an interdependent world.**

Isolationist Independence ←→ *Interdependence*

■ **Greater numbers of people will seek personal meaning in their lives in response to an intense, high-tech, always-on, fast-moving society.**

Personal Accomplishment ←→ *Personal Meaning*

■ **Understanding will grow that sustained poverty is expensive, debilitating, and unsettling.**

Sustained Poverty ←→ *Opportunity and Hope*

■ **Pressure will grow for society to prepare people for jobs and careers that may not currently exist.**

Career Preparation ←→ *Career Adaptability*

■ **Competition will increase to attract and keep qualified educators.**

Demand ←→ *Higher Demand*

Compiled by Gary Marx, president, Center for Public Outreach, Vienna, Va. (Published by Educational Research Service).

- Are we so intently focused on the bottom line that we've taken our eye off the future?

- Do we accept the status quo, or do we challenge it?[6]

- Are we doing things well?

- Are we doing the right things?

- What even greater benefit could result from our efforts?

- Do we have the right answers?

- Are we asking the right questions?

Richard Feynman, a fellow educator who won the 1965 Nobel Prize for Physics, said in his own challenging way, "I can live with doubt and uncertainty and not knowing. I think it is much more interesting to live not knowing than to have answers that might be wrong."[7]

This philosophy should not be confused with herd mentality or "group-think." In *The Wisdom of Crowds*, James Surowiecki warned against giving "too much credence to recent and high profile news while underestimating the importance of longer-lasting trends and less dramatic events."[8] Instead, we need to open our minds to the knowledge, experience, and ideas of diverse groups of people, turning them loose to consider possibilities, to learn from each other, and to help us, across all disciplines, as we think about and plan for the future. (See "Twelve Guiding Principles for Leaders Capable of Creating a Future" in figure I.2.)

■ Sixteen Trends

How was this book developed?

In 2000, the author, working with Educational Research Service, conducted a study and produced a book titled, *Ten Trends*...

Educating Children for a Profoundly Different Future.[9] That publication has stimulated discussions about the implications of those trends for schools, school systems, colleges and universities, work force developers, communities, states, nations, governmental and nongovernmental organizations, professional and trade associations, foundations, businesses and industries, media organizations, futurists, and politicians. Many volunteered that working together to address those trends was just what they needed to reenergize their organizations and bring people together in common purpose.

Since then, the author has continued to observe those trends and to identify others. The process engaged a Creating a Future Council of Advisors—34 thoughtful people who agreed to take part in a modified Delphi process. Responding to a first-round questionnaire, they individually identified three top societal trends and three issues that could be expected to affect education and the whole of society. In a second-round survey, members of the Council speculated on the implications of a cluster of no more than three trends each and were asked to comment on the premise that leaders, among other things, should be connected generalists. Their responses helped guide both this book, published by ERS, and a companion book, *Future-Focused Leadership: Preparing Schools, Students, and Communities for Tomorrow's Realities*, published by the Association for Supervision and Curriculum Development (ASCD).

The survey responses were coupled with ideas that emerged from an intensive review of trends, issues, ideas, and processes noted by futurists, forecasters, demographers, leadership experts, educators, business people, governmental and non-governmental agencies, journalists, and many others. As part of this sustained process of exploration and information gathering, the author identified the Sixteen Trends included in this book. Obviously, there are many other trends that are simultaneously affecting society.

What next? First, it is our hope that readers will seriously consider how they will deal with the trends we've highlighted. Second, we hope they will then use their curiosity and persistence to identify and address a multitude of other trends that are shaping our future. Perhaps, in the process, they will even set some trends of their own.

How is this book organized?

After setting the scene by addressing the importance of connected leadership and the need to constantly stay in touch with the internal and external environment, the book immediately cuts to the chase. A full chapter is devoted to each of the Sixteen Trends. Specific, fact-filled essays present a rationale, research, and an explanation of possible implications both for society at large and education in particular. A concluding chapter focuses on how educational systems and other organizations and institutions might deal with trends head-on as they think about and plan for the future.

As you study each of the trends, you might ask, "What's the difference between → and ←→?" The → mark indicates a clear, nearly unmitigated trend. A designation of ←→ indicates a trend that can be expected to develop or continue based on both evidence and the reality that certain conditions are likely unsustainable. For example, we can expect a tug between planetary security and self-interest, and between polarization and open-mindedness.

How can I use this publication?

When *Ten Trends* was published in 2000, the book suggested educational leaders and others in society would "need to become increasingly proactive and collaborative" in shaping the future. That's because we do have a choice. We can sit back and take "whatever happens." Or, rather than limiting our response to the latest mandates, we can blaze our own trails. Using these Sixteen Trends as a starting point, we can pave a better pathway to the future. In the process, we'll generate the energy and commitment we so deeply need to ensure students get an excellent education and our communities and nations thrive.

Your challenge is to turn this book into an action publication. It is meant to stimulate planning, breakthrough thinking, risk taking, and thoughtful action. Put copies of this publication in the hands of educators, parents, and students, as well as community, business, government, and other leaders. Use it to stimulate discussion, even debate, about how schools, school systems, colleges and universities, and other institutions need to be reshaped for the future. You might even want to create a network of Futures Councils that are asked to read this and other books and articles suggested throughout the text, hear presentations, and engage in generative thinking about the implications of these and other trends.

Build professional development programs around the need to constantly renew what we do and how we do it. Make the book required reading for staff, board, and key members of the community. Hold community-wide leadership seminars that take a look not only at the future of the education system but also at other quality-of-life issues, as well as economic growth and development. Use what this book has to say and the processes it suggests as a starting point for your planning and a key part of your environmental scan. Devote agenda time to serious study of one trend a month. Seriously study each trend. Consider implications, and take action that will keep the organization in tune with society and poised for the future.

We expect professors to use this book as a text or subtext, perhaps required reading, for both regular classes and as a basis for developing new courses. The courses might, for example, address trends, issues, planning, communication, or education futures.

We expect teachers to draw from the ideas and research included in each chapter to refresh their classes and further excite students about what they are learning. We also expect a growth in futures studies courses or units that help students better understand how to deal with issues and consider the implications of trends. Taking on the future enhances thinking and reasoning skills, contributes to active learning, and makes every other course more interesting and connected to the larger world. The future, after all, is where those students—all of us for that matter—will live our lives.

You'll find even more suggestions for putting ideas into action in the final chapter of this book. However you use them, we hope these ideas will ignite interest that challenges the status quo and encourages imagination.

■ Thriving in an Age of Renewal

The world is changing at warp speed. Education systems are expected to prepare their students for the future. They answered the call to get students ready for an agricultural society. Schools and colleges were transformed again as we moved into an industrial age. Today, we are entering what seems like the rarified atmosphere of the global knowledge/information age.

Our education systems, often working against great odds, have traditionally been among the most consistently successful institutions in our society. While schools and colleges continue their heroic efforts, often against a backdrop of higher expectations and limited resources, a sense of urgency is growing. An exhibit at the National Building Museum in Washington, D.C., carried this caption, "Companies come and go with the lightning speed of a computer's delete button."[10] That could apply to more than companies—all the more incentive for us to stay ahead of the curve.

Many schools and colleges are discovering that industrial-age schools are fighting an uphill battle in trying to prepare students for life in a whole new era. "Change" can be a nasty word to some. Say it, and someone is likely to respond, "Are you telling me I'm not doing a good job? Change makes me uncomfortable."

Rather than talk about change, then, let's focus our energies on developing descriptions of the system we need to help create an

We can't do that....

Don't you know we're...?

It's an all too typical reaction. In authoritarian nations where people are ruled with an iron fist, a common response to ideas is, "That is not possible." Even in nations where "all things are possible," some people put up their defenses whenever they're presented with an idea or an opportunity. It goes something like this. "We can't do that. Don't you know we're . . . too small, too large, urban, suburban, rural, rich, poor, already developed, underdeveloped, highly diverse, not at all diverse...?"

The fact is that we can usually go a long way toward accomplishing whatever we have the will to do. Trends we've included in this book will affect all of the above . . . and more. Universally, they have a variety of implications for everyone, and it's likely we'll be able to do something about them.

Here's a story for the naysayers. "When newfangled Great Western Railway steam engines left London in 1844 to pull coaches at 45 miles per hour, commentators expressed horror at such unnatural swiftness, while physicians urged passengers to avoid the trains on grounds that anyone moving so rapidly would surely suffocate," according to Gregg Easterbrook in *The Progress Paradox*.[11] Imagine what they'd think about today's super-fast bullet trains!

even more effective future for our schools and our students. It's one of the most uplifting things we could ever do and will become a part of our legacy. This book will help us on our journey toward an increasingly successful and satisfying future.

Figure I.2
12 Guiding Principles for Leaders Capable of Creating a Future

Sixteen Trends . . . Their Profound Impact on Our Future, published by ERS, and *Future-Focused Leadership: Preparing Schools, Students, and Communities for Tomorrow's Realities*, published by ASCD, are companion publications. In this book, we directly address massive trends and consider their implications for education and the whole of society. In *Future-Focused Leadership: Preparing Schools, Students, and Communities for Tomorrow's Realities*, we zero in on leadership and communication and provide an in-depth look at the many ways we can scan the environment and develop a vision for the future. In that book is a chapter devoted to "Twelve Guiding Principles for Leaders Capable of Creating a Future." Here is a brief listing of those items.

- Curiosity, persistence, and genuine interest are the main power sources for futures thinking.

- Breadth and depth are both important.

- Leaders connect the dots and seek common ground.

- There are more than two sides to most issues.

- The future is not necessarily a straight-line projection of the present.

- Enlightenment and isolation are becoming opposites.

- Peripheral vision can help us avoid being blind-sided.

- A belief in synergy can spark knowledge creation and breakthrough thinking.

- Collateral opportunity and collateral damage both deserve our attention.

- Bringing out the best in others is basic.

- Courage and personal responsibility need to overcome fear and self-pity.

- The role of strategic futurist is part of everybody's job.

(Source: *Future-Focused Leadership: Preparing Schools, Students, and Communities for Tomorrow's Realities*, Gary Marx, published by the Association for Supervision and Curriculum Development, 2006.)

■ Questions and Activities

1. Use the trends as a first step in creating a future for your organization. To begin, read one or more chapters of this book. Then, gather a group of colleagues or classmates together to brainstorm the implications of the trend or trends for how we run our education institution, what students need to know and be able to do, and possibly for the future of the community, for economic growth and development, or for the future of a city, county, state, or country.

2. Study trends related to aging, minorities, generations, and poverty. In light of the information provided, prepare a somewhat similar analysis or demographic profile for your own organization, community, and/or constituency.

■ Readings

1. Marx, G. (2006). *Future-focused leadership: Preparing schools, students, and communities for tomorrow's realities.* (The companion book to this publication.) Alexandria, VA: Association for Supervision and Curriculum Development.

2. Gladwell, M. (2000). *The tipping point . . . How little things can make a big difference.* NY: Little, Brown, and Co. (First Back Bay paperback, 2002).

3. Surowiecki, J. (2004). *The wisdom of crowds.* NY: Doubleday, a Division of Random House.

4. Bennis, W., & Goldsmith, J. (2003). *Learning to lead.* Cambridge, MA: Basic Books.

5. Easterbrook, G. (2003). *The progress paradox.* Trade Paperback Ed. NY: Random House.

6. Petersen, J.L. (1999). *Out of the blue . . . How to anticipate big future surprises.* Lanham, NY, and Oxford: Madison Books.

7. Cornish, E. (2004). *Futuring . . . The exploration of the future.* Bethesda, MD: World Future Society.

8. Coates, J.F., Mahaffie, J.B., & Hines, A. (1997). *2025 . . . Scenarios of U.S. and global society reshaped by science and technology.* Greensboro, NC: Oakhill Press.

9. *The Futurist* magazine. (Various issues.) Bethesda, MD: World Future Society. Available at http://www.wfs.org

Hold it just a minute. What about our heritage?

"We're proud of our community. The population is dwindling, but we don't want to lose our heritage." That type of concern should be a part of any discussion focused on creating a brighter future. Some communities and various organizations simply die, and their heritage is largely lost. Without sensitivity, the past and the future can collide. Rather than engaging in warfare, the past and the future need to coexist. To insist on either/or may be to put both in jeopardy. That's why we need to weave into our planning a discussion of what we want to keep and what we want to emphasize about our history and character. It can be a huge strength, but maintaining our heritage takes a conscious future-focused effort. To do nothing may be to lose it all.

Trend 1

We're not as young as we used to be!

For the first time in history, the old will outnumber the young.

Younger → Older

Worldwide: In developed nations, the old will substantially outnumber the young. In underdeveloped nations, the young will substantially outnumber the old.

Younger → Older   Older → Younger

The handwriting is on the wall. In 2000, 27 percent of the U.S. population was 18 or younger, and 21 percent was 55 or older. By 2030, when the Baby Boom Generation is between 66 and 84 years of age, 25 percent will be 18 or younger, and 31 percent will be 55 or older.[12]

■ Why Is Aging an Issue?

The aging of the population in some parts of the world and the expanding youthfulness in others will continue to raise issues of seismic proportions. The solvency of pension programs and competition for resources between those who are older and those who are younger will shake the political and economic foundations of numerous countries, including our own.

Whole new industries will develop to provide for the expanding needs of an aging population in most of the developed world. Education systems will be caught in a tug between growing enrollments of "regular students" on one hand and a swelling wave of "lifelong learners" on the other. Masses of teachers, administrators, and other school personnel will retire, creating shortages and heightening competition with other industries for qualified people.

Many historically successful organizations, which have simply trailed their constituencies into retirement, may end up retiring with them, unless they innovate and constantly rethink their missions.

Enjoy this joke . . . while you can.

Reporter: "What is the best thing about being 104?"

The 104-Year-Old: "Very little peer pressure."

Soon, centenarians will have even more "peers." We're not sure about the "peer pressure."

■ Six Key Factors that Affect the Aging of the Population

Why are some parts of the world getting younger and other parts getting older?

The question of the century is not even a head-scratcher. Putting it simply, the answer is directly connected to the balance among six key factors: life expectancy, average age, birth rates, fertility rates, death rates, and immigration.

When life expectancies and average ages go up and birth rates and death rates go down, a society becomes inevitably older. On the other hand, when life expectancies and average ages go down and birth rates and death rates go up, a society becomes inevitably younger. There is a major caveat, of course: immigration.

The following items include brief data for the United States. A breakout of those statistics, plus international information, is presented in figure T1.1.

Life Expectancies

In 1789, when the United States was taking its first steps as an independent nation, life expectancy was about 35. Jumping ahead to 1930, life expectancy had moved up to 59.7 years. [13] By 2001, it had reached 77.2, according to the National Center for Health Statistics. [14] Dramatically, the child born in 2001 is expected to live 29.9 years longer than the child born in 1900. [15] Despite the steady rise, Professor Jay Olishansky at the University of Illinois predicts a decline in life expectancy in the United States by mid-century resulting from an "obesity epidemic that will creep through all ages like a human tsunami." [16]

"I have a wish to die young . . . but as late in life as possible."

Anonymous Greek Sentiment

Average Ages

In 1800, the average age of people in the United States was 16. [17] By 2000, that figure had more than doubled to 36.5 years. The U.S. Census Bureau is predicting an average age of 40.7 in 2050 and 42.1 in 2095. [18] Admittedly, no one knows for sure what breakthroughs in extending life, cures for diseases, or natural or human-caused disasters might intervene.

Birth Rates

While life expectancies and average ages continue their relentless climb, U.S. birth rates have taken a steady nosedive. In 1910, the United States registered 3.01 live births per 100 population.[19] In 1960, there were 2.37. By 1990, the rate had fallen to 1.67 and in 2002 dropped even further to 1.39.[20]

Fertility Rates

As noted, birth rates reveal the number of live births per 100 population, while fertility rates reflect the average number of live births per 100 women of normal childbearing age, 15 to 44.

In 2001, the fertility rate dropped to 6.53 from 7.09 in 1990. From 1946 to 1964, when the Baby Boomers were being born, the rates were substantially higher—10.6 in 1950 and 11.8 in 1960. That compares with a spare 8.92 in 1930, at the beginning of the Great Depression.[21]

Death Rates

Of course, death rates play a key role in the shift toward an aging population. In 2001, the United States reported 8.5 deaths per 1,000 population, compared to 14.7 in 1910.[22]

Immigration

A population factor that ameliorates the effect of all the others is immigration—and it's having a profound impact on the very face of the planet. It is a known fact that people, if they have the fortitude, will use any means available to pursue opportunity—the opportunity for education, economic advancement, and the freedom to fulfill their dreams. They often flee repression and economic hardship.

Births Compared with Deaths

According to the U.S. National Center for Health Statistics, there were 4.02 million births and 2.41 million deaths in the country during 2002. That's a natural increase of 1.60 million.[23] At the turn of the 21st century, the U.S. Census Bureau reported one birth every eight seconds, one death every 13 seconds, and a net of one international migrant every 30 seconds, yielding a population gain of one person every 12 seconds.[24]

While U.S. society is feeling its age, it is, on average, a bit younger than some developed countries, largely because of immigration. If there had been no immigration to the United States since 1990, the population in 2000 would have been 262 million—19 million less than the 281 million who were counted. In fact, the U.S. Census Bureau reports that post-1990 immigrants and their children accounted for 61 percent of the nation's population growth during the 1990s.[25]

■ Dependency Ratios

What portion of the population is of working age?

Dependency ratios are defined as the ratio of people who are of *working age (15 to 65)* compared with those who are *under 15* and those who are *65 or over*.

The U.S. Census Bureau is predicting that, by 2025, "the world's elderly population, ages 65 and above, will more than double, while the world's youth population, under age 15, will grow by six percent." As a whole, the world will face "an elderly support burden nearly 50 percent larger in 2025 than it did in 1998," according to the bureau's *World Population Profile*.[26]

Figure T1.1
Data Bank
A Digest of Demographics

LIFE EXPECTANCIES
Average lifespans in years:
United States[27]

1789	35.0
1930	59.7
2001	77.2

Internationally
Figures are for 1998.
(U.S. did not rank in the top 20 countries.)

Andorra	83.47[28]
Macao	81.69
San Marino	81.23
Japan	80.80
Singapore	80.17
Canada	79.56
Nigeria	41.00[29]
Sierra Leone	37.00

AVERAGE AGES
Based on average age of people living at the time:
United States[30]

1800	16.0
2000	36.5
2050 (Projection)	40.7
2095 (Projection)	42.1

Worldwide[31]

2000	22.5
2050 (Projection)	38.0

BIRTH RATES
Live births per 100 population:
United States[32]

1910	3.01
1960	2.37
1990	1.67
2002	1.39

Birth Rates (cont.)
Internationally[33]
2002 Data for Comparison:

Niger	4.99
Afghanistan	4.10
Japan	1.00
Bulgaria	.80

Note: Replacement rate is 2.1 births per 100 population.

FERTILITY RATES
Live births per 100 women of normal childbearing age, 15-44.
United States[34]

1930	8.92
1950	10.60
1960	11.80
1990	7.09
2001	6.53

DEATH RATES
Deaths per 1,000 population.
United States[35]

1910	14.70
2001	8.50

Internationally[36]
2002 data for comparison (est.):

Kuwait (Lowest)	2.46
Botswana (Highest)	26.20

BIRTHS COMPARED WITH DEATHS
United States[37]
2002: 4.02 million births and 2.41 million deaths, a natural increase of 1.60 million

Births/Deaths (cont.)
Worldwide[38]
2004 Estimated: 128.97 million births and 56.20 million deaths, a natural increase of 72.77 million.

TOTAL U.S. POPULATION[39]
Actual and Projected:

2000	275.3 million
2020	324.9 million
2050	403.6 million
2100	570.9 million

Percentage 65-Plus

2000	12.7 percent
2010	13.2 percent
2020	16.5 percent
2050	20.3 percent
2100	23.0 percent

Numbers 85-Plus

2000	4.3 million
2020	6.7 million
2050	19.3 million
2100	37.0 million

Numbers 100-Plus

2000	65,000
2010	129,000
2020	235,000
2050	1,095,000
2100	4,783,000

WORLD POPULATION[40]
Actual and Projected:

1950	2.5 billion
2000	6.07 billion
2020	7.5 billion
2050	9.08 billion

Social Security

Worker-to-Beneficiary Ratio

In 1950, 16 people were working for every person drawing benefits from the U.S. Social Security system. By 1960, the ratio stood at 5 to 1. In 2000, it dropped to 3.2 to 1. By 2020, it is expected to drop even further to 2.4. In 2040, it is projected that only two people will be working for every person drawing benefits from the system.[41]

■ U.S. Population Growth

Make Room. There'll be twice as many of us by 2100.

The population of the United States is expected to grow from 275.3 million in 2000 to approximately 403.6 million in 2050 and 570.9 million in 2100. During that time, the 79 million strong Baby Boom Generation, born between 1946 and 1964, will move into its advanced years, increasing the numbers of those 65+ from 12.7 percent of the total population in 2000 to 20.3 percent in 2050. In 2030, the Boomers will be between 66 and 84 years of age. While people who make products for mature consumers are salivating, those working to keep Social Security solvent are wringing their hands.

Among the fastest-growing segments of the population on a percentage basis will be those who are more than 100 years of age, whose ranks are expected to increase from 65,000 in 2000 to 1,095,000 in 2050. Similarly, those 85+ are projected to go from 4.3 million in 2000 to 37 million in 2100.[42]

While demographics may not be our destiny, the aging of the population will continue to present a plethora of challenges and opportunities for the nation and virtually all of its institutions.

Figure T1.2*
U.S. Population Projections[43]

Mid-Year, Middle Series Projections, 2000-2100
U.S. Census Bureau
Percentages of Total Population

Year	Total U.S. Population	Under 5 Years	5-17 Years	18-24 Years	20-54 Years	55-64 Years	65+ Years	Total 0-18	Total 55+
2000	275,306,000	6.9	20.1	10.0	51.6	8.7	12.7	27.0	21.4
2010	299,862,000	6.7	18.6	10.0	49.4	11.8	13.2	25.5	25.0
2020	324,927,000	6.8	18.2	9.1	45.5	13.0	16.5	25.0	29.5
2050	403,687,000	6.7	18.3	9.1	43.9	10.8	20.3	25.0	31.1
2100	570,954,000	7.6	17.6	8.8	41.3	10.0	23.0	25.0	33.0

*A variety of age ranges has been developed for the benefit of readers. Some overlap. Therefore, adding the items across the chart should not be expected to provide a total of 100 percent.

■ U.S. Population Pyramids[44]

These illustrations have been used for several years to graphically show five-year cohorts of the population moving up the age ladder. Take a look at the pyramids for the United States in figure T1.3. You'll be able to see the Baby Boom Generation as it begins its climb, creating bulges as it moves along from 2000 to 2025 and 2050. Similar illustrations are available for most other countries.

■ World Population Growth

Earth's population was approximately 2.5 billion in 1950. By 2000, it had reached 6.07 billion. International experts are projecting a world population of 7.5 billion by 2020 and 9.08 billion by 2050. That's a 363 percent increase in 100 years.[45]

Figure T1.3
Population Pyramid Summary for United States

United States: 2000

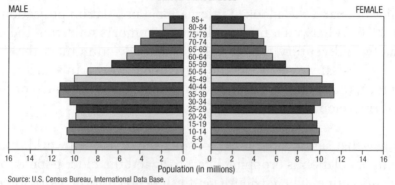

Source: U.S. Census Bureau, International Data Base.

United States: 2025

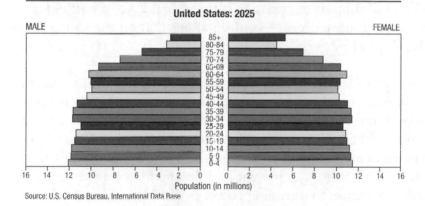

Source: U.S. Census Bureau, International Data Base.

United States: 2050

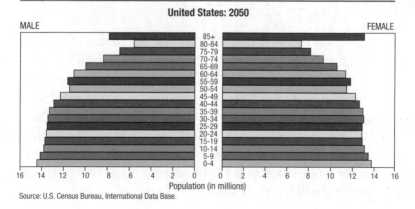

Source: U.S. Census Bureau, International Data Base.

■ Facing the Facts

One way or the other, everyone will be outnumbered.

Enjoy drama? Take a look at international population projections for 2050! What you'll find are dramatic numbers reflecting the fact that, by mid-century, the old will substantially outnumber the young in what we today call the "developed" world. In sharp contrast, the young will grossly outnumber the old in much of the "underdeveloped or developing" world.

Why is that significant? First, consider the developed world. If the youth population is dropping like a rock and the older population is skyrocketing, where will we get fresh people for the work force? Who will support our pension plans? What kind of battles for resources can we expect—confrontations that pit the young against the old, and vice versa?

Next, consider the underdeveloped or developing world. For the most part, those nations will see massive increases in their youth populations but have few people older than 55. When there are huge numbers of young people who might be un- or under-educated and unemployed, with little obvious opportunity, anger grows. That anger can present itself in anything from an enlightened revolution to unending chaos, civil wars, and international terrorism.

Contemplate figure T1.4. By 2050, 26 percent of the U.S. population will be from birth to age 19, and 31 percent will be 55 or older. Now look at Italy. By mid-century, the population is expected to drop by more than 20 percent. In 2050, only 15 percent of the population of Italy is expected to be from birth to age 19; 48 percent will be 55 or older. Now, check out Yemen. Its population is expected to increase more than four times by 2050, when 42 percent of the population will likely be from birth to age 19, and only 11 percent will be 55 or older.[46]

Figure T1.4
Worldwide Projections
Old Outnumbering Young; Young Outnumbering Old
U.S. Census Bureau, International Statistics and Projections, 2000 and 2050[47]

Country	Population in Millions 2000	Population in Millions 2050	2050, % of Population Birth-19	2050, % of Population 55+
Italy	57.6 m.	45 m.	15	48
France	59.3 m.	61 m.	20	38
United Kingdom	59.5 m.	63.9 m.	19.6	38.7
Russia	146 m.	118 m.	19	41
Japan	126.7 m.	99.8 m.	17	46
China	1,262 m.	1,417 m.	20	38.6
India	1,002.7 m.	1,601 m.	26.6	26.4
United States	275 m.	403.6 m.	26	31
Canada	31.2 m.	41.4 m.	20	37.6
Mexico	100 m.	153 m.	25	29
Argentina	36.9 m.	50.1 m.	35	28
Nigeria	123 m.	303 m.	38	19
Iraq	22.6 m.	53.6 m.	30	20
Saudi Arabia	22 m.	91 m.	44	11
Yemen	17.5 m.	71.1 m.	42	11

■ Education

Growth of Students v. Shortage of Educators

In 2000, kindergarten through grade 12 enrollments in the United States stood at 53.16 million. Those numbers were expected to grow to 53.86 million by 2005 and then relax somewhat to 53.49 million in 2010 and 53.69 million in 2012, according to the National Center for Education Statistics (NCES).[48]

At the turn of the millennium, approximately 3.1 million people comprised the U.S. elementary and secondary teaching force. The number of teachers needed was projected to increase to 3.46 million by 2008. According to Said Yasin, writing for the *ERIC Digest*, "school systems would collectively have to hire about 200,000 teachers annually over the next decade to keep pace with rising student enrollments and teacher retirements."[49]

Here's where the aging of the population comes in. As enrollments are increasing, Boomer generation teachers are quickly moving toward retirement. The same is true for administrators. In a report published in 1999, the U.S. Department of Education was predicting a need for 2.2 million new teachers over a 10-year period, just to close the gap created by retirements and people leaving the profession.[50] A 2000 study indicated a shortage of candidates for superintendencies, principalships, and other central and building-level administrative positions.[51]

Bottom line—Unless education systems become increasingly competitive for the people they need, they will simply lose them to other employment opportunities.

■ Implications for Society

Aging

The impact of aging on society will be massive. Now is the time to plan ahead. Demographic facts and projections lay before us a case that is open and shut, barring some microscopic, seismic, or astrophysical cataclysm, such as a killer virus, volcano that shrouds the planet, or asteroid striking the earth. Whatever happens, the time has come to pay more attention than we have so far to the political, economic, social, and technological implications posed by the aging of our population.

Consider the following possible implications of the aging trend for society as a whole.

- Pension programs will likely be strained beyond their limits as the ratio of retirees closes in on the number of actual workers contributing to those funds.

- Older citizens will cringe at the very word, "old." They will, as a group, constantly seek a fountain of youth and opportunities to improve the quality of their lengthening lives through pharmaceuticals, diet, and exercise.

- Demand will accelerate for products and services directly related to the needs and desires of older citizens.

- Industries that provide services for older citizens will continue to grow. Entrepreneurs will see this "demographic group" as a market with increased buying power.

- Financial service companies will burgeon as retirees and those soon to retire try to get the very best return on their investments.

- As Boomers move even closer toward and into retirement, their political clout will reverberate. Seniors often have the time and the inclination to vote and the life experience to make their case exceedingly convincing to decision makers.

- As older citizens have more time they can call their own, demand will increase for personalized lifelong learning. They will want to pursue the interests and curiosities they may have put on hold when they went into the workplace decades before.

- School systems, community colleges, and four-year colleges and universities will be expected to offer continuing education courses for people who are retired or about to retire—courses that stimulate the intellect and provide counsel on issues connected to aging.

- Former members of the "regular" work force will give birth to new consultancies that offer their customers a wealth of wisdom and experience that they don't currently have on staff.

- Even more ocean liners will take to the seas. Family vacations, such as grandparents and grandchildren spending a few weeks away together, will become even more common.

- At the very time the Social Security system anticipates that people will stay in the work force longer, companies will downsize many older citizens from their jobs at what might have been, in the past, the peak of their working and earning years.

- Growing numbers of organizations will adjust schedules and working conditions to attract and keep some older citizens on the job, even part time.

- In many developed countries, immigrants will become an even greater portion of the work force, particularly in the professional and service sectors. Older citizens will see the work and the contributions of these immigrants as vital to maintaining benefit programs such as Social Security, Medicare, and Medicaid.

- Communities will need to plan ahead for quality geriatric medical care, assisted living, nursing homes, geriatric day care, and other services for an aging population.

- The greatest transference of wealth in the history of humankind will take place as the Boomers will their life savings to the young or to fortunate charities.

- Resentments are likely to grow as older citizens purchase second homes, while younger people, who fear loss of Social Security benefits for themselves, struggle to pay the rent.

- The gap will grow between the haves and the have-nots, who are retired and live on relatively fixed incomes. Society will be hard pressed to address what will increasingly appear to be an injustice.[52]

■ Implications for Education

Aging

The issue of aging is spawning education issues that demand our attention. In every community, educators and leaders in other industries should be identifying the implications of trends such as this one as they accelerate the process of creating a sustainable future. Just a few of the implications of this trend include:

- **Balancing the political demands of the young and the old.** "Will a population that is both aging and growing press for expensive health and security programs of their own, or will they coalesce with the young and with families to provide adequate resources for education?" asks Arnold Fege, president of Public Advocacy for Kids in Annandale, Va. Ted Stilwill, former director of the Iowa Department of Education, warns of a possible "clash between the needs of those of us headed into retirement with the needs of young children for education and other services." If the country is not able to deal effectively with this issue, Stilwill cautions "our country will become less competitive economically, and the potential for exacerbating the negative spiral increases."

  "There will be tremendous competition for resources among schools, municipalities, and other taxing entities," predicts Keith Marty, superintendent of the School District of Menomonee

Falls in Wisconsin. He adds, "School leaders and communities that collaborate and come together for children will be able to garner resources and public support" and better balance the political demands of the young and the old. They'd better!

- **Recruiting and retaining older citizens for service as educators.** In this chapter, we've pointed out that growing enrollments expected during the early part of the 21st century will run squarely into massive retirements from education.

The system must face head-on the problem of gaps created by retirements and movement from the profession. The National Education Association (NEA), in an issue paper addressing the teacher shortage, applauds efforts to bring more young people into the profession. "But," the paper emphasizes, "too little attention has been paid to holding onto the quality teachers already hired—both the beginning teachers as well as the more seasoned ones."[53]

One choice is to become more flexible, to make it easier for older educators who are taking early retirement to stay on the job part-time. Some suggest that many who have worked in other professions for much of their lives would like to move into teaching careers. Futurist David Pearce Snyder suggests "a growing number of white collar workers will be available for recycling into teaching."

A choice we don't have is to *not* deal with the problem and end up with a decline in the number of educated people capable of driving our democratic society and free-market economy.

- **Expanding community and career education, adult education, community and four-year college and university programs, and other opportunities for lifelong learning.** School systems and community colleges, as well as many four-year colleges and universities, have been working together in fits and starts to make the education system somewhat more seamless. Some call it the P-16 movement—prekindergarten through the fourth year of college. Those efforts will likely be accelerated by the increasing demands of an aging population.

The K-12 system may not cover enough ground to meet the expanding needs of older citizens who are pursuing new later-in-life careers, satisfaction for their intellectual curiosities, or upgrades in their technology/computer skills. However, K-12 schools are located in every community and could provide a home for not only their own adult and continuing education courses, but also for courses offered by higher education institutions. E-learning also offers opportunities for growing numbers of people to pursue courses online and on their own schedules.

• **Promoting cross-generational communication.** Schools and colleges will be focusing on how to build services and constituencies across all or parts of five generations. At the same time, they will be considering how to prepare students for intergenerational understanding—an essential for maintaining a civil society and for students' success later in life.

As society ages even further, "Grandparents Day" at school might be expanded to "Great-Grandparents Day." Schools will likely invite even more older citizens into the classroom to share their wisdom and life experiences. A retired engineer, for example, might be just the right person to explain to students how exciting math can be. In visits to the classroom or through electronic connections, GI, Silent, Boomer, Xer, and Millennial generation space scientists and engineers, either in person or through distance learning, could excite students about a career in astrophysics.

Some schools may set aside part of the building as a senior center, where older citizens can come to read the paper, connect to the Internet, visit with friends and colleagues, and get to know students and staff. While there, they can also help teachers make some of those important connections between the textbook and real-life applications. One school superintendent has even suggested making

Figure T1.5
The Way We Were, 1900 v. 2000

A collection of facts from "American Ingenuity . . . The Culture of Creativity That Made a Nation Great," *U.S. News and World Report,* **Collector's Edition, "Amazing Journey," by Roger Simon and Angie Cannon.** [54]

How has the United States changed in a century? Plenty. It might change even more during the 21st than it did during the 20th, but then, everything is relative. Here are a few comparisons.

	1900	2000
Population	76 million	275 million
Minorities	9 million	87 million
Five Biggest Cities by Population Size	New York, Chicago, Philadelphia, St. Louis, Boston	New York, Los Angeles, Chicago, Houston, Philadelphia
Five Biggest States by Population Size	New York, Pennsylvania, Illinois, Ohio, Missouri	California, Texas, New York, Florida, Illinois
Foreign-Born Population	14 percent	10 percent
Top Sources of Immigration by Numbers of Immigrants	Austria-Hungary, Italy, Russia, United Kingdom, Germany	Mexico, Philippines, Russia, Dominican Republic, India
Average Household Size	4.76 persons	2.59 persons
Infant Mortality Rate (Deaths in first year of life, per 1,000)	165	7
Households Headed by Married Couple	80 percent (1910)	53 percent (1998)
Urban Dwellers	50 percent	80 percent
Share of Income Spent for Food	43 percent (1901)	15 percent (1997)

space available for limited geriatric day care. Of course, any of these approaches involves policy, budgetary, and security issues.

- **Communicating with people who don't have kids in school.** One question likely to crop up even more frequently within the education system at all levels will be, "How can we inform, involve, and serve people who don't have kids in our schools?" Reaching out may be at least part of the key to maintaining political support.

As noted earlier, older citizens can be magnificent resources for the schools. They are potentially an education system's greatest gifts or worst nightmares. If the more age-mature people in our communities have an opportunity to be engaged, they'll likely feel a sense of ownership. If contact is limited, battle lines could be drawn between the needs of older citizens and the needs of young people.

That's why effective communication is essential with empty nesters, who may no longer have children in school, and with those who may never have had children in the first place. Sharing information through newsletters, Web sites, targeted email, cable television, podcasting, and special events will likely be essential.

Listening can make that communication even more effective. Thoughtful communicators will ask what members of this important constituency would like to know, what they understand, what they don't, and how they prefer to get their information. They will look for communication gaps and close them.[55]

- **Maintaining the solvency of pension funds.** The growing phalanx of people poised for either early or on-time retirement, coupled with reduced return on pension fund investments, has placed a growing strain on retirement systems. Those systems are further stressed by the fact that people are living longer after they leave regular employment. Threats about cutbacks or structural changes in Social Security have raised the level of concern about maintaining the integrity of that program. Education institutions can expect this ongoing issue to move to the critical list during the early decades of the 21st century.

■ Bridging the Gap

What was once called the "generation gap" has become a complex web of gaps as people live longer. More generations are occupying the planet at the same time. New technologies have given them the capacity to readily rally support for their particular age group.

Will our institutions, including our schools, be able to coalesce the support they need from such divergent groups with such a variety of attitude-changing life experiences? Will clefts develop or intensify? Will our nation become a house divided? These questions have far-reaching implications for society.[56] An entire chapter of this book is devoted to generations. (See Trend 5.)

■ Questions and Activities

1. What are six key factors causing some parts of the world to get older and other parts of the world to get younger?

2. On a percentage basis, which of the following groups will grow most rapidly between 2000 and 2100: 65+, 85+, or 100+?

3. Explain dependency ratios. Gather needed information and compute the dependency ratio for your community, state/province/canton, or country.

4. Study the figure devoted to "Worldwide Projections, Old Outnumbering Young, Young Outnumbering Old." Develop three one-sentence observations about aging trends across nations. Identify four possible implications of these international aging trends for what students will need to know to be prepared for the future.

5. Develop a demographic profile of your community, including age, gender, race and ethnicity, social and economic, and any other factors you consider important.

6. Develop a list of 10 ways schools or colleges in your community could better reach out to and serve older people.

7. If you were developing a legitimate new product or service that would be helpful to older people, what would it be? In what way would it be helpful?

■ Readings

1. U.S. Census Bureau (various dates). *National population projections, summary files by age, sex, race, and Hispanic* origin. Available at http://www.census.gov/population

2. Wallace, Paul. (1999). *Agequake: Riding the demographic rollercoaster shaking business, finance, and our world.* London: Nicholas Brealey Publishing Ltd.

3. Population data from a recent world almanac.

Trend 2

Highly diverse ... and looking good.

Majorities will become minorities, creating ongoing challenges for social cohesion.

Majority/Minority → Minority/Minority

Worldwide: Growing numbers of people and nations will discover that if we manage our diversity well, it will enrich us. If we don't manage our diversity well, it will divide us.

Diversity = Division ↔ Diversity = Enrichment

The face of the United States of America is changing. Look ahead to just past mid-century, and what will you find? We'll be a nation where everyone will be a minority.

■ Getting a Take on Diversity through the Majority/Minority Lens

In the late 1990s, *Time* magazine devoted its cover to the emerging face of the U.S. population, and it's a new look. That computer-generated face reflected volumes about a country of immigrants whose motto is *E Pluribus Unum*— "of the many . . . one."

Today, the streets of free and open societies have become rainbows, a melange reflecting the combined characteristics of many racial, ethnic, tribal, or other groups. In the democracy of our dreams, a country doesn't belong to any one of them. It belongs to all of them.

Thanks to U.S. Census Bureau projections, we can hold up a magic mirror and get a glimpse of the population all the way to 2100, the dawn of the 22nd century. We'll start with a wide-angle shot of the general population, then take a close-up of young people.

■ General Population

As the opening of this chapter makes clear, the United States is becoming a nation of minorities. Shortly after 2050, no single racial or ethnic group will constitute more than 50 percent of the population. While that shift will take place around 2040 among young people—ages birth to 19—it will be somewhat more gradual among the total population.

In 2000, 71.4 percent of the nation's 275.3 million people were non-Hispanic White. By 2050, 52.8 percent are likely to be in that category. In 2100, the number of non-Hispanic Whites is expected to drop to 40.3 percent. While Blacks and Native Americans will show growth in numbers, they are expected to remain about the same as a percentage of the total population. Asians and Hispanics will increase dramatically.

■ Youth Population (Birth to Age 19)

The youth population in the United States, ages birth to 19, is projected to increase from 78.4 million in 2000 to approximately 106.4 million in 2050 and 144.6 million in 2100. While 64 percent of the 2000 youth population was non-Hispanic White, that number will drop to 49.1 percent by 2040, 46.2 percent by 2050, and 36.1 percent by 2100.

*Figure T2.1**
Projected U.S. General Population by Race/Ethnicity
Numbers and Percentages[57]
U.S. Census Bureau

Numbers in Thousands and Percentages of Total

Year	Total (Numbers Rounded)	Non-Hispanic White (in 000s)	Black (in 000s)	American Indian/ Eskimo/ Aleut (in 000s)	Asian/ Pacific Islander (in 000s)	Hispanic (in 000s)
2000	275,306,000	196,670 71.4 %	33,490 12.2 %	2,048 .74 %	10,620 3.9 %	32,479 11.8 %
2010	299,862,000	201,956 67.3 %	37,483 12.5 %	2,300 .77 %	14,436 4.8 %	43,688 14.6 %
2020	324,927,000	207,145 63.8 %	41,549 12.8 %	2,550 .78 %	18,527 5.7 %	55,156 17 %
2030	351,070,000	210,984 60.1 %	45,567 13 %	2,787 .8 %	23,564 6.7 %	68,168 19.4 %
2040	377,350,000	212,475 56.3 %	49,618 13.1 %	3,023 .80 %	29,543 7.8 %	82,692 21.9 %
2050	403,687,000	212,991 52.8 %	53,466 13.2 %	3,241 .80 %	35,760 8.9 %	98,229 24.3 %
2100	570,954,000	230,236 40.3 %	74,361 13 %	4,237 .74 %	71,789 12.6 %	190,331 33.3 %

*Because of rounding, totals do not precisely equal 100 percent.

During the 21st century, Hispanic Americans are expected to move from 16.2 percent of the youth population in 2000 to 37.6 percent in 2100. Blacks and Native Americans are expected to grow in numbers but drop slightly as a percentage of the total youth population. Meanwhile, Asian youth are expected to move from 4.2 percent of that group in 2000 to 12.7 percent in 2100.[58]

Figure T2.2*
Projected U.S. Population of Children
Resident Population, Birth through Age 19[59]
U.S. Census Bureau

Numbers in Thousands and Percentages of Total

Year	Total Population Children, Birth-19 (Numbers Rounded)	Non-Hispanic White (in 000s)	Black (in 000s)	American Indian/ Eskimo/ Aleut (in 000s)	Asian/ Pacific Islander (in 000s)	Hispanic (in 000s)
2000	78,451,000	50,414 64 %	11,384 14.5 %	751 1.0 %	3,285 4.2 %	12,618 16.2 %
2010	81,113,000	47,955 59 %	11,550 14.2 %	757 0.9 %	4,321 5.3 %	16,530 20 %
2020	85,724,000	47,601 55.5 %	12,052 14 %	809 0.9 %	5,287 6.2 %	19,974 23.3 %
2030	92,643,000	48,720 52.6 %	12,707 13.7 %	840 0.9 %	6,554 7 %	23,822 25.7 %
2040	99,043,000	48,674 49.1 %	13,380 13.5 %	873 .88 %	8,135 8.2 %	27,984 30.2 %
2050	106,498,000	49,246 46.2 %	14,193 13.4 %	915 .86 %	9,763 9.1 %	32,380 30.4 %
2100	144,619,000	52,331 36.1 %	18,379 12.7 %	1,091 .75 %	18,379 12.7 %	54,439 37.6 %

*Because of rounding, totals do not precisely equal 100 percent.

■ Social Cohesion . . .

Overcoming the tension between coming together or falling apart.

What is social cohesion? It's the glue that holds us together as families, as nations, as a world. What we have in common helps us form our sense of community. If we accept diversity as part of the norm, it will enrich us, bind us together. If we don't, our diversity can divide us.

Diversity should be an inclusive word, but defining diversity is not a simple matter. Generally, we think of it as encompassing racial and ethnic groups. However, the richness of inclusion has been stretched to recognize differences in age, gender, social and economic conditions, national or political affiliation, religion, and a host of other factors. Some communities have taken steps to see minorities based more on social and economic differences than on racial and ethnic ones.[60] In the future, minorities and majorities might be singled out based on the quality of education they've received.

In a technology-driven, "market-of-one" society, advertisers often lump us by the demographics of our zip code. People and communities are reduced to market niches. Targeted messages are developed to appeal to the needs of each possible customer. However, demographics, the statistical characteristics used to describe people, has now been extended to encompass psychographics, or the identification of what motivates them.

As a world, we sometimes come together despite longstanding disagreements or other conflicts. We can be united by common threats, such as a pandemic, a lethal attack, natural disaster, possible environmental devastation, or a lack of support for education.

An ongoing challenge in any society is to constantly seek common opportunities. These opportunities, if we pursue them together, can act as a social adhesive. In a world that is shrinking each day, those opportunities could be a common commitment to improving education, promoting the well-being of children, building a park, ensuring social justice, launching and maintaining weather satellites, or working as a team across national boundaries to help humanity explore the vastness of space and the mysteries of the atom. With enough commitment to pursuing common opportunities, to moving toward common ground, perhaps even the threats will become more manageable.

The Danger of Dominance

When domination by one or more groups replaces an acceptance of diversity as the norm, people generally engage in conflicts that involve: tribal, racial, and ethnic divisions; religious differences; and a variety of other social and economic divides. Without some sense of democratic inclusiveness, people who identify with divergent groups will either feel "in power" or "out of power."

■ Factors Driving This Trend

A number of factors are having a profound impact on turning the United States from a majority/minority into a minority/minority society. Some of the more prominent are immigration, birth rates, and an interesting phenomenon called "multi-country nations." These and other forces are also affecting population diversity in other countries.

Immigration

The United States is largely populated by families of immigrants. Even Native Americans are widely thought to have emigrated across the Bering Strait from Asia.

In the1920s, most immigrants to the United States came from Germany, Italy, the Soviet Union, Poland, Canada, Great Britain, Ireland, Sweden, Austria, and Mexico. In 2000, most came from Mexico, the Philippines, China and Hong Kong, India, Cuba, Vietnam, El Salvador, Korea, the Dominican Republic, and Canada.[61] While some immigrants move directly into high-paying, traditionally prestigious careers, a majority bear great hardship as they reach for the first rung on the ladder of opportunity and begin their climb.

Most developed countries have declining or very slowly increasing populations. One exception is the United States, which is expected to show steady gains, at least through 2100. In 2000, the total foreign-born population in the United States was approximately 31.1 million, a record 57 percent increase during the decade of the 1990s.[62] The country had a net immigration of 980,000 in 2000 alone. That number is now expected to decline to 757,000 in 2020, then increase to more than one million annually between 2028 and 2046.[63]

Immigration, of course, has had profound implications for education systems in the United States and several other countries. Those implications include the need to pool resources to provide education for expanding enrollments in immigrant-rich areas of the country. As with earlier waves of immigration, many students will continue to come to school speaking an array of languages, but not necessarily the language of the local marketplace. Georgia Congressman John Lewis, addressing an Education Writers Association annual conference in 2000, summed up the situation. He intoned that many of "our foremothers and forefathers came to this great country in different ships, but we're all in the same boat now."[64]

Birth Rates

Across the board, birth rates have been going down in the United States and other "developed" countries. Average rates, however, tend to vary among racial and ethnic groups. In 2002, according to the National Center for Health Statistics, the overall birth rate stood at 1.39 children per 100 population, down from 1.41 in 2001 and 1.67 in 1990.[65] A 1998 report illustrated the discrepancies in rates among various groups: Whites averaged 1.23 children per 100 population, Asians 1.64, Blacks 1.82, and Hispanics 2.43. Over time, slight variations in those rates can have a profound impact on the total make-up of a population, locally, nationally, and world-wide.[66]

Cosmopolitans and Multi-Country Nations

Concentrations of wealth often bring lower birth rates and lower death rates. That means a good share of developed countries are aging, their labor forces dwindling. People of many races, cultures, and nations see these countries as "opportunity magnets."

Because of a lack of employment opportunities, low wages, or red tape that stifles creativity in their home country, people head for nations that are eager for their talents. Not constrained by political boundaries, companies have been expanding far beyond the country where their home office is located. This global phenomenon took on a whole new head of steam following the end of the Cold War. The tendency has been for people to move toward those countries that feature market capitalism, political pluralism, and cultural diversity.

In the global marketplace, people who come to work and raise their families in countries such as the United States, Canada, the United Kingdom, India, China, Australia, or South Africa, for example, don't necessarily want to give up their culture and connection to their homeland. In short, for growing numbers of people in the world, shared culture and history have become greater unifying factors than political boundaries.

People from the United States live and work in other countries, but they consider themselves an extension of the United States. Growing numbers of people from Japan, China, India, Iraq, Mexico, and El Salvador, to name just a few, also live and work in other countries but still consider themselves an extension of their homeland. Resources sent back home to relatives have become a significant portion of the gross domestic products of some countries. While many hope to melt into a new nationality, others don't.

We are seeing "the emergence of another kind of tribalism, one forged by globally dispersed ethnic groups," says Joel Kotkin, an international fellow at Pepperdine University School of Business and Management. "These global tribes are today's quintessential cosmopolitans, in sharp contrast to narrow provincials," he concludes. Therefore, the United States is becoming the "Greater U.S." India is becoming "Greater India." Mexico is becoming "Greater Mexico."[67]

Of course, the children of these cosmopolitans take their seats each and every day in schools around the world. That raises questions and fires debates in family conversations and international councils, but it's nevertheless an exciting and enriching phenomenon that's a fact of life.

■ Whatever happened to the melting pot?

When Irish, German, Italian, and other European immigrants came to the United States during a wave of immigration at the turn of the 20th century, the idea of the melting pot had reached mythic proportions. These Europeans were captivated by "the promise that all immigrants can be transformed into Americans, a new alloy forged in the crucible of democracy, freedom, and civic responsibility," according to William Booth of *The Washington Post*.[68]

Invitations to the melting pot turned out to be limited. "Separate but equal," a myth enshrined in law, excluded certain groups, such as African Americans. Even schools and universities were segregated. Then, in May of 1954, the U.S. Supreme Court handed down its landmark decision in *Brown v. Board of Education*. Journalist Juan Williams, writing in the *American School Board Journal*, called it the ruling that changed America. Ten years later, the Civil Rights Act became the law of the land. Affirmative action appeared. The struggle for equal rights continues.[69]

At the turn of the 21st century, observers began questioning whether growing numbers of immigrants were still willing to give up their

Multicultural Marketing . . . Another View

Jeff Yang is CEO of Factor, Inc., a company focusing on the Asian American market. In a special supplement to *American Demographics* magazine, he predicts marketers will need to become more multicultural in their approach. Targeting messages to certain traditional racial or ethnic groups may not work in the future. Yang expects multicultural groups to emerge. He calls them:

- **The Plural Mainstream.** With the White majority in the United States slipping to less than 50 percent shortly after mid-century, the new mainstream will be much more diverse, melding perhaps several ethnicities, races, and cultures.

- **The Outward Bounders.** These, Yang says, are "young people (mostly immigrants and the children of immigrants) who define themselves primarily by transnational affinities—memberships in networks and interest circles that span continents."

- **The Transient Internationals.** These are "temporary U.S. residents from abroad, both students and professionals," Yang notes. "While they have always been difficult for marketers to reach, they enjoy a greater degree of infrastructure today than ever before and are a viable niche market."[70]

national and cultural identities. Is "one nation, indivisible" still a logical outcome? If not, is it possible to maintain a polyglot nation that is "fractured into many separate, disconnected communities" or Booth asks, will we "evolve into something in between, a pluralistic society that will hold on to some core ideas about citizenship and capitalism, but with little meaningful interaction among groups?"[71]

Samuel Huntington expressed similar concerns in the March/April 2004 issue of *Foreign Policy* Magazine. While many Hispanics have been U.S. citizens for centuries, concentrated migration from the south has accelerated dramatically during the latter part of the 20th and the early 21st centuries. Huntington observes that many of these immigrants "have not assimilated into mainstream U.S. culture, forming instead their own linguistic enclaves, from Los Angeles to Miami."[72]

Business Week, in a 2004 article by Brian Grow, presented "three broad possibilities" for newly arrived Hispanic immigrants. Similar scenarios could have applied to many groups during historic waves of immigration. Grow's scenarios include:

- **Melting In**—Following the path of most other immigrant groups and gradually melding into American life, giving up Spanish, and marrying outside their ethnicity.

- **Acculturation**—Speaking both Spanish and English and retaining much of their own culture and ties with their home country, even as they adapt to U.S. lifestyles.

- **Mexifornia**—Remaining in Spanish-speaking enclaves and setting the cultural and political agendas in soon-to-be majority-Hispanic states, like California and Texas.[73]

■ Constantly Reframing Our Community and National Identities

Unless we celebrate and honor differences, we will likely become— or reinforce an already established—cleft community or cleft nation. A shared identity will come only from celebrating and honoring our differences and by constantly looking for what we have in common. Each community and nation, in an increasingly mobile world, will be challenged to constantly reframe its identity or face division, dissension, and lost potential.

Concern about Enclaves

At the turn of the 21st century, approximately 81 percent of people in Hidalgo County (McAllen, Tex.) were Hispanic; 62.3 percent of people in Honolulu, Hawaii, and 36.2 percent of people in San Francisco, Calif., were Asian.[74] In Detroit, Mich., 83.5 percent were Black.[75]

Will the United States and other countries become cleft nations, with people living in enclaves? Will our communities become—or remain—cleft communities? Or will they experience a Diaspora, as people come together in a more unified way? The Civil War treatise, "A nation divided against itself cannot stand," still echoes.

Yet, we have seen another phenomenon that can be described as melding, melting, and mixing. Demographer Harold Hodgkinson points out that world-renowned golfer Tiger Woods is a good example of the multiracial/multi-ethnic world citizen, since he is Cablinasian—Caucasian, Black, Native American, and Asian.[76]

Former President Jimmy Carter eloquently observed, "We are, of course, a nation of differences. Those differences don't make us weak. They're the source of our strength."

Whether the United States or any other nation hopes to be a melting pot or just a magnificent salad or stew, people young and old need to understand the importance of equal opportunity if they hope to maintain some sense of sustainable progress and domestic tranquility. One of the greatest challenges facing the United States and other "democratic" societies is the responsibility to prove to the world that people from all over the globe can live together in harmony.[77]

Stereotypes . . . Complimentary or Downright Mean?

Consider the following terms we too often use to describe certain groups: pushy and aggressive, cheap, great singers, clannish, family-oriented, great athletes, chauvinistic, lazy and shiftless, hardworking and ambitious, heavy drinkers, great imitators, smart, sly and sinister, very religious, dumb, uneducated, wealthy and powerful, warm and expressive, big on machismo, or violent and hot-tempered.

"Basically, a stereotype is an exaggerated belief, oversimplification, or uncritical judgement about a category," says William Helmreich in his book, *The Things They Say Behind Your Back*. Why do we use stereotypes? "Frequently, they eliminate the need to learn about people, especially for those who do not, either because of fear or sheer laziness, wish to make the effort," he speculates.

"Do stereotypes actually cause prejudice?" Helmreich asks. "Not necessarily. More often, they justify prejudice, but in doing so they reinforce prejudice. It's difficult to separate one from the other," he concludes.[78]

One thing is certain. Stereotypes—while often the basis for jokes that even those who are being stereotyped sometimes enjoy—can cause pain, lead to crimes and even genocide, become self-fulfilling prophesies, create a sense of exclusion, and form a roadblock to social cohesion.

■ News Stories . . . Today and Tomorrow

Issues raised by society's ability to refresh itself with first-generation immigrants will likely create lead stories for decades to come.

The following are topics of both recent and possible future articles and news reports. A few scenarios include:

- Immigrants move to generally large gateway cities while long-time residents of those cities move to the South, the Northwest, or a variety of smaller cities in various parts of the country.

- Tensions grow between and among ethnic groups over political power and claims to the local marketplace.

- Children of some first-generation immigrants, whose parents work endless hours to support their families, find their children caught up in the pop culture. Yet, some of those children are frustrated, sensing that they can't afford to be a part of what surrounds them.

- Racial or ethnic groups, who feel under-served, create their own institutions, for their exclusive use.

- Cinco de Mayo joins St. Patrick's Day as a day of celebration in growing numbers of communities.[79]

- Great American success stories celebrate leading members of society whose parents or grandparents paved the way for them by spreading acres of concrete, laying miles of bricks, hanging a sea of drywall, clearing bins of asbestos, mowing millions of acres of lawns, harvesting mega-tons of fruits and vegetables, and digging ditches whose combined depth will never be measured or celebrated.

■ Educators and Students . . . A Demographic Disconnect

"Minority children make up about 40 percent of the nation's elementary and secondary student enrollment, while just 13.5 percent of teachers are members of racial or ethnic minorities," reported *Education Week*, citing data from the National Center for Education Statistics (NCES).[80]

In the same article, Mildred Hudson, CEO of Recruiting New Teachers, noted that while an estimated 2.5 million teachers would be needed over a 10-year period, only limited resources have been aimed at making sure those teachers reflect the United States' growing racial and ethnic diversity.[81] In a January 1998 column, Bob Chase, then-president of the NEA, declared, "Classrooms everywhere are starved for good teachers of color, particularly black and Hispanic men."[82]

Studies have shown a similar pattern for school administrators. Some of the most recent data come from a 2000 *Study of the American School Superintendency*, conducted by the American Association of School Administrators. That study indicated only about 5 percent of superintendents were "persons of color" up from 4 percent in 1992.[83]

■ Minority Student Achievement

Equal educational opportunity for *all* is a continuing quest. In some ways, it is at the heart of our commitment to a truly pluralistic society. Whether we call it "minority student achievement" or "the need for a level playing field," the urgency is intensifying with the growing diversity of the population. It is a fact that we need to fully develop the talents and abilities of all students, whatever their races, ethnicities, or social and economic backgrounds. As we realize the gravity of the situation and the penalty that comes with the cost of neglect, concern will deepen about our ability to ensure all students succeed.

Test scores of traditional minority groups have shown improvement over time, but the challenge continues to be urgent. Education systems constantly disaggregate testing information in attempts to analyze problems and develop solutions, which often lie outside the school and sometimes seem beyond their grasp. Many educators are increasingly concerned about an over-reliance on testing, which can lead to self-fulfilling prophecies.

Even though college entrance exams are highly influenced by the percentage of students who actually take the tests, the American Youth Policy Forum (AYPF), in a 2004 publication *Raising Minority Achievement*, reported that "minority" students scored, on average, 45 to 100 points lower than their "majority" counterparts. [84]

The Urban Institute noted a similar finding in a 2001 report. Of White students who entered ninth grade in U.S. schools, nearly 75 percent graduated with a regular diploma in 12th grade. That compared with 50.2 percent of Black, 53.2 percent of Hispanic, 76.8 percent of Asian/Pacific Islander, and 51.1 percent of Native American/Alaska Native students.[85] The AYPF report indicates that by the time young people reach their mid-twenties, those graduation rates are somewhat higher, because some obtain General Equivalency Degrees (GEDs).

In 1999, according to the AYPF report, 36.1 percent of White, 16.5 percent of African American, and 14.4 percent of Latino high school graduates went on to complete bachelor's degrees. In that year, "whites were twice as likely to obtain a bachelor's degree than their African American and Latino peers. Asians out-performed all other subgroups in the competition of postsecondary degrees, except for the associate's degree."[86]

The Minority Student Achievement Network, in June 2003, addressed the question, "What is the relationship between race and achievement in our schools?" Noting gaps, the Network also pointed to substantial numbers of high-achieving students in what have traditionally been called "minority" groups. "Causes of achievement gaps are complex and include school, community, home, and societal factors," the Network concluded. "Eliminating the gap is not only the right thing to do, but it is essential to ensure the future of our democracy."[87] (Readers can find more information on this issue in the chapter focusing on the poverty trend.)

Whatever the demographics of any student's community, each will be expected to live, work, and thrive in a highly diverse world.

That's a reality with monumental implications for every education system, community, and nation.

■ Implications for Society

Diversity

The move from a majority/minority to a minority/minority society has substantial implications for our individual and collective futures. Here are just a few.

- Immigration will continue to be a hot-button issue as society ages, creating an ongoing need to welcome people who will enhance the work force. Many will become full-fledged citizens.

- Thoughtful political leaders will realize the imperative of emphasizing inclusion and diversity, versus exclusion and division.

- Political consensus may become more difficult as candidates and office-holders target their appeals for support to those groups whose numbers are expanding, pitting one group against another, rather than focusing on the common good.

- "Ethnic societies" will likely increase, sharing information and bringing people of similar backgrounds together to enjoy the food, dance, and other cultural glue that binds them.

- Communities and nations will wrestle with the need to adjust their identities to more closely match the reality of current and future demographics and ensure people regularly celebrate not only their differences, but also what they have in common.

- Media and marketers will appeal to language and cultural groups in an ongoing quest to sell their products and services.

A Class Picture

If we could have taken a national class picture around the turn of the 21st century, it would have looked like this.

- In **elementary and high schools**, 31.1 million students would have been non-Hispanic White; 7.9 million would have been Black; 2.1 million would have been Asian or Pacific Islander; and 7.3 million would have been Hispanic (of any race).

- At the **college level**, 8.4 million were non-Hispanic White; 1.7 million were Black; 743,000 were Asian or Pacific Islander; and 1.1 million were Hispanic (of any race).

- Moving to **graduate school**, 2.4 million were non-Hispanic White; 271,000 Black; 298,000 Asian or Pacific Islander; and 170,000 Hispanic (of any race).

Not in the picture: Dropout rates varied from 3.8 percent for non-Hispanic Whites to 6 percent for Blacks, 4.8 percent for Asian and Pacific Islanders, and 7.1 percent for Hispanics (of any race). Nine percent of students with families earning less than $20,000 dropped out of the picture, compared with 3.8 percent of those earning from $20,000 to $39,999, and 2.3 percent of those earning $40,000 or more.[88]

- Diversity within racial and ethnic groups will lead to serious questioning of those who say they "represent them." Demographics will likely be joined by psychographics, which is more focused on attitudes, values, and what motivates people.

- Minorities will increasingly affect the well-being of the majority, as non-Hispanic Whites (as well as others) get older and become more dependent on the productivity of minority workers to support everything from pension plans to geriatric services.

- Public-policy concerns such as equal opportunity, equal access, segregation/integration, fair housing, job discrimination, affirmative action, student loans and scholarships, concentrated poverty, and equal treatment under the law will continue to command significant attention.

- Demand will grow for the resolution of immigration issues raised by homeland security.

- Understanding will grow about the international marketplace and the key roles played by people who live in one country but whose cultural and social ties are in another.

- Foreign policy, international economic growth and development, human rights, and other issues will require a substantial understanding of the people, histories, and cultures of the world. The handling of those issues will increasingly reflect the stark realities of interdependence in a world that is shrinking because of advances in transportation and communication.

- Communities, states/provinces/cantons, and nations will focus increased attention on a balance between "what divides us and what unites us."

■ Implications for Education

Diversity

- **Improving achievement for *all* students.** Perhaps no other issue raised by this trend is as critical as making sure each and every student has an equal opportunity to receive a sound education. Challenges, even conflict, will likely grow as some students and their schools fail to meet benchmarks on high-

Exercising Power . . . Responsibly

"The U.S. and Western Europe, accustomed for the past 300 years to running the world, are a tiny percentage of the world's markets and labor pool. They continue to exercise power that is disproportionate to their size, but court disaster if they do not exercise that power responsibly. Anyone who does not believe that things can change should consult the histories of the Soviet Union and South Africa."

Douglas Greenberg, President and CEO, Survivors of the Shoah Visual History Foundation

stakes tests. Schools will continue to disaggregate test scores, hoping to focus on filling achievement gaps. Debate will escalate around whether the tests are a fair measure for individual students. Public Advocacy for Kids' Arnold Fege comments that at least two types of students might suffer disadvantage, those who "do not experience success," and those who "do not have an opportunity to learn in diverse settings."

• **Providing inclusive, multicultural education.** Why should we be concerned about multiple cultures, especially if our own community is not very diverse? The answer is simple. Wherever students grow up, they ultimately will have to survive and thrive in a multicultural world, made even smaller by instant communication and rapid transportation. Betsy Rogers, 2003 U.S. National Teacher of the Year, declares that an education that helps students understand multiple cultures "must become a part of our curriculum K-12."

• **Pursuing social cohesion, seeking common denominators, and adjusting our identity.** While we are learning about and celebrating our diversity, we also need to help students, staff, and communities find common denominators. Communication that helps diverse people discover what they have in common promotes social cohesion, the glue that holds us together. Seeing the world as an extended neighborhood is a good place to start.[89] Many communities and their education systems will need to consider adopting new, even more inclusive identities to match their evolving demographics.

"Clearly, big city school systems have already begun to make this transition," Fege says, "but diversity is moving into the suburbs and rural areas of the nation, and school districts need to be prepared." He adds, "Integration of the public space, as well as private spaces, will be essential, and local communities as well as nations will need to engage in activities leading to cultural understanding. Town meetings, community conversations, interfaith communication, and tolerance for differences, especially religious differences, must be pursued."

- **Attracting and keeping excellent teachers and role models.** The percentage of minority students will continue to increase, but many education systems have been hard-pressed to adequately tap the talent pool of minority teachers and administrators to serve as role models for students. Marc Ecker, 2004 president of the National Middle School Association, sees "the recruitment of ethnic minorities" as a continuing challenge. In an effort to fill the gap, some education systems are refocusing their recruitment efforts, encouraging members of minority groups to pursue careers in education, and even attracting teachers from other countries.

- **Helping students, parents, educators, and community members understand a rapidly changing world.** Ignorance is not an excuse. Students, parents, educators, and communities need to be prepared for the educational implications of a society that is becoming even more plural and a world that is increasingly complex. Rick Kaufman, former executive director of public engagement and communication for the Jefferson County Public Schools in Colorado, points out the need to build community-wide understanding quickly because "societal issues spill over to schools as well."

- **Insisting on preparation and professional development programs that address diversity.** We need to be sure that preparation programs at colleges and universities and professional development programs at local, state, national, and international levels change with the times. Everyone needs to understand how to work with students, staff, and community in a highly diverse world.

- **Catching up with the students.** Growing numbers of students are ahead of the curve in understanding the need for an education that prepares them to constructively engage with people who might seem different from themselves. "Students will require adults to make a transition to the new minority/minority world," suggests Rosa Smith, president of the Schott Foundation in Cambridge, Mass., and a former superintendent in Columbus, Ohio, and Racine, Wis.

- **Developing an international focus.** The student who is prepared for the future will need a grounding not just in the pop culture of his or her own country but in the histories, cultures, people, and languages of the world. All students, wherever they live, need a more global perspective. What happens thousands of miles away has repercussions for our lives, our security, our economy, and our happiness. Tolerance and an appreciation for diversity will become more important than ever, if we hope to achieve a peaceful world.

- **Developing language and other communication skills.** Immigrant students, in varying degrees, are often fluent in more than one language, through sheer necessity and will, if not through language courses in their native or adopted countries. Rosa

Smith recommends that all students eventually be required "to be fluent in at least three languages." She also notes that, in preparing for this international focus, schools will need updated and honest versions of world and American history and religions.

Making this shift will require effort. "Language diversity is actually lower now than it was at the beginning of the 20th century, and strategies for coping with it are weaker," according to the Shoah Foundation's Douglas Greenberg.

And not all immigrant students are fluent in English either. "Schools need to continue to improve programs designed to help English language learners (from other countries) become successful in competitive school environments," urges Carol Peck, president and CEO of the Rodel Charitable Foundation in Arizona and a former school superintendent. She warns, "Early failures lead to discouragement and dropouts."

• **Becoming culturally sensitive.** C. Lynn Babcock, 2000 president of the National Association of Elementary School Principals, points out the challenge of dealing with "continued lack of understanding, acceptance, and tolerance of those who are different."[90] While many educators are well traveled and have extensive international experience working with people of all ages in many cultures, others are not. Education systems need to declare the importance of cultural sensitivity as a basic requirement for all educators, even those whose interests have traditionally stopped at the edge of the desk, the classroom door, or the boundaries of their community.

• **Communicating effectively with the community.** "Let's send a note home." It's still a legitimate way to send a message, but it's far from a guarantee that we've actually communicated. Many school systems are facing a virtual explosion of diversity. Today, if we hope to get a message through, we need to consider everything from language to preferred media as well as the cultural weight of what

From the Papers:

- "Today . . . more than one-third of the 439,000 students attending the Chicago Public Schools are Hispanic. The enrollment of the nation's third-largest school district . . . is now 51 percent black, 36 percent Hispanic, 9 percent white, 3 percent Asian-American, and less than 1 percent Native American."
Education Week, March 10, 2004 [91]

- "The Maryland counties nearest Washington accounted for 80 percent of the state's growth over the past decade, powered by huge increases in the number of Blacks, Asian Americans, and Hispanics, the Census Bureau reported today."
Washington Post, March 20, 2001 [92]

- "Despite the ruling of the U.S. Supreme Court nearly a half-century ago that school segregation was unconstitutional, the nation's schools became increasingly more separated by race in the 1990s, according to a report by the Harvard Civil Rights Project."
Education Week, August 8, 2001 [93]

- "The growing number of Hispanics is a catalyst, not only for discussing the changing face of our national demographics, but also for discussing the changing face of our democracy" suggests Juan Figueroa, president, Puerto Rican Legal Defense and Education Fund.
The Seattle Times, May 10, 2001 [94]

we say and how we say it. The same is true for listening as we try to understand needs and deal with problems. Cultural sensitivity and effective communication go hand-in-hand.

- **Considering categories.** Certainly since Aristotle, most people connected with the Western world have been committed to putting things and people into categories. We do it with race, ethnicity, and other demographic characteristics as we try to ensure equal educational opportunity for all. However, those lines have become blurred because of melding, melting, and mixing. The education system and society-at-large will feel continuing pressure to better understand that students might be a blend of several races, ethnicities, and cultures, and don't fit easily into any preconceived category.

- **Investing in all children.** We simply cannot afford to lose the talents, abilities, interests, and energies of any child anywhere in the world because of a lack of opportunity for education. Let's start by seeing education as a worthwhile investment, not as a mere expense.

■ Questions and Activities

1. Study Figures T2.1 and T2.2 in this chapter devoted to "Projected U.S. Population by Race/Ethnicity" and "Projected U.S. Population of Children." Despite the demographic makeup of your own community, what implications do these trends have for education in general? For business and industry? For government? For individuals?

2. In your own words, describe social cohesion. Why is it important? What can we do to improve social cohesion?

3. What is likely to happen when one group dominates all others in a diverse society?

4. Identify and briefly discuss three factors that affect the diversity of a population.

5. Compare immigration patterns in the United States in 1920 and 2000.

6. Consider your own community. How would you describe its "identity" compared with 30 years ago?

7. Suggest six ways you would improve intercultural understanding within a school or college.

8. In a few paragraphs, what does "inclusion and diversity" v. "exclusion and division" mean to you?

■ Readings

1. U.S. Census Bureau. (various years). *National population projections, summary files by age, sex, race, and Hispanic origin.* Available at http://www.census.gov/population

2. Kotkin, J. (1992). *Tribes . . . How race, religion, and identity determine success in the new global economy.* New York: Random House, Inc.

3. Huntington, S.P. (2004). The Hispanic challenge. *Foreign Policy Magazine.* March-April 2004, 30-45.

4. Population data from a current world almanac.

Trend 3

Knowledge! It's the engine of the new economy.

Social and intellectual capital will become economic drivers, intensifying competition for well-educated people.

Industrial Age → Global Knowledge/Information Age

We often long for "the good old days," and nostalgia takes us back to the golden moments. But as generations pass, memories continue to fade of those days when most workers earned their living by the sweat of their brows and the strength of their backs.

Millions of people continue to strain their bodies to make a living, but today they also often have strained bank accounts. That's because social and intellectual capital have become the prime sources of wealth in our new economy. Today, who you know and what you know both count.

■ Intellectual Capital

"Intellectual capital is the intellectual material—the knowledge, information, intellectual property, experience—that can be put to use to create wealth." This now-classic definition, penned by author Thomas Stewart, first appeared in a 1997 issue of *Knowledge Inc.*[95] Many who read it found the idea of intellectual capital "an interesting concept."

Today, more and more people are discovering that this accelerating trend has a direct impact on their bottom line, in industries ranging from manufacturing cars to improving student achievement in schools.

Stewart, in his 1999 book, *Intellectual Capital*, zeroes in on what he calls the "educational pay premium" and singles out one demographic group to make his point. In 1979, he says, "male college graduates commanded income 49 percent greater than men with just high school diplomas." In 1993, just 14 years later, he observes, "the education premium was 80 percent." It is a fact that education generally pays for people in every demographic group, even though equity remains somewhat elusive. Stewart's revelation is another indication that intellectual capital, fueled by education, is becoming an even more powerful centerpiece of a sound economy.[96]

Once upon a time, we referred to them as "the intangibles" or "blue sky." Now, we've discovered that these hard-to-measure phenomena have value that exceeds anything that could be contained in a warehouse, observes University of Southern California distinguished professor and leadership expert Warren Bennis. Even when people claim they have no way of measuring intellectual capital, he muses, "[W]hen you ask them how much of their brainpower they think they are using on the job, the standard response is about 20 percent." He adds, "So if we only added another 10 percent to that, just think what our organizations would be like." It's a side of "efficiency" that deserves our attention.[97]

■ Efficiency Redefined

Tension grows between "do more of the same" and "innovation"

Consider for a moment that you are visiting with a traditional efficiency expert. Here are a couple of things you might hear.

- "How many widgets did we move today? If each person moved five more widgets, our productivity would increase, and we'd need fewer people."

- "Let's squeeze out that higher paid, experienced person and bring in someone who'll work for a third the salary."

That's part of the logic that has driven the efficiency movement.

Efficiency has another side, however; if everyone is so busy moving widgets that they don't have time to think, what new ideas, what innovations might we be missing that could take our organization successfully into the future? What do we lose when experience and insight go out the door? What happens when hidebound commitment to the status quo drives creativity out?

In business, competitive intelligence has become a major issue. Whatever our institution, we need to attract the best people we can and encourage them to think beyond what's currently on top of the desk. In short, we need to continuously expand our intellectual capital.

Thomas Stewart credits new technologies, coupled with innovative management, as keys to addressing 21st-century efficiency. "The power of Amsterdam, when it was the richest city in the world, was in its warehouses," he says. Since then, telecommunications and computer technology, coupled with creative genius, have made the idea of just-in-time manufacturing and delivery a reality. "GE Lighting has replaced dozens of warehouses with databases. A big saving," Stewart remarks.[98]

■ Social Capital

Everything starts with relationships. While we form relationships because it seems like the right thing to do, we seldom consider their value to our bottom-line success. "The problem facing almost all leaders in the future will be how to develop their organization's social architecture so that it actually generates intellectual capital," Bennis points out.[99]

Harvard Professor Robert Putnam placed social capital directly in the spotlight in both his classic work, *Bowling Alone*, and presentations at numerous conferences. For example, at a 2000 White

House Conference on the New Economy, Putnam told a gathering of leaders that, "The basic idea of social capital is that networks have value . . . for transmitting information . . . for undergirding cooperation and reciprocity."[100]

What often "inhibits people from exploiting economic opportunities that are available to them?" Francis Fukuyama, in his now classic book, *Trust*, explains it as "a deficit of what sociologist James Coleman has called 'social capital': the ability of people and organizations to work together for common purposes in groups and organizations." Fukuyama adds, "The concept of human capital, widely used and understood among economists, starts from the premise that capital today is embodied less in land, factories, tools, and machines than in the knowledge and skills of human beings."[101]

"Economic development is fueled not just by stocks of land, labor, and financial capital but also by education (human capital) and healthy ecosystems (ecological capital)," says Gary Gardner, director of research for the Worldwatch Institute. "By the 1990s, many theorists added social capital (community building) to the list because of its importance as a lubricant and glue in many communities: it greases the wheels of communication and interaction, which in turn strengthens the bonds that community members have with one another," Gardner adds.[102]

We often think of "the team" as the cabinet, the faculty and staff, the leadership council, or give it some other title to limit or explain its scope. However, to capture the brilliance—the intellectual capital—that exists in the organization and community, we need to broaden the social circle. John Hoyle, professor of educational administration at Texas A&M University and a noted education scholar, cautions colleagues that "communications technologies will become smaller," meaning more portable. With their own miniature base station, people might become "even more independent and less interested in improving social capital," Hoyle suggests.

Limit the circle, and you narrow the range of ideas that will refresh the organization. Broaden it, and intellectual wealth blossoms, paving the way for creating a future.

■ Entrepreneurs at Work in the New Economy

Intellectual entrepreneurs are constantly pursuing ideas. They create a climate that stimulates creativity and innovation and welcomes the challenge of new thinking. Everyone, including students, needs to understand what it will take to constructively move forward in a world of accelerating change.

So, what is an entrepreneur? According to the National Council on Economic Education (NCEE), an entrepreneur is a person who, in essence, does the following things: sees an opportunity, makes a plan, starts an organization/business, manages the organization, and receives a profit/creates a benefit.

NCEE aims to help students "develop the real-life skills they need to succeed: to be able to think and choose responsibly as consumers, savers, investors, citizens, members of the workforce, and effective participants in the global economy."[103] A study by the Gallup Organization found that nearly seven out of 10 youth ages 14 to 19 are interested in becoming entrepreneurs or learning more about entrepreneurship, Stephanie Bell-Rose and Steve Mariotti reported in an *Education Week* commentary.[104]

Let's get a glimpse of a few entrepreneurs at work.

Microsoft: "Major companies such as Microsoft own nothing of value except knowledge," says MIT economist Lester Thurow. "Fighting to defend and extend the domain of their intellectual property is how they play the economic game," he adds in his book, *Building Wealth*.[105] Microsoft's primary value consists of copyrights, trademarks, patents, and relationships with its employees, customers, and suppliers. It is a classic example of a company whose value is based on social and intellectual capital.

Bristol-Myers Squibb: This leading pharmaceutical company installed new intellectual capital management software, recognizing "that the success of its research hinges on how quickly and easily its scientists can harness its fast-growing wealth of knowledge." Verity, Inc., which helped the company find a solution to managing its intellectual wealth, was recognized by the data management community as one of the nation's top leaders in handling business intelligence.[106]

Century 21 Real Estate: This company has long franchised what it knows through offices in communities across the United States and in other parts of the world. Its parent company, Cendant, has had a franchise in Taiwan for several years called Senyi Real Estate. As of 2004, the company was franchising its pool of intellectual capital in China, one of the world's fastest growing markets. A *Forbes* Magazine report from Shanghai notes that the names of these Chinese companies translate to "Happy Rise Real Estate" and "Great Rainbow Real Estate."[107]

General Electric: After Tom Stewart wrote a seminal 1991 article about this phenomenon, he met with GE Chairman Jack Welch, who told him, "Intellectual capital is what it's all about. Releasing the ideas of your people is what we're trying to do, and what we've got to do if we're going to win."[108]

■ Creating Intellectual Entrepreneurs

A New Focus for Education

Educators sometimes recoil when they hear, "We need to increase the entrepreneurial skills of our students." They are concerned that they're being instructed to simply turn out workers who have a laser focus on the bottom line. But entrepreneurial skills are essen-

Kodak: "Film, Digital, or Both?"

That is the question.

Say the word "Kodak," and you immediately think of pictures. It's a company with an enviable history of innovation and service and a commitment to continuous improvement. Until recently, however, photography was a study in composition and chemistry.

Then along came digital photography. Kodak was faced with a choice, go one direction or the other or follow both paths—chemical and digital. The company has done the latter, and was flexible enough to do it because of its longstanding dedication to innovation and improvement.

The educational system is going through a somewhat similar challenge as the world moves from an industrial to a global knowledge/information age.

tial in both the for-profit and nonprofit sectors. It helps to be entrepreneurial if you want to do well economically; however, if you want to improve education or get support for a park in your neighborhood, you also need to have that entrepreneurial spirit. As educators, if we hope to produce students who will be reasonably well prepared for the rest of their lives, we need to help them become intellectual entrepreneurs who are both curious and persistent as they pursue a world of possibilities.

MIT economist Lester Thurow makes clear that "without entrepreneurs, economies become poor and weak. The old will not exit; the new cannot enter." The emerging knowledge/information age encourages people to go over, around, or through barriers to get things done.[109]

■ Getting Educators and Community on Board

Capturing the Ingenuity

Schools and colleges have a golden opportunity to capitalize on the social and intellectual capital that surrounds them. For example, increasing numbers of educational institutions are bringing diverse groups of people together to hear about societal trends. They're asking them to pool their thinking about the implications of those trends for the educational system, for what students need to know and be able to do, and even for economic growth and development and quality of life in their communities. They are using enlightened, future-oriented leadership to capture the ingenuity of staff and community, and focusing their intellectual capital on the pressing challenge of constantly creating a future. At the same time, by using the process, they are building broader understanding of social and intellectual capital—forces that are increasingly at the heart of economic value.

Let's face it, school systems, colleges/universities, and other educational institutions have been in the intellectual and social capital business for a long time. What should be a major source of intellectual capital in every community? Where do we develop relationships that often last us the rest of our lives? The answer, of course, is "School!" The educational institution should be among the key venues where divergent ideas coalesce to form new knowledge.

■ Key Considerations

For social and intellectual entrepreneurs

Here are a few considerations for education and other institutions as the need to create entrepreneurs hits the workplace and the classroom:

- **Teamwork, plus Management and Entrepreneurial Skills.** Many graduates of our schools will likely spin off from large and small companies to become freelancers, free agents, or consultants. To function effectively, they will need management skills, including some idea of how to manage their time and a budget. They'll also need entrepreneurial skills to help them figure out how to take an idea to market, whether it is in the for-profit or nonprofit sector. In addition to having an opportunity to use their own unique talents and abilities, they'll need to be adept at working as a member of a team.

- **Information, Relationships, and Economic Value.** In November of 1999, *beauty.com* went online. In February 2000, *beauty.com* was sold to *drugstores.com* for $42 million.[110] What was on the block when one bought the other? Intellectual and social capital . . . information and relationships.

- **Staying in Touch . . . and Flexibility.** Organizations need to stay in touch to avoid freezing themselves around that one product or service "that has always worked for us." McDonald's discovered people were moving toward healthier diets. Levi-Strauss had to deal with the drift of people toward softer fabrics. Nike had to contend with a movement toward the brown shoe. For educators, the blackboard morphed into a whiteboard and PowerPoint presentations; filmstrips became flat-screen 16:9 aspect ratio digital video; and information frozen on a page was supplemented by constantly updated Web pages and sophisticated computer software. On one hand, those who provide education are faced with a growing demand to meet certain standards and prepare students to do well on often narrowly focused high-stakes tests. On the other hand, they are asked to personalize, to provide an education that considers each student's interests, talents, and abilities. Flexibility is fast becoming a virtue.

A Note of Caution: Drew Allbritten, former executive director of the Council for Exceptional Children, cautions that too firm a connection to social and intellectual capital could seem to limit value to academic-related intelligence, overlooking "the skill sets of those who are vocationally oriented." Too narrow a definition of social and intellectual capital could prove to be counter-productive, he warns. Albritten's concern is a good reminder that information and relationships are important in every discipline and every walk of life.

■ Knowledge Workers

The whole idea of knowledge workers isn't new. In 1910, Norman Angell claimed in his book, *The Great Illusion*, that "brainpower has replaced manpower, horsepower, and material power as the main force of our age." Peter Drucker planted seeds for popularizing the idea in the 1960s, according to Bill Emmott, editor in chief of *The Economist*, in his 2003 book, *20:21 Vision*.[111]

Education has been a driving force in supporting the development of knowledge workers. Even though the system itself is largely based on an industrial model and is in the process of making needed change, it has promoted equal opportunity. That direction alone has extended the circle and opened the door for growing numbers of people who must be capable of thriving in a global knowledge/information age.

Concerns mushroomed in the early 2000s about the slow growth in jobs, even as the economy showed signs of expanding. Manufacturing jobs seemed to be going overseas. Few were sure, as they looked to the future, whether the economic sun was rising or setting.

Yet, the March 2004 issue of *Business 2.0* carried an article listing the "Top 10 Boom Towns in America." These were metropolitan areas that focused on attracting knowledge workers for knowledge industries. Wisely, these communities established themselves as magnets for people capable of using their know-how to expand often longstanding and traditional industrial bases. They also hope to serve as magnets for people who might use their know-how to not only lift traditional industries but also invent new ones. However, Paul Kaihla, who wrote the article, cautioned, "Far more than in previous rebounds, job demand will favor the 'haves'—the most skilled, best educated segments of the work force—over the 'have-nots' in low skills, low impact, rote professions."[112]

The Rise of the Creatives. Richard Florida, in what may become a classic work titled *The Rise of the Creative Class*, notes that, as we began the 21st century, knowledge workers made up about 30 percent of the U.S. work force but accounted for about 50 percent of total wages.[113] In charting these "creatives," Paul Kaihla points out they comprised about 35.8 percent of employees in Raleigh-Durham, N.C.; 38.7 percent in San Jose, Calif.; 39.6 percent in Washington, D.C.; 34.3 percent in Austin, Texas; and 28.7 percent in Atlanta, Ga. Those were his top five boomtown picks.

"Hot professions," Kaihla reports, will include computer scientists; cardiology technologists; lawyers; public relations professionals; civil engineers; biological scientists and technicians; security and commodity brokers; architects, surveyors, and cartographers; civil engineers; interior and exterior designers; and a host of others.[114]

The intensifying demand for knowledge workers poses a growing challenge for the education system and society at large. If a country doesn't meet the education need, people from other parts of the world will line up for the jobs. If a country doesn't produce jobs for knowledge workers, then they will likely look for another place on the globe where they can profit from their creative genius.

■ Cool Ideas and Hot Potatoes

It's all pretty exciting. In this new economy, driven by social and intellectual capital, we'll be able to move in new directions and develop products and services that are beyond our imaginations. In the process, we're likely to raise the dander of some people who "don't want to go there."

New generations of technologies are speeding up everything. What once may have taken decades is now accomplished in minutes.

Urban Warfare . . . American Cities Fight for Talent....

"Brain-Gain Cities Attract Educated Youth"

That was a front-page headline in the November 9, 2003, *Washington Post*. Writer Blaine Harden wasted no time in making his point: "In a Darwinian fight for survival, American cities are scheming to steal each other's young. They want ambitious young people with graduate degrees in such fields as genome science, bioinformatics, and entrepreneurial management skills." Harden observed, "Migrants on the move to winner-take-all cities are most accurately identified by education and ambition, rather than by skin color or country of birth. They are part of a striving class of young Americans for whom race, ethnicity, and geographic origin tend to be less meaningful than professional achievement, business connections, and income."[115]

With less time to fully understand and adjust to new and exciting ideas that will open a panoply of economic possibilities, we can expect a range of reactions. Here are a few:

- Early adopters are likely to say, "This is the coolest thing I've ever seen. Count me in."

- In an economy driven by intellectual capital, property rights will grow as an issue. Perhaps the most profound of these concerns at the turn of the 21st century was, "Who owns the genome?" Expect disputes over intellectual property.

- The world's greatest researchers are largely online. Sharing of information that might have taken 80 years at the time of Copernicus now takes eight minutes or eight seconds. Because of nearly instant exchanges of ideas and information—powered by both personal and cyber relationships—medical, transportation, communication, and other technologies are developing in quantum leaps, far outpacing the ability of some people to understand and adjust. In some cases, so many people worldwide are involved in scientific development that it is often difficult to pinpoint who exactly should be credited with an idea or an invention.

- Astute communities and countries will consider how they can attract industries that serve as magnets for knowledge workers. In some cases, communities will work with their education systems to grow their own.

- Public and private partnerships may form to encourage targeted investments that lead to improvements in local economies and quality of life but, at the same time, generate concerns about the delicate balance among business, government, and civil society.

- Conflicts will likely develop as new knowledge, which gives birth to innovative products and services, runs headlong into existing values, beliefs, biases, traditions, and lifestyles. Some who are offended will feel the world is moving too fast for them, or even that it's out to get them.

- Corruption may increase as some entrepreneurs who have little commitment to ethics try to make a fast buck at everyone else's expense.[116]

- Concerns about fairness will become a bottom-line issue that will bear on the reputation of a company or a country. For example, our commitment to bridging the gap between the technology-rich and technology-poor in our communities will increasingly stretch worldwide. Legitimacy will depend in large part on our commitment to strengthening civil society and empowering citizens with new economic tools.[117] Of the more than six billion people who occupied the planet at the turn of the century, half lived on less than $2 a day," according to former World Bank President James Wolfensohn. Fairness must be built on a foundation of encouraging rather than hoarding economic opportunity.[118]

■ Social and Intellectual Capital . . .

Our economy and future depend on it

Let's say it again. The future of any economy is tied directly to its ability to grow its social and intellectual capital. Our crystal ball tells us that setting the stage for the constant development of ideas and the free flow of information will be essential. Our individual and collective futures depend on it.

■ Implications for Society

Social and Intellectual Capital

The bottom line, whether it's establishment of a democratic society; improving education; enhancing the quality of life; ensuring justice; addressing issues such as security; promoting sales of products and services; or growing local, national, and world economies, will increasingly depend on social and intellectual capital. The following implications are meant only to stimulate further thinking and, we hope, even heated conversation.

- The education system, at all levels, will be expected to become a center for social and intellectual capital and to prepare students for life in a global knowledge/information age.

- Leaders will be expected to regularly update employees and citizens about trends and issues affecting society and to engage them in discussions about possible implications for an even better future.

How can we measure the value?

A discourse on measuring the value of intangibles, such as social and intellectual capital, could fill volumes. While a full discussion of that topic is beyond the scope of this work, there are key questions that can help shed light on their contributions. Intellectual Capital Services, a firm with offices in London, is known for helping clients explore value creation in the new economy. ICS suggests questions such as:

- What are your organization's most valuable intellectual resources, and how do they contribute to sustainable value creation?

- Do you know what the return is on your investments in intellectual capital?

- Do you have appropriate tools for measuring and managing these intellectual resources to ensure maximum value is extracted from them?

- How do shareholders and other stakeholders perceive the value of your organization's intellectual capital? How could you maximize the value you deliver to them?[119]

- Those already in the work force will require constant professional development to help them contribute most effectively to the new economy.

- Communities will consider how they can become magnets for knowledge-based industries and produce the creative knowledge workers who can sustain them.

- Leaders will need to understand chaos or complexity theory, create and operate in a culture that accelerates and rewards the production of ideas, and thrive on the constant process of creating a future.

- Nations and communities will be challenged to constantly expand their technological infrastructure.

- Those who thrive will likely be those who never stop developing and/or providing the next generations of products and services.

- Imagination will become a key resource.

- Mindsets, which tend to be static, will need to be replaced by a mentality that the economic pie is not limited by its present dish. It can actually get larger.[120]

- Economic indices and factors that affect them—such as wholesale and retail sales, the cost price index, inflation, employment/unemployment, productivity, interest rates, and tax policy—will continue to be important. However, they will be joined by concerns about protection of intellectual property and quality-of-life issues for all people.

- Disputes about the ownership of intellectual property and ethics will help determine the nature, extent, appropriateness, and sustainability of certain types of progress.[121]

- As communication and transportation shrink the globe, society must realize that what affects one part of the world affects everyone—that the world is now interconnected.

■ Implications for Education

Social and Intellectual Capital

- **Preparing students for the future, not for the past.** Concern has grown that stringent standards and tests can create a box that actually inhibits the expansive education needed to thrive in a global knowledge/information age. While having clear expectations is important, "meeting the current standards may not provide kids with all of the conceptual and social skills that will be needed," says Jane Hammond, superintendent-in-residence at the Stupski Foundation in California and former superintendent of the Jefferson County Public Schools in Colorado.

  "Simply put, more kids need higher levels of education," adds Carol Peck, president and CEO of Rodel Charitable Foundation in Arizona and a former National Superintendent of the Year. "We need to continue to drive the accepted norms to higher levels, placing a greater percentage of students in what were once considered classes reserved only for top-level students," she suggests.

  Thinking and reasoning will be accepted as basic skills, not only for students, but also for teachers/professors and administrators. School leaders need to "start with the future conditions our young people will inevitably face and then build back from there," says William Spady, president of Change Leaders, a Dillon, Colo.-based education consulting firm.[122]

- **Creating a new knowledge/information-based model for schools.** Tell someone that today's schools were created to mirror the needs of an industrial society, and you get little argument. What's needed is a system capable of preparing students for a global knowledge/information age. Considering that the world outside is moving at mind-bending speed, however, can schools and colleges make that change fast enough?

The best possible scenario is that educational institutions will actually lead the change, using futures tools to help redefine themselves. Schools will prepare students to be both employable and contributing members of society in a new era. Educators will adapt to working in a culture that expects them to stay in touch and find excitement in constantly creating the education system of the future. That is not likely to happen by simply freezing the system and demanding even more from an industrial-age model.

As a way of priming our thinking, Michael Silver, director and assistant professor of education administration at Seattle University, offers some suggestions. They include: learning at higher levels in intellectually challenging areas of knowledge, such as math and science; revising often longstanding schemes for curriculum tracking and student ability grouping; and helping students learn even more strategies for conflict resolution, problem solving, and communication that will lead to heightened emotional intelligence.

- **Getting students ready for the new economy.** One thing is becoming increasingly clear. People who are not prepared for an economy based on social and intellectual capital will stand a good chance of becoming "the new disadvantaged" in society. That means students will need to possess basic management and entrepreneurial skills. They will need to be able to collaborate with others, work in teams, and separate truth from fiction as they explore conflicting information that is expanding exponentially.

Students will need to be prepared to engage in critical and creative thinking, use a vast array of technological tools, understand and respect people of cultural backgrounds that may be different from their own, and possess high levels of perseverance and curiosity. On top of all that, they will need to be keenly aware of and sensitive to the ethical dimensions of their discoveries, conclusions, and actions.

A full understanding of the principles of democracy, learned through civic education and actual practice, will serve as a foundation for releasing the talents and abilities of students. Those principles, and the experiences schools provide in putting them into play, should increase the eagerness of students to consider the creative ideas of others.

- **Insisting on preparation and professional development that challenges habits and mindsets.** "We're no more effective than our people!" We've said it over and over again, and it's basically true. That's why we need to be sure we are preparing not only aspiring teachers and administrators but also seasoned veterans to understand the implications of the knowledge/information age for them, their students, and their communities.

Preparation programs are too often "out-of-touch with the realities of today's students and schools," says Carole Kennedy, who served for some time as principal-in-residence at the U.S. Department of Education.[123] Professional development programs will need to be frequent, with plenty of advice from thinkers and researchers and spirited peer-to-peer interaction, which is at the heart of a learning organization. Delivery systems? They will likely range from presentations and face-to-face interaction to online and other computer-assisted learning, including virtual reality.

Do we use research to improve education programs? Not enough. "One of the big problems in educational research is that people haven't understood the need to take it one step further and translate it into usable knowledge," Ellen Condliffe Lagemann, dean of the Harvard Graduate School of Education, told *Education Week*.[124] Obviously, the research needs to be relevant, readily available, and user friendly to have a chance at positively affecting practice.

- **Serving as a prime source of intellectual leadership for the community.** A credible intellectual leader sees things in context, understands both the big and little pictures, engages in both critical and creative thinking, and helps people understand not just what is happening but why it is meaningful and important.

Every educator should make a commitment to becoming an intellectual leader. We shouldn't even have to say it. Too often, however, people in education and other fields try to freeze the status quo rather than model behavior that stimulates creative thinking.

A good place to start is engaging staff and community in an informed discussion about how our education system and curriculum need to be shaped to effectively prepare students and the community for a new economy. This book is designed to stimulate those spirited conversations.

■ Questions and Activities

1. What is "intellectual capital?" "Social capital?"

2. Why are many communities trying to develop and attract more knowledge workers?

3. What are the characteristics of knowledge workers? Why is growth in the need for these workers important for education?

4. What are the six most important things you believe a school or college should do to prepare students for life in a global knowledge/information age?

5. How can we teach students to become more entrepreneurial in either or both the for-profit and nonprofit sectors?

6. What must happen for educational institutions to become more entrepreneurial in creating their futures?

7. Develop an agenda for a professional development program that will help educators better understand why and how they should move from industrial age toward information age schools and colleges.

8. Identify six characteristics of an intellectual leader.

■ Readings

1. Florida, R. (2004). *The rise of the creative class.* New York: Basic Books, a member of the Perseus Books Group.

2. Stewart, T. (1999). *Intellectual capital . . . The new wealth of organizations.* New York: Doubleday.

3. Gibson, R. (2002). *Rethinking the future.* London: Nicholas Brealey.

4. Fukuyama, F. (1995). *Trust . . . The social virtues and the creation of prosperity.* New York: Free Press Paperbacks.

5. Thurow, L.C. (1999). *Building wealth . . . The new rules for individuals, companies, and nations in a knowledge-based economy.* New York: HarperCollins.

6. Putnam, R. (2001). *Bowling alone.* New York: Simon & Schuster.

Trend 4

Convergence and miniaturization ... less is becoming more.

Technology will increase the speed of communication and the pace of advancement or decline.

Atoms → Bits

Macro → Micro → Nano → Subatomic

It's not just the technology. It's what it does to release the genius of students, staff, and community that will really make a difference.

■ The Dizzying Pace of Change

One of the most newsworthy weddings in the history of our planet celebrated the marriage of computing and telecommunication. Those life-changing nuptials spawned an entirely new era. The sharing of information and creation of new ideas that may once have taken 80 years or more is now happening in eight minutes or sometimes even in eight seconds. Forecaster Marvin Cetron reminds us that 80 percent of all the scientists who have ever lived in the history of humankind are alive today, and they're on the Internet.

The pace of change, fueled by technology, is unrelenting. In an interconnected world, educators, scientists, politicians, journalists, and people in general have access to instant information. No longer do we have to wait for the mail. We can send and receive messages, hold

A Personal Story

The morning after one of my speaking engagements with a school system, organizers arranged for me to meet with fourth-, fifth-, and sixth-graders, because teachers had created a futures unit based on my earlier trends book.

After meeting individually with some classes, I moved to an auditorium completely filled with elementary students. They'd been discussing the trends, and they were loaded with questions. The first student who came to the microphone, a fifth-grader, looked me in the eye and asked, "What are the limits of technology?"

I've learned a lot of things as a result of addressing audiences worldwide, including leaders in education, business, government, and other fields, including many students. One of those lessons is that we should never underestimate the inquisitiveness and wisdom of children. They are, after all, our future.

cyber conversations, and explore a cascade of data and ideas at the click of a mouse.

To revisit the fifth-grader's question (above): "What are the limits of technology?" We don't really know. We do know this, however: Those schools and colleges, communities, businesses, and countries that make appropriate use of technology to help unleash the genius of their people will likely move forward at an unprecedented rate. Those that don't will likely fall backward at the same dizzying pace.

■ The Art or Science of Being Wired

Remember when being "wired" meant you'd had one too many cups of coffee? Today, people are virtually wired. They are connected to their home, their office, and the world by cell phones, headsets, pagers, global positioning systems, and an expanding number and type of personal digital assistants (PDAs). They are pursued by email and drawn into electronic listserves, chatrooms, and virtual conferences, even as they surf the World Wide Web for key information. We're going wireless with Wi-Fi (wireless fidelity) and creating our own Web logs, widely known as blogs. Some bloggers, whose sites attract a great deal of attention, are into selling BlogAds at prices up to $5,000 a week as part of an emerging "blog economy."[125] With high-speed computers, we can now originate our own equivalent of a personal television network. We can also do "podcasting," creating our own radio shows that we upload on the Web for grateful fans who download our handiwork to their iPods.

The convergence and miniaturization of technologies, once confined to an office or lab, first made these devices luggable. Then, they became portable. Now, we can carry a single device, with more uses than most of us will ever discover, in a pocket, purse, backpack, or fannypack.

It's not all science. As technology affects our lifestyles, it is also creating new art forms. For some people, such as clothing or virtual set designers, these new technologies are at the intersection of art and science. Some people purchase cell phones that match their clothing or car interiors. Using picture phones, we can snap creative digital images and email them to our friends, and even put them on the Internet for anyone—anywhere in the world—to see.

■ Computing: How did we get here? Where are we going?

Perspective is important; we need to stand back every now and then to observe where we've been.

Any discussion of technology might legitimately start with the first lever, the invention of the wheel, or the discovery of fire. Instead, we'll leapfrog all of that and trace a thumbnail history of the

20th Century Technologies

At the turn of the 21st century, the Pew Research Center released results of a poll that asked respondents to identify major "technologies of the 20th century" and "technologies of the 1990s." Here are some of the results of that poll:

- **Technologies of the 20th century:** radio, automobile, home computer, highway system, airline travel, television, birth control pill, space exploration, nuclear energy, and nuclear weapons.

- **Technologies of the 1990s:** email, the Internet, cellular phones, cable television, fertility drugs, Prozac, Viagra, and cloning.[126]

The results pull into sharper focus what has been happening to us. Take a look at communication, transportation, and medical technologies. It's relatively easy to conclude that they have all had an exponential impact on the pace of change.

evolution of today's and tomorrow's computers, focusing on computer speed, capacity, and portability.

ENIAC, the Electronic Numerical Integrator and Computer. While this was not the first working computer, it was the first to gain substantial notoriety.[127]

When it became operational in the mid-1940s, ENIAC filled an entire room; weighed 30 tons; had 19,000 vacuum tubes, 1,500 relays, and hundreds of resistors, capacitors, and inductors; and consumed 200 kilowatts of power. At the time the epitome of worldwide technological development, the computer was programmed using wire cable connections and by setting 3,000 switches on the function tables for each and every problem.

Mobility? Of sorts. The device featured 42 panels, each nine feet tall, two feet wide, and a foot thick. All of the individual panels were on wheels. They could be moved around. In 1955, 10 years after it began operation, ENIAC was shut down and is now an interesting museum display at the Smithsonian and at the University of Pennsylvania, where it was born.

Transistors, Solid State, Silicon Chips, and Microprocessors. The development of solid-state electronics, transistors, and integrated circuits (silicon chips) caused sales of vacuum tubes like those used in ENIAC to plummet. These technological advances revolutionized computing and paved the way for the first microcomputers, according to Dilys Winegrad and Atsushi Akera, in a paper they titled, "A Short History of the Second American Revolution."[128]

Then came the microprocessor, and the rest is history. In fact, as part of a 50th anniversary celebration for ENIAC, a group of Penn students recreated that historic computer . . . on a single chip.[129]

The growing speed and versatility of microprocessors and the convergence of numerous technologies into single, portable, handheld devices continue to simplify certain functions while making our personal and professional lives even more productive . . . and even more complex.

What's next? The quantum computer? Concern has been building about the limits of the silicon chip. Nanotechnologists are working on this challenge even now, developing, among other things, quantum materials. Inside labs at research universities such as Cal Tech, scientists are working on processes they believe will take us down the road toward the quantum computer.

According to *Business Week*, "some of the theoretical possibilities boggle the mind." Quantum mechanics is already at work in lasers and MRI machines. If carried over to a new generation of computers, it could lead to unbreakable codes and completely secure communication, powerful tools for seeing individual molecules and peering into the human body, and new insights into fundamental physics, such as the science of superconductivity. That's not all. "The mathematical challenge of factoring a 400-digit number—which would take 10 billion years on today's supercomputers—might be cracked by a quantum computer in 30 seconds."[130]

Moore's Law states that computer power will double every 18 months. As we entered the new millennium, we were into the process of moving beyond this challenging benchmark.[131]

■ Macro → Micro → Nano → Subatomic

The Issue of Size

Macro and Micro

We've discussed ENIAC. As computers go, that would be macro. Transistors and then silicon chips/microprocessors helped us go micro, to converge and miniaturize while increasing computer speed and capacity.

Nano

What technology will drive the economy of the future? It will be nanotechnology, which gives us the ability to manipulate atoms and molecules, promising stronger, lighter-weight materials than the world has ever known, faster computers, and unprecedented medical breakthroughs. Michael Roco, who has provided leadership for an Interagency Working Group on Nanotechnology at the National Science Foundation (NSF), calls nanotechnology "the next revolution."[132]

McLuhan on Technology and the Briskness of Communication

Welcome to "Global Village!"

He is legendary. Marshall McLuhan was a noted futurist, University of Toronto professor, author, thinker, and spellbinder. He wrote books such as *The Medium is the Message* and coined terms such as "global village." A 2002 film, *McLuhan's Wake*, is based on his last scholarly work, *Laws of Media*.

In a review for the *American Communication Journal*, Wendy Hilton-Morrow reports that the movie restates some of the sage's better known theories on the effects of technology, including "its numbing effect, its potential for creating a global village, its retribalization of man, and its incompatibility with a passive model of education."

McLuhan's four laws of media, generally driven by technology, include: "(a) any medium amplifies or intensifies some situation; (b) any medium makes part of the environment obsolete; (c) any medium recreates or revives any older structure or environment; (d) and any medium, pushed to its limit, can reverse to create the opposite of its intended function."[133]

"Nanotechnology is where technology is going," says Eric Drexler of the Foresight Institute, which publishes an online newsletter on the topic. "Nanoscale science and technology includes the frontiers of chemistry, materials, medicine, and computer hardware—the research that enables the continuing technology revolution," he remarks.

As nanoscale technologies advance, they will enable the development of molecular manufacturing . . . "using nanoscale machines to build large-scale, atomically precise products cleanly, at low cost," Drexler predicts. "Its products will cure cancer and replace fossil fuels, yet those advances will, in retrospect, seem a minor part of the whole," he adds. Nano will likely bring huge benefits for medicine, economic productivity, and the earth's environment. However, he warns that, "hostile forces may use it to produce new, decisively powerful weapons."

Drexler feels national government leaders have generally paid too little attention to the nanotech issue. Specifically, he calls for significant research, honest information, and grants that are directed more toward science than politics, "because it matters whether we go down the right path in developing and applying these powerful capabilities."[134]

Subatomic

We're not there yet, but we're hearing more and more discussions of subatomic particles, neutrinos and quarks. If we are ever able to build subatomic machines, we'll be beyond the level of mechanical friction. That will speed things up even more.

■ Technology . . . It's More than a Computer

Even though high-speed computing and telecommunications continue to jolt our economy and make other technological advancements possible, the computer isn't the only game in town. It has spawned hundreds of other computer-based technologies.

The **Internet** and **World Wide Web** have become treasure troves of information and instant connections for everyone, including students. Once, the challenge was finding enough information for that research report. Now, it's a matter of sorting through a cyber-library (cybrary) of materials growing at more than a million pages a day, then figuring out what is authentic . . . and what isn't. Educational institutions have their own Web sites and intranets. They use general and targeted

Reaching Out

As nanotech allows us to move atoms and then move more deeply into them, astrotech is helping us reach into outer space. While more powerful microscopes peer in, more powerful telescopes peer out. Every discovery reminds us of how much we have yet to learn.

Pluto was long thought to be our solar system's most distant planet. Then, during November 2003, a 171-megapixel camera at Mount Palomar Observatory in California caught a glimpse of an even more distant "planetoid." As if that weren't enough, the discovery reignited debate about whether Pluto meets the criteria for actually being called a planet. In July 2005, Mike Brown of Cal Tech said astronomers had discovered another object about 45 degrees off the main plane of our solar system approximately 1-1/2 times the diameter of Pluto, which they called our 10th planet.[135]

Then, the Hubble Space Telescope gathered light from one of the most distant and chaotic galaxies ever seen. Astronomers everywhere took note. "To me, it's as if the Earth were growing a new sensory apparatus, consisting of hundreds of telescopes linked at almost the speed of light through the Internet," Timothy Ferris, author of *Seeing in the Dark,* told *The Washington Post.* Some astronomers estimate there are about 50 billion galaxies. Some are likely to harbor solar systems and planets like ours.

Schools will be getting more powerful telescopes and microscopes, helping students study everything from microbes to spiral nebulae. Expect the number of students interested in bioinformatics, astrophysics, and other related fields to take off like a rocket.[136]

email, while portable computer-driven communication devices and services such as cell phones, instant messaging, pagers, Blackberries, and other types of PDAs have made a growing number of educators and students eager to participate. But there are also downsides, chief among which are an alarming "digital divide" between the haves and have-nots and the sense that there is never any downtime.

Consider **virtual reality**. Nothing new here if you're training for the military or learning to fly an airliner or space vehicle, or for that matter, playing a video game, or enjoying a high-tech amusement park ride. Now, the challenge is to incorporate it into our schools. Because the entertainment industry has popularized virtual reality and its special effects, those who see its benefits for schools classify it as "edutainment," part of the growing category of goods and services that meld education and entertainment.

Printing has taken on an entirely new dimension. While traditional forms of putting words and pictures on a page continue, digital printing and digital imaging now allow for affordable mass customization of both products and publications. Marketers, communicators, and merchants can now target increasingly smaller and more diverse subgroups with messages and materials customized to reflect geographic, demographic, or other differences. As the digital printing revolution continues, on-demand printing of books and garments will become commonplace. Interior design products will be easily customized. For example, custom wallpaper can be created to match a favorite throw pillow or piece of art. Using our computers, we can now, with some ease, produce digital drawings; modify digital photographs; work with typography and page design; and readily combine several elements into a single composite image. "Pixel counts" have become a normal part of our conversations. Changes in anything from type to color can be made on a computer screen and transmitted around the world.[137] We are experiencing another Guttenberg moment.

The word on **television** is "high definition, plasma, digital, and liquid crystal display (LCD)." Early in the 2000s, most of what we see on television will be in a wide-screen, 16:9 aspect ratio format. Schools and colleges are doing sophisticated programming that is often shared via satellite or cable with their communities and their colleagues who are a school, a county, or a world away. There was a time when school systems hurried to get a board report out before morning so that the staff "would not have to read what happened in the paper." Now, people can watch board meetings live, in real time, in their own homes. Virtual board meetings may be on the way.

Distance learning is no longer an innovation; it has become a staple. Many schools and colleges have run television and radio stations for decades. Even more might soon have their own low-power FM radio outlet. Several already have broadcast channels, and many more have their own public access cable channels. The use of satellite, computer systems, and microwave channels designated specifically for educational purposes (ITFS)[138] is expanding the ability of educators to offer distance learning programs. Online courses are burgeoning. The need is growing for upgraded computer systems, cameras, recorders, switchers, and monitors, as well as cablecasting and broadcast equipment. During the 2002-03 school year, one-third of students in U.S. public schools took a distance learning course, according to a National Center for Education Statistics study, reported by *Education Week*. "Through the Internet or through video or audio conferencing, with teacher and student in separate places," the report noted, "nearly one in every ten public schools in the country had students enrolled in such courses."[139]

In **general transportation,** we're seeing a new generation of telematic e-cars, featuring global positioning systems (GPS) and miniature electronic metering systems (MEMS). "Smart" highways will signal breakups in roads and weaknesses in bridges. They'll also provide guidance systems to keep people from running into each other.

Robotic technologies, powered by computers and stimulated by developments that help us maneuver vehicles on the moon and

Mars, will guide us down our streets and highways. Of course, the uses of robotics will proliferate, with implications for everything from home care to searching narrow passages of mines after a cave-in or a flattened building after an earthquake.

Medical and biotechnologies. High-speed computers made it possible to map the genome, and medicine will never be the same. A definition of biotechnology shared by the United States with the Organization for Economic Cooperation and Development (OECD) focused on "the application of molecular and cellular processes to solve problems and create goods and services." Types of companies involved ranged from human and animal health to agriculture, aquaculture, and environmental remediation. The Brookings Institution states, "The biotechnology industry is built upon fundamental breakthroughs in the understanding of genetic and biological processes to develop new means of diagnosing and treating diseases."[140]

Medical marvels have become household words. For example, MRIs (Magnetic Resonance Imaging), CT Scans (Computed Tomography), PET Scans (Positron Emission Tomography), ultrasound, and nanobots are highly sophisticated technologies that can assist in diagnosis of conditions that might require treatment using other medical technologies. Of course, all depend on the spirit of invention of those who created them and the knowledge and skill of those who use them.

Science and technology labs will open new opportunities as students have access to tools that help them pursue subjects ranging from astrophysics to biotechnology. There may be even further benefits. For example, Ted Blaesing, superintendent of the White Bear Lake Area Schools in Minnesota, sees biotechnology not only as a career path, but also as a source of discoveries that "could lead to numerous changes in how we teach our students."

At this point, we're not sure whether technology drives our values or whether our values drive technology. However, we are quite sure that our pursuit of new technologies will continue. Students will be investigating and reporting on those developments using PowerPoint, or whatever replaces it.

An Observation from a Junior High Student

"The nation and planet are becoming increasingly dependent on computer technology. Perhaps it will get to the point where, should all the computers and electronics cease to operate around the world, the earth would be plunged into a state of chaos, confusion, and disarray. We may already have reached that point. The way we live changes with the things we create. Each new invention affects us in a new way, for better or for worse, depending on our perspective. New technologies that the world once dreamed impossible to achieve and invent change the world a million times over. As businesses and homes are forever altered by these new technologies, so too will be the schools."

Ryan Hunter, Junior High Student, New York State

■ What else is on the drawing board?

There is inherent danger in listing what's in the works in a world of exponential change. Chances are it will either fall on the ash heap of unrealized dreams or become so much a part of daily life so quickly that few will see it as an innovation. Taking a peek at what's entering the theater or waiting in the wings can be instructive for us, however, as we consider education, careers, and possibilities for making our lives better . . . or perhaps worse. Check out these possibilities:

- Satellites the size of footballs that can be launched with cannon rather than traditional rockets.[141]

- Pharmaceuticals tailored to our genetic makeup.[142]

- A computer the size of a cube of sugar with more computing power than all of the computers currently operating on earth.[143]

- Molecular manufacturing done in nanofactories that could help reduce chemical pollution.[144]

- Brain cell and nerve tissue transplants to aid those with mental handicaps, head trauma, or other neurological disorders.[145]

- A high-tech interpreter that will listen to what is being said and convert it first from speech to text, then from text to speech, in another language. As of 2004, IBM's prototype software was set up to handle English and Mandarin Chinese.[146]

- A king-sized, double-decker aircraft capable of seating 555 passengers, about 155 more than current jumbos.[147]

- Automobiles energized by solar power and hydrogen, whose emissions consist of pure water. (During 2003, a prototype made a grueling 4,000 km. trip across Australia.)[148]

- Advances in automobile technology such as road-condition sensors, continuously variable transmissions, automated traffic management systems, night-vision systems, and smart seats that tailor airbag inflation to the passenger's weight.[149]

- Further development of non-lethal weapons such as sticky foam, high viscosity oil additives, malodorous substances, electromagnetic pulses, strategically directed bright light, and strobes that cause disorientation.[150]

- Biometrics readers that will increasingly be used as a key to your car and your admission to a school or other public building, maybe even the lunch line, a school bus, or other public transportation. A reader will likely match your thumbprint to the one stored in a computer's memory.

Of course, this is just a short list.

Technology Careers

Technology is multidisciplinary. What dazzles us are the technologies that drive what we hope will be constructive progress in many fields: education; communication; transportation; government; business; aviation and space exploration; physical, chemical, and biological sciences; and the social sciences, to name just a few. Here are some of the careers that are either currently or soon will be a part of the work scene: water quality specialist, cryonics technician, space mechanic, tissue engineer, smart home technician, and, as we noted earlier, cybrarian. The list goes on.

■ Who will develop the next generations of these and other technologies?

Who will develop commercial applications for nanotechnologies? Who will use contemporary and emerging technologies to create music, write novels and poetry, do research, work as team members with colleagues half a world away, test scenarios, discover or invent pharmaceutical products and medical procedures that will prolong and improve the quality of life, develop new sources of energy and propulsion, take a deeper look into outer space and the inner world of the atom, find cures for major diseases, preserve the environment, design assistive technologies to enable the disabled, formulate ways to improve education, and develop superconductors that will make today's technologies seem ancient within a few decades?

Where We've Been . . . Where We're Going

Noted futurist Graham T.T. Molitor is a master at framing a macro perspective of where we've been and where we might be going. He is president of Public Policy Forecasting and vice president and legal counsel for the World Future Society.

In a recent article, "Beyond the Fourth Wave," Molitor traces a continuum of past, present, and possible future eras or ages:

- **Agriculture:** crop production, animal husbandry . . . declining since the 1880s.

- **Industrial:** textiles, steel, machinery, rail, motor cars, chemicals . . . declining since the 1920s.

- **Services:** retail, professional, specialties, menial . . . declining since 1956.

- **Information:** knowledge, information, education, computers, communication, and silicon . . . dominant since 1976.

- **Leisure:** hospitality, recreation, entertainment . . . dominant commencing in 2015.

- **Life Sciences:** biotech, genetics . . . dominant by 2100.

- **Megamaterials:** quantum physics, nanotechnology, high-pressure physics . . . dominant by 2100-2300.

- **New Atomic Age:** fusion, lasers, hydrogen and helium isotopes . . . dominant by 2250-2500.

- **New Space Age:** spacecraft, exploration, travel, resource gathering, astrophysics . . . dominant before 3000.

Granted, the characteristics of each of these eras will likely co-exist. Agriculture, for example, while a current key to our survival, is heavily influenced and made more productive by a variety of technologies, and each worker is producing food and fiber for more people than ever before. Some of what Molitor suggests for the moderately deep future is already here, at least in its covered wagon stage. Note that he points out when certain technologies and characteristics might become "dominant" and deserve an era of their own. [151]

Who will take that further step and create technologies that are currently beyond our imaginations? It will be the students who are in our schools today. So, the question is, "What are the implications for education?"

■ The Two Edges of Technology

The same technologies that can shed light can also produce darkness. An aircraft that can take us to nearly any part of the world can be used as a missile to bring down office buildings filled with humanity. The bacteria or viruses used to produce vaccines can be used to infect, inflict illness, and create pandemics. Computer geniuses capable of using their knowledge and skill to enlighten the world can also hack into bank accounts or school records and spread havoc with viruses and worms.

"Digital technologies," cautions Douglas Greenberg of the Shoah Foundation, "will not only speed the transmission of educational information, they will also speed the transmission of intolerance and hatred."

The ethical dimensions of technology deserve our attention. Those dimensions range from how polite we are to others as we use our technological marvels to making sure that the intended or unintended consequences of our actions tilt toward creating a better world and away from plunging it into an abyss.

■ Implications for Society

Technology

- Our success in a global knowledge/information age, including economic growth and environmental sustainability, will depend on our ability to develop entirely new or new generations of existing technologies.

How soon is too soon?

A 1999 article in the *Philadelphia Inquirer* raised eyebrows when it observed that "more kindergartners learn to point and click before they can spell M-O-U-S-E." The newspaper reported, "America is in a frenzy to wire its tots." In at least one nursery school, the two- and three-year-olds finish their snacks, listen to a favorite story, and then, some still in diapers, head not for the blocks or finger paints, but to the computers.

While some parents, when choosing a preschool, put computers near the top of the list, at least one educational psychologist, Jane Healy, writes, "It's nonsense. It does not prepare them for the future. It prepares them to be droids." One toddler's mother remarked, "We're thrilled." Her son, 2-1/2, has "got his little mouse skills down . . . In today's society, I think it's essential."[152]

You decide.

- Competition will intensify to attract and keep talented people who are capable of applying technologies in numerous industries. Their discrete professions might range from computer scientist and database administrator to software engineer and biological scientist or technician. "The integration of information technology throughout all functions of all private and public enterprise will substantially increase the basic communication, calculation, and systematic thinking skills required by all except minimum wage jobs," says Consulting Futurist David Pearce Snyder.

- Countries and communities will become more sophisticated in high-tech law enforcement as technologies intended to help are used to deceive or inflict harm.

- Thoughtful leaders will be needed to minimize growth of the digital divide, which could create social and economic rifts and lead to conflict within communities and between nations that are technology rich and those that are technology poor.

- Because telecommunications can further divide people by their specific interests, their narrow biases, or their points of view, society will be pressed to develop techniques or rituals that help us discover what we all have in common.

- A worldwide knowledge base will be readily available to anyone with the technology to access it, creating strains on our ability to separate truth from deception, information from misinformation or disinformation, and fact from fiction or opinion.

- Leaders will no longer be able to "rule" by hoarding information, because those they lead might have access to the same information . . . or even more. Of necessity, new forms of increasingly inclusive leadership will blossom.

- Computing power, networks, and portability will continue to make physical place less important as cottage industries develop, consultants and freelancers provide growing numbers of services, and employees of large and small firms spend part of their time working at home.

- Routine functions such as having a doctor check vital signs, shopping for anything from groceries and clothing to books, or purchasing theater tickets without leaving the home or office will become even more commonplace.

- For both economic gain and social responsibility, individuals and organizations will develop new technologies that will lead to new sources of energy and propulsion, reduce the trend toward environmental degradation, discover cures for major diseases, counter acts of violence and terrorism, lengthen and improve the quality of life, and develop new forms of entertainment.

- Civic and government leaders will develop even more technology-driven approaches for listening to their clients or communities and determining their personal needs. In turn, they will provide information that is of particular interest to various individuals or groups.

- Identity theft and intellectual property disputes will proliferate, stimulating new laws, methods of enforcement, and courses such as "ethics and technology" and "computer etiquette."

- The educational system, at all levels, will be reshaped, as people gain even greater access to ideas and information traditionally taught in schools and colleges. As a philosophy, "possibility" will largely replace impossibility.

■ Directions for Education

Technology

The impact of technology will be widespread, touching all other trends that have implications for schools and colleges and the individuals and societies they serve. Those implications include:

- **Capitalizing on the benefits of distance education.** As noted in this chapter, distance education is fast becoming an important part of the learning mix. For example, curriculum and instruction are supplemented through the Internet and various types of computer networks, satellite communication, and audio and video conferences. Educational systems will continue to select these programs wisely and provide professional development for teachers in how to use them most effectively. Many teachers will sit or stand before the cameras or computer screens to offer these courses. For many smaller education

How do new technologies take off?

It's like "the process for spontaneous combustion: A pile of greasy rags sits in the corner, occasionally emitting a wisp of smoke before it suddenly bursts into flame," Glover Ferguson, chief scientist with Accenture, Ltd., a consulting firm, told the *Wall Street Journal.* "You're not quite sure what is the tipping point. But when it gets hot, it takes off."

Ferguson was describing how new technologies break into the market. High-definition television, wall panels, utility computing, wireless fidelity (Wi-Fi), DVD players and recorders, TiVo, ReplayTV, and a host of other consumer electronics products were just gleams in our eyes a few years ago. Today, the newspaper reports, these products "have crossed the line—from possible to the real."

What pieces come together to launch a product? "Prices must fall. Consumers need to see, and understand the value of the product. It helps to have heavyweight backers. An infrastructure needs to be in place. And, the new technology has to work better than anything it hopes to supplant, with a minimum of bugs and hassles," the *WSJ* reports.

Read this item again, and find the wisdom for any community or business developing a new industry or product or for any education system launching a new program or creating a future.[153]

systems, distance education has long been a source of programs that were hard to offer locally because of the lack of critical mass. Now, these sophisticated programs are bringing the world into the classroom. Some of the directions that follow are in some way related to distance education.

- **Meeting the demand for higher-level teaching skills.** Growing numbers of students will come to school with more information on some topics than their teachers. A student might have a keen interest and may have devoted hours to mining the Internet and other sources for information.

  The insecure teacher could see that kind of enterprise as a threat or the student as overly precocious. The masterful teacher, however, will find the ideas and information interesting and perhaps even offer cautions or suggest that the student dig even deeper.

  As technologies increase student access to information, the teacher who is a subject-matter or grade-level specialist will also become a facilitator and orchestrator of learning, taking on a role as partner in the learning experience. The astute teacher, who often has more life experience, will also help the student move from raw data and information toward usable knowledge and, then, in the direction of wisdom.

  "Teachers are becoming mentors and catalysts whose job is not to lecture, but to help students learn to collect, evaluate, analyze, and synthesize information," according to noted forecaster Marvin Cetron and teacher Kimberley Cetron.[154]

- **Making the school a learning community and a learning center for the community.** Schools will increasingly become centers of learning for their communities. Their Web sites will carry not only education information but also link to other community- and worldwide sources. Before and after school, students and parents will connect to the school's Web site to access learning resources, check on assignments, and get help with homework.

  While the Internet connects educators and students with a world of ideas and information, intranets will offer everything from policies to crisis plans. "Laptops and more Internet access will extend the learning day and close the gap between home and school," says Charlotte Frank, a long-time executive with The McGraw-Hill Companies.[155]

"Technological advances in learning and telelearning will lead us toward redefining what we mean by learning communities, what we teach, and how we deliver education," says Kenneth Bird, superintendent of the Westside Community Schools in Omaha, Neb. He adds, "The next generation of school leaders will need to develop a more expansive view of their learning communities."

- **Opening the classroom to the world.** The examples are everywhere—from watching rovers traverse the surface of Mars to conversing with astronauts aboard the International Space Station or scientists probing the ocean depths. Students and teachers have been able to "go along for the ride" with scientists, archaeologists, and explorers.

Information about the world is so accessible that intense debates have followed events such as the space shuttle *Columbia* disaster, the shootings at Columbine High School, and the devastating attacks of September 11, 2001. "How much should our children experience these kinds of things?" some have asked. There is little shelter from world events. Now, the challenge is to incorporate these widespread resources into curriculum and instruction appropriately.

- **Considering the implications of nanotechnology for education?** We've already said it: The people who will develop new products and services using nanotechnology are students in our schools and colleges today. Education systems need to think about the benefits of getting involved in nano at the ground floor. Consider, for example, a 2002 report in *Newsweek* magazine estimating a need for 800,000 to one million nanotechnology workers in the United States alone as we move nanotech from the lab to the marketplace. The article also reported that the National Science Foundation (NSF) was requiring its six university nanotech centers to sponsor K-12 outreach programs.[156]

- **Investing in science education.** To stay ahead of the curve, any community or country will need to ensure students have an understanding of and appreciation for science in its many forms. Their economies and the personal health and well-being of their people may depend on it. Those who are prepared for scientific careers will be drawn to areas of the country and world where they are encouraged to conduct their research and engage in development. "Brain gain" v. "brain drain" will take on added significance. All people should be grounded in a basic understanding of science so that they can make reasoned judgments about budgetary allocations or the benefits and possible consequences of scientific projects.

- **Offering preparation and professional development that breaks habits and mindsets.** While computer power doubles on the average of every 18 months, some say that organizational change can take up to 20 years. That challenge hits home for many educational institutions, especially since they are charged with preparing their students for the future.

Educators need to know how to use existing technologies. They also need an introduction to new technologies as they emerge. Bottom line—preparation and professional development programs should focus on how to adapt quickly to new opportunities posed by technology. "Rapid technological advances require earlier identification of skill building needs," suggests Graham T.T. Molitor, president of Public Policy Forecasting and vice president and legal counsel for the World Future Society. He points out the need for educators to develop skills essential for coping with demands posed by "new jobs, careers, and livelihoods."

- **Reaching agreement with parents on responses to questions and concerns.** Growing numbers of parents, when they want information about how their students are doing in school or have complaints, are sending emails or leaving voicemail messages for teachers. They often expect an instant response, just as they do when working with a business or professional colleague. Teachers, meanwhile, are committed to keeping their classes on task. *Time* magazine, in a 2005 article, "Parents Behaving Badly," cites a Syracuse University professor who has experienced students using their cell phones to call parents directly from the classroom to complain about a grade, and then passing the phone on to her.[157] Mutual expectations will be needed between schools and parents to ensure the communication system is reasonable and effective in light of new technologies.

- **Engaging educators and students in continuous self-learning.** We've all said it: "If education is truly important, then educators need to demonstrate they are continuing to learn." It isn't always necessary to go somewhere else to learn, because the learning can come to us. Educators, in fact, can help their students make self-learning even more useful and connected to their interests. An exciting prospect is to help students create new knowledge as they find relationships among the scattered information and ideas they encounter.

- **Teaching the ethical dimensions of technology.** Starting with etiquette, how and when should we use certain technologies if we are at a meeting or carrying on a face-to-face conversation? Moving on to safety, should we let certain technologies distract us when we're driving?

Technology can help us develop new generations of mind-bending processes and devices, such as the quantum computer. It can help us conquer diseases and make it possible for us to exchange messages with someone half a world away. Intentionally or unintentionally, it can also help us spread diseases and wage attacks.

Many school systems once banned cell phones. Some now allow them, because they played a key communication role during the attack on Columbine High School in Colorado. Today, many technologies are converging into single small instruments that might include not only a cell phone but also instant messaging and the ability to connect to email and the Internet. Some include a digital camera. Occasionally, a student takes a compromising picture of a teacher or another student and uploads it to the Web for all to see, creating disciplinary actions and policy debates that were inconceivable just a few years ago.

Educators and students desperately need a solid grounding in the ethical dimensions of technology in what has become a very fast-moving world.

- **Discovering technologies to assist in both instruction and administration.** Taking a step back, we can readily see how far we've come using new technologies. Because of constant developments, however, we are never finished. The minute we install hardware or software and train people for one generation of computer or telecommunications technology, the next generation is knocking at our door. One indication is that Internet and Intranet sites will need to constantly be upgraded as staff and community demands become even more sophisticated.

We're concerned about charting student progress, disaggregating test scores, perhaps using virtual reality as a teaching tool, maintaining even more accurate and secure student records, listening to student and community ideas and problems, and using technology to help us level the playing field for a growing diversity of students. The business office is pressed to produce even more discrete financial information. We're confronted with the prospect of computer-based voting. We want comput-

The New Cyberculture

The future is not a direct line-projection of the past or present. We should know that from the technological interventions that have virtually changed our capabilities and our attitudes, almost overnight. Some thoughtful people have made the case that the automobile, the airplane, and the Internet, among many other technologies, have made us more eager to develop a cyberculture, a seemingly natural progression.

Darren Tofts, Annemarie Jonson, and Alessio Cavallaro, in their book *Prefiguring Cyberculture: An Intellectual History*, even speculate that since the first human scratched a picture on a rock face we have been on the road to even more advanced and complex forms of literacy.

Since we have become dependent on a constellation of technologies for our learning, comfort, and long-term survival, speculation has grown that, in the process, we may have already turned ourselves into cyborgs.[158]

ers that will help us do everything from stage simulations to improve our transportation scheduling and computer-operated indoor environmental and security systems.

All educational institutions are on a fast track as they try to stay ahead of the technological curve. While time and budget often get in the way, the demand is unrelenting to develop, adopt, adapt, and effectively use new generations of technology.

Of course, it all costs money, and growing numbers of educational institutions are working overtime to help their constituencies understand the need for support. Creative financing through approaches such as performance contracting remain an option.

Biotech in the Classroom

Bringing biotechnology into the classroom, Peter Petrossian, a science teacher at Pyle Middle School in Bethesda, Md., has had students extract DNA from a number of sources, such as fruit, animal tissue, even their own cheek cells.

In a January 2004 article, *The Washington Post* reported the class also had a lesson devoted to DNA fingerprinting. Here's the scenario: A dog has been dognapped, and the students are asked to solve the crime. In the process they collect DNA found at the crime scene and compare it with known suspects.

Petrossian says, "Twenty years ago, these procedures weren't even available to anybody—now I've got seventh graders doing it!"[159]

- **Offering leading-edge career, technical, and vocational education.** As noted earlier, with some fits and starts, demand will continue to grow for knowledge workers. That means schools and colleges need to prepare students to understand and use new and more sophisticated technologies more effectively. This type of education and training also helps students connect what they're learning with what is important in the outside world and encourages them to consider career possibilities.

"A rapidly changing job market is fueled by meteoric changes in technology," observes George Hollich, retired director of curriculum and summer programs for the Hershey School in Pennsylvania. Forecaster Marvin Cetron suggests "a new kind of vocational education, suited for tomorrow's medical technicians, computer programmers and repair workers, and other technology specialists."

- **Building an understanding of the need to develop new technologies.** Students will need to develop a firm understanding that they are the ones who will be expected to develop entirely new generations of existing technologies. Education systems will likely include at least a unit on the history of technological development. When students graduate, they should understand the social, economic, political, environmental, and scientific demand for these technologies, the career opportunities they present, and the role each of them might play in bringing them to fruition.

- **Increasing the use of biometrics as a security measure.** As noted earlier, biometric products come in several forms, but they have one thing in common—they try to identify a person through various biological features. In the future, to start a car or enter a building, you might have to place your thumb against a device that reads your print. If there is a match, you'll be able to start your engine or go to class. This type of technology can even be used to take attendance. There are other forms of hardware and software, as well. Some match up with your eye, your voice, your hand's vascular system, or your face.

Taking a step beyond biometrics, the global positioning system is being used in a growing number of vehicles, including some school buses. Some have even suggested that children/students be equipped with individual GPS devices so that they can be easily located and don't get lost. The tug between privacy and security will stir growing numbers of discussions as these technologies become more common in our lives.

- **Encouraging the restructuring and redesign of schools.** To paraphrase a very old saying, putting new wine in old flasks is not good for the wine. In today's world, growing numbers of schools are changing their industrial age structures to meet the needs and opportunities posed by the global knowledge/information age.

In some cases, a school's conversation about systemic change gets rolling during an update of the technology plan. That's just one more reason why key technology professionals should be seen as members of the leadership team. While technology should not necessarily be the tail that wags the dog, it can serve as a strong starting point on the road to creating 21st century schools.

Updates of the school facility should make way for state-of-the-art technologies that help improve the learning environment. Air quality, acoustics, temperature, humidity, and lighting can be controlled to enhance rather than interfere with learning and to improve overall indoor environmental quality.

Here's an all-too-familiar example of how environment affects learning. A teacher and her students are not feeling very well. Allergens are taking their toll. So is the flickering fluorescent light and the unit ventilator that makes so much noise, people have called it "the shaker." The teacher exerts herself to be heard above the noise. So do students. Carbon dioxide levels rise, and everyone gets tired. Achievement suffers.

■ Questions and Activities

1. How is convergence affecting technologies and our lives?

2. What was ENIAC?

3. What promise do you see for nanotechnology in building the economy of your community? What are the implications of nanotechnology for what we teach in our schools and colleges?

4. Develop a plan for transforming laboratories in schools to accommodate fast-moving developments in science and technology.

5. Assess the digital divide in your community. Develop a brief five-point approach for overcoming it.

Gearing Up

Plans, Concerns, and Opportunities

Plans: Most educational institutions have sophisticated technology plans. They have learned, often through experience, that their plans need to be flexible since the world is moving so quickly. They involve people in planning and professional development and pay attention to the design of system architecture. They try to be open, yet meticulous, in the selection of hardware and software and in designing technologies into the learning process and the environment.

Concerns: Maintenance, professional development, and funding continue to be concerns. Some people, after all these years, rebel against using high-tech resources to enhance education. In some cases, the technology is there, but it is only used for repetitive, not higher-level tasks such as problem solving or scenario development. Closing the digital divide that separates the technology rich from the technology poor is an ongoing battle. Even though there's benefit to setting up targeted email lists to parents and others in the community who are interested in certain topics, it might not be done. Web sites might not be as user-friendly as they could be.

As we race to stay ahead of the curve, we're confronted by cyberporn and debates about Internet filters. We need protections against spam (unwanted email) and computer viruses, worms, and hackers. With so much information readily available, we need a deeper understanding of copyright laws, the Fair Use Doctrine, and intellectual property rights. As regular students focus on biotechnology and nanotechnology projects as part of their basic education, some people will very likely pose questions about what we're teaching and why. Flares sometimes illuminate the sky as people raise concern that our investments in technology may come at the expense of other things we need to do to ensure a sound education for each and every student. We'll be taken to task for our ability "to do what has never worked even faster"—all because of our new technologies.

Opportunities: For our education system, technology is a gift that will keep on giving—a Pandora's box, filled with surprises. "School people need to live in the real world and to understand the far-reaching nature of new technologies," suggests Texas A&M Education Leadership Professor John Hoyle. "Today's students are plugged into the new and turned off by the old. Teaching strategies must be revamped and teachers given the help they need to begin to know their students."

■ Readings

1. Negroponte, N. (1996). *Getting digital.* (First Vintage Books ed.) New York: Random House.

2. Cetron, M. (2003). Trends shaping the future. *The Futurist* magazine. (March-April 2003).

3. Drexler, F. (2004). Why care about nanotechnology? *Foresight Institute Nanotechnology Newsletter.* (March 31, 2004). Retrieved from http://www.gmail.foresight.org

4. Recent works by many authors, as technologies develop rapidly.

Trend 5

The future is already here.

The Millennial Generation will insist on solutions to accumulated problems and injustices, while an emerging Generation E will call for equilibrium.

GIs, Silents, Boomers, Xers → Millennials, Generation E

"Think of us as a midpoint between no tolerance and loving everyone."

Avy, 11, United States[160]

"We just want to keep going, keep going, pushing the limits on things. That's our job really."

Tsipora, 16, Canada[161]

■ Like to see the future?

Look around you.

"The people who will run our country 40 years from now are already here." With that dramatic announcement, demographic expert Neil Howe unveiled a panoply of generations that have walked the earth and are about to take their first steps.

Howe and colleague William Strauss were addressing an annual conference of the World Future Society. Their book, *The Fourth Turning: An American Prophesy*, was in its first stages of igniting the interest of sociologists, demographers, educators, and planners of every stripe.

A generation, Strauss and Howe observe, usually covers a period of 17 to 24 years. In some ways, every fourth generation has a tendency to repeat itself. [162]

The Four Turnings

For centuries, the seasonal rhythm of growth, maturation, entropy, and destruction is a cycle that will likely continue into the future. Strauss and Howe describe the Four Turnings:

- The *First Turning* is *High*, an upbeat era of strengthening institutions and weakening individualism, when a new civic order implants and the old value regime decays.

- The *Second Turning* is an *Awakening*, a passionate era of spiritual upheaval, when the civic order comes under attack from a new values regime.

- The *Third Turning* is an *Unraveling*, a downcast era of strengthening individualism and weakening institutions, when the old civic order decays and the new values regime implants.

- The *Fourth Turning* is a *Crisis*, a decisive era of secular upheaval, when the values regime propels the replacement of the old civic order with a new one. [163]

■ Move over Boomers. Look over your shoulders Xers. Here come the Millennials.

"Have it your way!" That commercial message appealed to Baby Boomers. Born right after World War II, their parents were ready to put depression and war behind and dote on their children. Born between 1946 and 1964, they became a formidable force.

The Boomers are likely to remain a force as they move into retirement. By 2030, they'll be between the ages of 66 and 84 and they'll be competing for services and attention with more than 90 million members of Generation X and more than 75 million Millennials. They will, to put it mildly, have their hands full, because the Millennials will be in hot pursuit of resources they need to solve the problems and deal with the injustices of the world.

The Millennials, born beginning in about 1982, have been in our elementary and secondary schools since about 1987. The first of them graduated from high school and headed off to a job or college in 2000. Like the GI Generation, four generations before them, they are expected to be assertive in solving problems and creating what they consider a more just civic order.[164]

Beginning in 2004, we saw the emergence of Generation E. "E" stands for equilibrium. In a 21st-century context, they'll try to cut the losses and consolidate the gains we've made during the previous four generations. They'll be showing up in kindergarten in about 2009 or 2010 and college in about 2022.

The cycle of life continues. Now, let's look at these generations in greater depth.

■ Who are we anyway?

GIs, Silents, Boomers, Xers, Millennials, and Es

Generational experts don't always agree on the exact span of years that defines each generation, nor do they fully agree on what to call them. They do, however, agree that there are certain core values that make one generation different from another. The actual characteristics are sharpened by human events.

Considering current life spans, we have the privilege of seeing significant numbers of four or five generations at any given time. This chapter begins with a look at our current generations.

GI Generation

They were born between 1901 and 1924. At the turn of the century, they were from 76 to 99 years of age. Widely known as "the generation of heroes," some of them braved two world wars and the Great Depression. Those who are still with us lived through the consciousness revolution of the '60s and '70s and saw the turn of the new millennium. They saw the dawn of radio, television, air travel, and computers. Many gave of their lives for democracy either on the home front or the battlefront. Civic minded, they demonstrated a willingness to make huge sacrifices.

Author and former NBC News anchor Tom Brokaw wrote about them in his book, *The Greatest Generation*. "They helped convert a wartime economy into the most powerful peacetime economy in history. They made breakthroughs in medicine and other sciences. They gave the world new art and literature. They came to understand the need for federal civil rights legislation. They gave America Medicare," Brokaw points out. "They became part of the greatest investment in higher education that any society ever made," as the GI Bill made it possible for soldiers to become scholars.[165]

John F. Kennedy, Ronald Reagan, Jimmy Carter, Richard Nixon, Louis Armstrong, Bob Hope, Lucille Ball, Thomas P. "Tip" O'Neill, Sidney Poitier, Billy Graham, John Glenn, Judy Garland, Ann Landers, Robert McNamara, Robert Oppenheimer, Jackie Robinson, Sam Walton, John Steinbeck, Rosa Parks, Nelson Mandela, Lauren Bacall, Frank Sinatra,[166] Jane Wyman, and Walt Disney were their contemporaries. *Keep in mind that generational experts are telling us that the Millennials have similar motivations.*

Silent Generation

Born between 1925 and 1945, the 49 million individuals classified as the Silent Generation make up the smallest generation of the 20th century. Their parents, largely members of the GI Generation, were busy, coping with the Great Depression and World War II. They wanted their families to have a sound home and the security they had yet to experience. Some Silents fought in WW II, Korea, and Vietnam.

Silents are known for their patriotism, hard work, willingness to sacrifice, patience, honor, loyalty, and varying levels of conformity. It's a generation that never had a U.S. president, but its outer conformity camouflaged an intense dedication to purpose.

While developing new generations of technologies that revolutionized computing and eventually took us to the moon, they were watching *The Ed Sullivan Show* and unveiling new forms of music and cultural icons. The voices of the Silents, from "I have a dream today . . ." to "You Ain't Nuthin' But A Hound Dog" continue to electrify the planet.

Their contemporaries include or once included people like Martin Luther King, Jr., Neil Armstrong, Gloria Steinem, Carl Sagan, Colin Powell, Joan Baez, Ray Charles, Lily Tomlin, Harry Belafonte, James Dean, Buddy Holly, Abbie Hoffman, Robert

Eavesdropping

Leonard Bernstein: "Elvis Presley is the greatest cultural force in the twentieth century."

Dick Clurman, an editor at *Time* magazine: "What about Picasso?"

Leonard Bernstein: "No. It's Elvis. He introduced the beat to everything, and he changed everything—music, language, clothes. It's a whole new social revolution—the Sixties comes from it."

A conversation between Time's *Dick Clurman and distinguished composer and conductor Leonard Bernstein, recounted by David Halberstam in his book,* The Fifties."[167]

Redford, Vaclav Havel, Mary Tyler Moore, Dustin Hoffman, Elizabeth Taylor, Elvis Presley, and Woody Allen. (see "Eavesdropping," above.)

Baby Boomers

Born between 1946 and 1964, theirs was the first generation of the century not to have experienced a world war or the Great Depression. They did experience unprecedented American prosperity, the Vietnam War, Watergate, the growing impact of television, the liftoff and splashdown of our first manned space flights and landings on the moon. They were also caught in the middle of the civil rights movement, women's liberation, and the assassinations of leaders who had become symbols of their time.

"Once boomers start to retire, they will do so at a rate of more than 10,000 a day for the better part of two decades," E. Thomas

Wetzel, president of the Retirement Living Information Center, told writers of an article devoted to "Great Places to Retire" in a March 2005 issue of *Kiplinger's* magazine.[168]

Boomers are often described as: optimistic; concerned about their health, wellness, and personal growth; dedicated to their work; and self-centered.

Contemporaries include George W. and Laura Bush, John Kerry, Bill and Hillary Clinton, Bill Gates, Dolly Parton, Michael Jordan, Michael Jackson, Jerry Seinfeld, Cher, Steven Spielberg, Oprah Winfrey, David Letterman, Michael J. Fox, and George Stephanopoulos.

Generation X

Born between 1965 and 1981, members of this generation were dazzling the world at the turn of the century with a kind of low-key genius. For example, their faces lit up our television screens as rovers landed on Mars.

The Xers experienced a growth in single-parent homes, the widespread use of computers, and the emergence of a new world order as the Berlin Wall came down and the Soviet Union disintegrated, ending the Cold War. They were the first recent generation to

Xers Disprove Bum Rap

Bruce Tulgan, author of *Managing Generation X: How to Bring Out the Best in Young Talent*, notes a "widespread misconception among the public that Xers are mostly slackers" who have decided to "drop out of the rat race." "The truth is," Tulgan says, "there are millions of star Xers doing critical work in important positions in every field imaginable."[169]

worry about whether their pension funds, including Social Security, would be there for them.

Xers, who felt the scars of the post-Vietnam era, are described as informal, self-reliant, technologically literate, practical, and accepting of diversity. They are often free-agents who will squeeze everything they can from a job and often want more control of their work schedules.

Contemporaries include Brooke Shields, Ben Stiller, Halle Berry, Janet Jackson, Mike Tyson, Julia Roberts, Sammy Sosa, Cameron Diaz, Kobe Bryant, Macaulay Culkin, Yao Ming, Shaquille O'Neal, Jewel, Serena and Venus Williams, and Christina Aguilera.

The Millennials

Born between 1982 and about 2003, they are the fourth generation out from the GI Generation. People who really listen to them tell us that they are or will be committed to solving the problems of the world and dealing with the injustices.

While most Millennials are, at this writing, working their way through elementary, secondary, and higher education, some have already hit the work force. All are having an impact on the marketplace. They have also hit the streets, raising their voices for the first time at world economic conferences in places like Washington, D.C., Seattle, Genoa, Quebec City, and Goteborg. Because of their civic commitment, expect them to play an active role in political campaigns.

During their lifetimes, many will benefit from the greatest transference of wealth in history. Of course, that depends on whether their Boomer and Xer parents have been able to accumulate substantial resources during their lifetimes and have not spent it all on long-term care as they reach advanced ages.

By the way, not everyone calls them Millennials. They are alternately known as: Generation Y, the Echo Boomers, Gen Tech, Dot Com, Nexters, and About To Bes.

Who are these Millennials?

To be specific, Millennials have earned the following description—confident, sociable, moral, street smart, optimistic, accepting of diversity, and civic minded. Typically, some of their motivations were in response to what they admired and what they found questionable in the values and behaviors of their parents.

What else do Millennials have in common?

- Whether in their own communities or through the media, Millennials have experienced the multicultural society. For them, it's not a stretch—it's the way the world ought to be.

- They've seen the emergence of a new world order. When the wall came down in Berlin and the Soviet Union came apart, conflicts that once took place along political boundaries began their shift to cultural and, some say, civilizational boundaries.[170]

- This turn-of-the-century generation has seen the rise of violence and terrorism. The 1999 shootings at Columbine High School and September 11, 2001, terrorist attacks will likely be defining events for them.

For Millennials, high-speed computers and satellite communication are not recent inventions. They are a normal part of the world they know. While GIs, Silents, and some Boomers struggled to adapt to high-tech devices like the computer, the Millennials and Xers took to them like fish to water. Most have never had to "walk across the room to change channels on the television set," a story some parents tell their children, the equivalent of "walking four miles to school, uphill, through snow four feet deep."

Because the population of our planet is burgeoning, Millennials don't want to get lost in the crowd. Individual identity is important. Body piercing, small artistic or message-laden tattoos, low cut or overly ample clothing, and monogrammed bags help set individuals apart.

Note: The optimism of the Millennials was dampened somewhat by the economic downturn of the early 2000s as they saw college costs going up and their savings, if they had any, either frozen or going down. Among other things, The Dot Bust, according to journalist Michael J. Weiss, writing for *American Demographics* magazine, "helped forge a sensibility that will last a lifetime in shaping expectations and entitlement, in determining what one will give to and take from society, work, one's community, etc."[171]

What are their concerns?

In 2004, Peter Zollo, president of Teenage Research Unlimited (TRU), published *Getting Wiser to Teens*. This classic work probes everything from income sources to aspirations and fears. It examines how at least a portion of the Millennials age group communicates with parents and gauges concerns and motivations.

When asked about social concerns, the 12- to 19-year-olds reached through Zollo's research pointed out long lists of issues, such as: child abuse, drinking and driving, prejudice or racism, education, abortion, drug abuse, terrorism, AIDS, cigarette smoking, war, sexual assault, suicide, animal rights, violence/gangs, the environment, women's rights, alcoholism, biological and chemical warfare, divorce, unplanned pregnancy, unemployment/the economy, nuclear warfare, eating disorders, homelessness, gay rights, and health care. Could this be the start of their social/political agenda as they move into positions of leadership?

Fairness is a big thing with Millennials. They are likely to have zero tolerance for intolerance. When asked about labeling people at school, dealing with the tendency to split students into groups, such as jocks, nerds, and preps, the teens said they didn't like it. "Once you're labeled as part of a group, it's hard to lose the label," 64 percent said, while 61 percent said, "being labeled in a group that you don't want to be in can cause a lot of stress." Perhaps that's why some would prefer not even to be called Millennials.

Their top five favorite things about school were friends, assemblies/ special days/field trips, sports, seeing a boyfriend or girlfriend, and extracurricular activities. Their least favorite were getting up early, tests, homework, the length of the school day, and peer pressure.[172]

Time passes

"The eldest Millennials will reach age 50 in 2032. Around that time, their generation will produce a majority of state governors and members of Congress and very likely its first serious presidential candidate," Neil Howe and William Strauss wrote in their 2000 book, *Millennials Rising*.

The 2030s "will be the Millennial's peak decade for buying houses, acquiring debt, and raising children. Their leading wave will pour into business leadership positions," say Howe and Strauss. At that point, "They will provide the leading producers but no longer the writers and performers, of the pop culture for the younger generation," they predict.[173]

Generation E . . . for Equilibrium

Just as the Silents followed the GI Generation, it's likely something akin to Generation E will follow on the heels of the Millennials. E, in this case, stands for equilibrium. Some members of this new generation, who might one day be called "leading Es," were born beginning in about 2004. Assuming a 20-year generation, the youngest will celebrate a 76th and the oldest a 96th birthday in 2100.

The Es will grow up experiencing and hearing stories from aging relatives, some older than 100, about the chaotic decades that

More Words to the Wise . . . from the Millennials

- "One thing I want to say about computers. The Internet cannot transfer our feelings to each other."
  Pooja, 14, India[174]

- "I think people of the future will be more sensitive about problems of the world. I hope. Otherwise, I'm moving to Mars."
  Marina, 14, Brazil[175]

- "The next generation that will command this world will be us."
  Mariangela, 13, Costa Rica[176]

- "Something unique about our generation is that we voice our opinions. If we feel something, we're going to tell somebody. We might shout it out. We yell."
  Ben, 14, United States[177]

- "If each generation could finish up what they start, then it would be fine, and the world would be a better place for children."
  Sasha, 9, United States[178]

- "Look on the bright side. We'll all get high schools named after us." *Andrea in the movie,* Deep Impact[179]

preceded them and feel a need to ease worldwide tensions. They'll ruminate about wars, brinkmanship, breaches of ethics, and technological developments that outstrip the speed at which they want to adapt. They will generally have great respect for the dedication and sacrifices of their Millennial and Xer parents.

As a group, the Es will probably be neither conservative nor liberal. In fact, they might blanch at the very thought of polarization, when civil discourse is so much more productive. High on their generational agenda will be a commitment *to cutting our losses and consolidating our gains.*

As the world takes a breath, the Es will likely spawn a new era for politics and world affairs, education, the environment, the arts, and culture, much of it beyond our imaginations. Part of their duty will be to explain us to ourselves and launch us on another generational mission of discovery.

■ Defining Moments . . . Defining Events

Do generations shape events, or do events shape generations? The answer is that both perspectives are correct. Certain events become defining moments in our lives. That's especially true when we're "coming of age," generally between the ages of 16 and 24.

To shape our values, "the events must have social consequences, and they must be known and experienced by relatively large groups of people," according to Geoffrey Meredith, Charles Schewe, and Janice Karlovich in their book *Defining Markets... Defining Moments.* These common experiences "become the glue that bonds certain age clusters together and separates them from contiguous but different clusters."[180]

"Defining events" generally are not natural disasters, such as hurricanes or earthquakes. Most often, they involve human affairs. Examples of events that have helped to define and give resolve to generations of people during the 20th and early part of the 21st century include: World War I, The Great Depression, World War II, Pearl Harbor, Hiroshima/Nagasaki, Sputnik, the assassinations of John F. Kennedy and Martin Luther King, Jr., the civil rights movement, walking on the moon, the Vietnam War, the rise of the personal computer, the fall of the Berlin Wall and disintegration of the Soviet Union, the advent of the Internet, the '90s economic boom, Columbine, September 11, 2001, and scandals involving companies such as Enron, WorldCom, and Arthur Andersen.

131

As time goes by, you can build your own list of defining events as we move through the 21st century and beyond.

■ Implications for Society

Generations

As the Millennials move toward center stage, they will insist on actions and lead initiatives that will likely have a profound impact on society.

- Millennials are likely to aggressively support their preferred candidates and run for office themselves. Whether they actually vote in substantial numbers may depend on whether, as individuals, they believe their vote "makes a difference."

- Ethical behavior and justice will become even greater issues at all levels. Businesses and professions will be expected to demonstrate their corporate citizenship and social responsibility.

- As members of this highly motivated generation attempt to get the support they need to make what they consider positive changes in the world, they will be outnumbered by retiring Boomers and others who will compete with them for resources.

- Just as communities try to promote communication and understanding across racial, ethnic, social, and economic groups, they will also feel compelled to create opportunities for cross-generational communication.

- Processes will need to be in place and widely understood for peacefully and democratically dealing with issues and solving problems. Without these processes, society will likely face more aggressive approaches.

- At all levels, from international organizations to national capitals, from the capitals of states and provinces to county seats and town halls, governments should expect thoughtfully prepared proposals for solving problems, righting wrongs, and pursuing opportunities to improve the quality of life for greater numbers of people. If consensus becomes elusive, we can expect well-organized street protests, electronic "mass mobbing" (forming large groups through Internet appeals), and other forceful means of expression.

- Enlightened countries and communities will be organized to tap the strengths of people from multiple generations, who bring to the table a melange of values, attitudes, and motivations.

- Multiple generations will come together to conceive of an even better future for their countries or communities. Their focus will include but not be limited to conceiving of even better neighborhoods and the shaping of schools and colleges to effectively serve the needs of a fast-changing world.

- Unless pension programs and social contracts, such as Social Security, are secure for the Millennials, it is less likely that they will enthusiastically support them for others. They may even politically punish those whom they believe deprived them of what might otherwise have been their benefits.

■ Implications for Education

Generations

- **Helping students, educators, and communities understand divergent views.** Combined, the students, teachers, administrators, and parents who are directly involved in a school or college could represent up to three or four generations. Improvements in health care that have allowed people to work longer, the fact that many people are having children a bit later in life, and the reality of grandparents sometimes playing a central role in raising their

133

grandchildren will bring increasing numbers of generations under the roof at the same time, each with its own clusters of values. Unless schools and colleges encourage cross-generational communication and understanding inside and outside their organizations, they should expect misunderstandings and even conflict.

- **Teaching students how to make change peacefully and democratically.** We said it earlier. The Millennials, as they move into positions of leadership at every level, will take on the problems and injustices of the world. They will have some very destructive weapons at their disposal. Unless we teach them how to make change peacefully and democratically, we could end up anywhere from Nirvana to Armageddon.

Thinking and reasoning skills, coupled with a sound code of ethics and an understanding of the value of others' opinions, will be basic. Civic educators will likely play a role that goes far beyond the classroom as they advise their educational institutions and communities on how to make the democratic process work.

Students will need to learn how the political/decision-making system works and have practice in identifying and exploring issues, involving people in developing solutions, and in drafting and promoting changes in public policy. They will also need to know how to find and use information, communicate effectively, test ideas, and rally support through personal persuasion. Some will practice persuasiveness through the Internet. Bottom line—Millennials will need to know how to channel their substantial energies constructively rather than destructively.

- **Paying attention to conflict management skills.** Susan Gorin, executive director of the National Association of School Psychologists, wants students to learn and practice skills that will help maintain safe environments, "such as learning tolerance, conflict resolution, and what to do if you're worried about someone else."[181]

A case can be made that some school violence is perpetrated by students and others who have been bullied, failed, dismissed, or jilted, and simply don't know how to deal with the conflict. We know from hard experience that "righting wrongs" can take many forms, some peaceful . . . and some violent. People in general, and students in particular, need to understand how to deal with their disputes short of ending in a gun battle at the OK Corral.

- **Developing student teamwork and management skills.** Schools will need to realize they are dealing with a generation committed to building what they consider a more just society. Educators will be pressed to offer what a recent study called "a curriculum for life that engages students in addressing real world problems, issues important to humanity, and questions that matter."[182]

Then, educators will be expected to make the connection between what students are being asked to learn and how it will be useful to them in their lives. Media-savvy students, with multiple connections to information and ideas, will become a much more discriminating group when it comes to learning.

Project-based learning will offer students an opportunity to practice teamwork skills and experience the benefits of synergy. Active learning will move even further along the continuum from theory into practice. Distinguished futurist Joseph Coates believes "systems thinking aimed at helping students understand problems and possible solutions should be a core of teaching from kindergarten through college."

- **Helping students understand their roles in the global community.** The Millennials may be the first generation in a century or two to "grow to adulthood in a world environment that is less centered on the United States," says Frank Method, director of education policy for Research Triangle Institute,

International. In this environment, he suggests that "critical thinking skills, problem-based approaches, and collaborative learning modalities may be increasingly important."

Method points out that "the current generation is coming to adulthood in an environment . . . that promotes confidence that U.S. ways are superior and that the rest of the world is evolving toward similar ways and expectations." That can lead to injustice that is imposed because of "a failure to achieve those expectations or defend those principles," he concludes. In short, Millennials will need a firm understanding of the histories, cultures, and people of the world, and the ability to become constructive citizens of a planet that extends beyond their national boundaries.

- **Listening to students . . . giving them a voice.** This animated, energetic, committed generation of students will expect their voices to be heard in decisions that affect their education and their individual and collective futures. Listening to students is not just a nice thing to do. They have good ideas. They'll feel a greater sense of ownership. And it is *their* future.

- **Getting ready for the hurdles.** In our high-tech society, schools will be excoriated for *having* Internet filters and for *not having* them to deal with cyberporn or terrorist tool kits. Educators will be challenged to deal with everything from what they might consider unusual clothing to tattoos designed to send a message. Some students, who may not feel accepted by the larger group, may continue to find their identity in gangs. A bad grade, loss of a boyfriend or girlfriend, or being bullied could trigger violent responses, as students with limited life experience try to deal with their frustrations. Counselors, school psychologists, resource officers, and peers will need to be prepared to offer help in resolving conflicts and disputes and in putting what has been happening into perspective.

- **Offering opportunities for intergenerational communication.** Consensus might seem elusive with so many generations having access to a world of information. That's why schools, school systems, colleges, and other organizations need to deliberately create opportunities for intergenerational communication. Advisory councils, targeted emails, newsletters, and "bring a grandparent to lunch day" will help.

An elementary school in Taichung, Taiwan, actually set up a place inside the building where older citizens could get together for tea, read the paper, and visit. Since they were there, these wise and experienced citizens could be called into the classroom to help students understand how what they are being asked to learn will be important to them later in life.

Conversations with Millennials leave the impression that they feel a sense of responsibility for shaping the future and, if given a safe opportunity, would like very much to exchange ideas with people who are older and have substantial life experience.

- **Building media literacy skills.** A click of a mouse, and the screen lights up with a treasure trove of data and information. Without media literacy skills, however, people are increasingly vulnerable. Is what we're seeing fact or fiction? Is it true or false? Is it someone's opinion? Is it an opinion that should command attention?

Our cyber-attic is filled with information. Our future depends on the richness and trustworthiness of that information as we use it to make decisions about the future of our community, our country, and the planet.

In a fast-moving world, often driven more by technology than values, we need guidelines as we think about what deserves consideration. That's true whether we're making personal, family, or societal decisions . . . or deciding what should show up in that end-of-semester term paper.

Looking ahead, Ted Blaesing, superintendent of schools in White Bear Lake, Minn., predicts, "The demand for information that is factual is likely to replace the infotainment approach of current news programs."

- **Helping students understand how to build a case.** As our students pursue a cause, they need to know how to logically build a case. Their agility in mining the Internet can be helpful. On the other hand, they need to know how to organize their ideas, using creative and critical thinking skills.

Our students should be instilled with the curiosity and persistence they'll need to conduct research, consider pros and cons, make reasonable decisions, develop recommendations, and pursue appropriate action.

Education will become even more exciting as students have an opportunity to regularly analyze and synthesize what they are learning. In the process, they are likely to develop new knowledge and engage in what leadership experts call breakthrough thinking.

- **Building an understanding of ethical behavior.** All institutions, including schools and colleges, will be held to high ethical standards. What is simply pragmatic or expedient will give way to the ethical—trying to determine the right thing to do. Staff will need training, and students will need to develop an understanding of ethics as we move into the post-Enron world.

- **Becoming a partner in students' learning.** As noted earlier, growing numbers of students will come to school with more information on some topics than their teachers have. Is this a threat? No! Expansion of the knowledge base always should be a cause for celebration.

In addition to helping students move from data and information toward usable knowledge and wisdom, teachers will become orchestrators and facilitators of learning. The best teachers already are. They see themselves and their students as partners, each learning from the other. To make that happen, the education system will need to engage in generation-spanning professional development.

- **Attracting Millennials into education careers.** Granted, no matter how real the need, this could seem like a selfish but totally legitimate implication for educators. If, indeed, members of the Millennial Generation want to make a positive impact on the future, they should consider careers in education. As teachers and administrators who are Boomers retire, the United States alone will need to attract more than two million new teachers to the nation's classrooms. The same type of scenario is playing out in countries around the world.

Education systems need to focus attention on this high calling. At the same time, those who prepare our future educators will need to constantly upgrade their programs. Educators, after all, will be dealing with the Millennials. As students, and later when they become parents, they will be discriminating customers.

■ Questions and Activities

1. Study Strauss and Howe's "Four Turnings." Prepare a presentation or paper on how this phenomenon has, does, or will affect your organization.

2. Review the general characteristics we've listed for the Millennial Generation. What additional characteristics have you observed?

3. Consider people in your organization who are members of various generations. List 10 things they could and perhaps should learn from each other.

4. Develop a strategy for helping students learn about, appreciate, and enhance communication with generations other than their own.

5. If Millennials truly are committed to solving the world's problems and dealing with injustices, how can we educate them to attempt to make those changes peacefully and democratically?

6. How can schools and colleges educate people for understanding across generations?

■ Readings

1. Strauss, W., and Howe, N. (1998). *The fourth turning . . . An American prophesy.* New York: Bantam Doubleday.

2. Strauss, W., and Howe, N. (2000). *Millennials rising . . . The next great generation.* New York: Random House.

3. Zollo, P. (2004). *Getting wiser to teens.* New York: New Strategist.

4. Meredith, G.E., and Schewe, C.D., with Karlovich, J. (2002). *Defining markets, defining moments.* New York: Hungry Minds.

Trend 6

Let's get personal.

Standards and high–stakes tests will fuel a demand for personalization in an education system increasingly committed to lifelong human development.

Standardization → Personalization

"To any action, there is an equal and opposite reaction."

Sir Isaac Newton[183]

■ Standards . . . Static or Flexible?

We all aspire to standards that guide us in our performance and our behavior. Thoughtful people know, however, that the world is in the midst of exponential change, driven by people with dazzling mixtures of knowledge, talents, skills, interests, abilities, and behaviors.

We have a choice. Our standards can be narrow or expansive; they can be static or flexible. In education, they can freeze the system and its curriculum in the past, or they can encourage a constant process of preparing students for a future that is beyond our imagination.

"Not everything that counts can be counted, and not everything that can be counted counts."

Albert Einstein[184]

When high-stakes tests connected to those standards stop the education system in its tracks, lead to public rewards and punishments, and ultimately limit the curriculum to those things that are easily tested, the hackles start to rise. That's especially true for growing numbers of students with interests that go beyond what is taught or measured.

■ The Personalization Scenario

More and more schools and students are being declared failures because they haven't measured up on high-stakes tests. Students are held back or not allowed to graduate. Young people are raising concerns that the education they're receiving has been narrowed, primarily to what is being tested—that it does not offer the depth and breadth they need to get into college or pursue their dreams. Many parents are beginning to worry that their children are not getting the personal attention they need to be prepared for the future.

Newton's law is at work: To any action, there is an equal and opposite reaction. The outcome of the standards movement likely will be an increased demand for personalization of education. In a world crying for creative, knowledgeable people who've had an opportunity to develop their multitude of talents and abilities, what could be more positive?

■ How did we get here?

Sometimes, we get so caught up in current demands that it's hard to find the time or energy to examine the road we've traveled to get us where we are. For perspective, let's review a bit of pertinent history.

Tailoring our Teaching

"Give me time, autonomy, supportive colleagues, and few enough students so that I can understand each one well enough to tailor some of my teaching to him or her—and I will show you students who perform well, today and tomorrow."

Theodore Sizer, founder, Coalition of Essential Schools [185]

Some trace education testing in the United States to the Boston school trustees. In 1854, the story goes, they were concerned about the quality of instruction students were receiving. As they thought about it, they hit upon the idea of administering a written test to supplement their oral exams.

Interest continued to grow in academic measurement. That led to standardized tests. Some were norm referenced. Others were more discrete criterion-referenced tests. They were followed by intelligence tests, aptitude tests, and minimum competency tests. The National Assessment of Educational Progress (NAEP) has been producing what many have called "the nation's report card" since 1969-70. [186]

States adopted tests to help ensure schools were reaching state and, later, national standards. Some, such as the SAT and ACT—often known as college entrance exams—resulted in another set of numbers that are used publicly to compare schools, even though the averages are highly dependent on the percentage of students in a school or system actually taking the test. (Also see chapters in this book devoted to trends affecting minorities and poverty.)

■ The Rise of Expectations

In a nutshell, here are some relatively recent markers along the road to standards and high-stakes tests.

- Driven by concerns about inequities that resulted from what many saw as an over-reliance on widely differing local property taxes for the support of education, states took on a greater role in "equalizing" school funding.

- Concerned about holding school systems accountable for the state funds they were getting, legislatures wanted to see test results.

- A back to basics movement got under way, claiming in large part that the curriculum was too expansive and that schools needed to focus on a narrower range of offerings. That movement sparked a growing debate about what is basic for an educated person. What literacies do we need?

- Some suspected that growing "attacks" on public schools were part of a concerted effort to promote privatization. State takeovers also became somewhat common. Testing would be used to make the point that public school students were not doing well. Concern grew that the "gotcha" game some teachers applied to students might now be applied to whole schools.

- As stakes got higher, concern grew about schools that might be "teaching to the test." Incidents of alleged and actual cheating seemed to become more frequent. Many teachers expressed concern that tests should be used to determine what students have or have not learned and help them guide instruction, not to sort students and schools as a means of declaring winners and losers.

- Noting a sharp increase in international competition, leaders in business and government called for education reform. Many didn't think U.S. students were capable enough to be competitive in the international marketplace. Some pointed to comparisons among several nations' student achievement tests. At conferences and summits, business and government leaders found growing support for standards and testing, most of it conducted at the state and local levels.

No Child Left Behind (NCLB)

The intent of this 2002 U.S. federal education act is to close the achievement gap between disadvantaged students and their peers through making all students "proficient" by 2014. Described as an accountability measure, based on data, NCLB expects schools to make "adequate yearly progress" (AYP). A prescribed percentage of students need to pass tests in math, reading, and language arts in grades three through eight, as well as once in high school. Science assessments, at least once in elementary, middle, and high school, are scheduled at this writing to begin by the 2007-08 school year. All students are expected to reach proficiency in math and reading by 2013-14. Those schools that consistently do not show adequate yearly progress are categorized as low-performing schools.[187] The law has many other provisions; however, it is largely based on a foundation of standards and testing.

- As education took its place as one of the most important political and economic issues facing our country and the world, the federal government stepped in, spelling out even more rules of the game. Standards and high-stakes testing were at the center of it. Comparisons were drawn between and among states and schools, and test results blazed across the front pages of newspapers. A federal law declared that if schools did not make "adequate yearly progress," they could eventually be declared as failing.

■ Standards . . .

What questions should we be asking?

If we were buying a car, we would very likely read all we could find about cars. We would want to be ready to ask good questions and be sure what we were considering was right for our needs. We would probably be concerned about quality, price, service, and whether the model we were test-driving had a record for breakdowns or reliability.

When we're considering something as important as standards for the education of our children, it just makes sense that we would also ask hard questions. Unfortunately, those who ask questions are often labeled as opposed to standards or "presumably content with lower standards," says high-stakes testing critic Alfie Kohn.[188] "Tests have lately become a mechanism by which public officials can impose their will on schools, and they are doing it with a vengeance," he remarks.[189]

Key Questions about Standards. Before appropriate standards can be developed, it is important to consider these key issues.

- Do the standards focus on preparing students for the future, or do they freeze the system and its students in the past?

- Will students who don't do well on the tests—who don't measure up—simply give up, drop out, or be pushed out of school?

- Will high-stakes tests narrow the curriculum?

- Will pressure created by imposing standards and high-stakes tests, without adequate resources to personalize education, drive talented teachers and administrators from the field and discourage aspiring educators from pursuing careers in education?

■ Let's get personal

Nothing really happens in school until it happens to a student.

Wherever they are, schools are often among the largest organizations in a community. It is perhaps ironic that such formidable

146

institutions deliver one of the most personal services in any society. That's just one reason why educators need to make every effort to consider individuals and their needs when working with their communities and educating their students.

Personalizing education is certainly not a new concept. It's the core idea behind schools-within-a-school; reductions in class size; summer school; alternative schools; magnet schools; charter schools; individualized instruction; teacher advisor systems; after-school programs; in-school and out-of-school tutoring; certain approaches to mastery learning and outcome-based education; Advanced Placement programs; individual education plans (IEPs) for special education students; attention to learning styles, teaching styles, and school climate; and a host of other approaches. Depending on how the effort is organized, the commitment of those involved, and the resources available, all of these can bring some success.

Most teachers and principals can readily recount how they have helped individual students succeed in academics and the development of unique talents, skills, interests, and abilities—even in shaping appropriate behaviors. Thoughtful school counselors and psychologists, working in tandem with caring teachers, have been trying to narrow the valley between individual students and the school for decades.

Students, like everyone, obviously come in a variety of packages. In the late 1980s and early 1990s, David Kolb, a professor of organizational behavior at Case Western Reserve University, identified and began describing four learning styles, including: imaginative, analytic, common sense, and dynamic learners.[190]

■ Essentials of School Climate

School climate is on nearly any list of characteristics describing effective schools, and it is an essential consideration in personalizing education. Jim Sweeney, a longtime distinguished professor at Iowa State University, who conducted school climate studies in hundreds of schools and worked with thousands of teachers, identifies 10 factors that are essential to a winning school climate:

- A supportive, stimulating environment

- Student-centered philosophy

- Positive expectations

- Feedback

- Rewards

- A sense of family

- Closeness to parents and community

- Communication

- Achievement

- Trust[191]

■ Personalizing Education

On-the-Ground Examples

Concern about personalizing education seems to be growing. The acceleration of interest, to some extent, is in direct reaction to the lack of flexibility in demands for students to demonstrate they have met certain standards by doing well on high-stakes tests. The problem with a one-size-fits-all approach is that each student is unique. These are not cookie-cutter kids. Round pegs don't fit into square holes, but that doesn't mean we don't need round pegs.

Here are a few of the myriad programs, and options that zero in on the need to offer more personalized education.

Multiple Intelligences. Perhaps the most focused contemporary approach to personalizing education has been driven by Howard Gardner's classic work, *Frames of Mind*, published in 1983. He expanded on that work in a later book, *Multiple Intelligences . . . The Theory in Practice*, published in 1993.

Gardner's premise is that each of us has some mix of seven or more "intelligences," which he defines as "the ability to solve problems or fashion products that are of consequence in a particular cultural setting or community."

The old definition of intelligence, Gardner says, was largely "the ability to answer items on tests of intelligence." Seven of the intelligences he identifies are: musical, bodily-kinesthetic, logical-mathematical, linguistic, spatial, interpersonal, and intrapersonal. Gardner's theories are based on actual cognitive research.[192]

Some parents and educators complain that schools too often teach to only a few of those intelligences, which leads to student frustration and a loss of a fully developed range of talents society needs to advance.

Coalition of Essential Schools. "In most high schools, teens do not develop relationships with adults, largely because of the typical teacher load of 150 to 180 kids," according to a paper devoted to high school reform produced by the Education Writers Association. Coalition of Essential Schools founder Ted Sizer recommends something closer to 50 students per teacher (overall load, not class size). "Give me time, autonomy, supportive colleagues, and few enough students so that I can understand each one well enough to tailor some of my teaching to him or her—and I will show you students who perform well, today and tomorrow," Sizer told ASCD's *Educational Leadership* magazine.[193]

Smaller Learning Communities. The Education Foundation of the Charleston, S.C., Chamber of Commerce has created a Smaller Learning Communities Coalition "to provide small, safe learning environments where all students feel known, supported, and moti-vated to succeed." The Coalition hopes to work with school systems in Berkeley, Charleston, and Dorchester counties to "implement smaller learning communities, improve student achievement through rigorous academics, increase the relevance of academics through contextual learning experiences, and engage students through build-ing meaningful and effective relationships." Hoped for results will be "a decrease in our failure rate, an increase in our graduation rate, and an effective effort to combat anonymity and alienation among our youth," according to a descriptive planning grant abstract.[194]

New York Networks for School Renewal. In New York City, through an Annenberg Challenge initiative, 140 small schools were created to focus on the needs of approximately 50,000 students. According to a report on the program, the schools were "character-ized by innovative, respectful, and collaborative learning environ-ments." According to the report, the schools typically had lower dropout rates, better student and teacher attendance, and less student mobility than schools citywide.[195]

After-school Technical Assistance Collaboration. The Mott Foundation, a longtime advocate of community education, has been at work stimulating development of a network of after-school centers. Particularly active in low-income and under-served com-munities, the program addresses a 2000 estimate by the U.S. Census Bureau and the Urban Institute that "between seven to 15 million children return to an empty house on any given school day." Students might gather with their teacher after school and head for a museum, learn fractions by following a recipe as they make cupcakes, or hop into a full-sized canoe in the middle of the classroom to paddle down an imaginary river." The March 2004 issue of *Mott Mosaic* reported the program was active in 18 states, addressing the needs of individual children.[196]

Advanced Math for Elementary Students. The Fairfax County Public Schools in Virginia, with 166,000 students and 241 schools, had been busing some elementary students to a high school for advanced math classes. Now, the students can log in to the class at their home school while their teacher is teaching math to everyone else. The new approach makes a personal service more accessible and negates the loss of instruction time while riding the bus.[197]

Smaller High Schools in Baltimore. With support of a grant from the Bill & Melinda Gates foundation and eight philanthropies based in Baltimore, that city's public school system planned "to retool nine struggling high schools as part of an ongoing effort by the Gates Foundation to decrease class size," according to *Education Week*.[198] Baltimore has also opened smaller-enrollment "innovation high schools." For example, one is a 600-student Talent Development High School (TDHS), a partnership involving the district, Johns Hopkins University, and the Academy for college and Career Exploration. The school features an intense curriculum, coupled with a personalized atmosphere, community involvement, and an emphasis on the arts, expression, and career academics. It was also designed to include Advanced Placement classes, set high expectations for students, and help staff and students focus on the same goals.[199]

The Complete Curriculum. A report, "The Complete Curriculum: Ensuring a Place for the Arts and Foreign Languages in America's Schools," asks people in charge to be sure these subjects are not given short shrift or dropped from the curriculum. Brenda Welburn, executive director of the National Association of State Boards of Education, in response to that report, told *Education Week*, "With our heavy focus on testing a limited number of subjects, schools are using all the available time to shore up kids' basic skills in order to have them show improvement on the tests." She added, "While we understand the need for every student to have strong fundamental skills, we are not providing a comprehensive education for all students."[200]

■ Standards and High-Stakes Testing

Many studies, news articles, and educators in the field support higher levels of achievement for all but express concern about the impact of the high-stakes environment on individual students, families, and schools.

A flurry of news reports have addressed concerns such as: the possible abandonment of the term paper in favor of required tests; the alignment of teaching, standards, and tests; a tendency to teach to the test, thereby letting "the tail wag the dog"; clarifying the meaning of "proficient"; the limits placed on learning by specific, uniform mandates; the tendency for some students who are having problems with the mandated tests to drop out of school; a bulge in the ninth grade as students are held back because of unacceptable test performance; and a report in March 2001 that states were already spending a half-billion dollars on testing.[201]

Student/Parent Reaction. "High stakes testing, standards-based education, and teacher accountability will result in longer hours, more homework, more pressure on kids, and in some cases increased parental displeasure as schools take time from the family and as it becomes apparent that students are not all outstanding," observes Susan Wooley, executive director of the American School Health Association in Kent, Ohio.[202]

Requirements that Thwart Efforts to Help Minority Students. Another flag is hoisted by Rick Kaufman, former executive director of public engagement and communication for the Jefferson County Public Schools, headquartered in Golden, Colo. "School districts continue to be barraged with state and federal mandates with little or no money to accompany these laws," he points out. "Therefore, some programs that have proven to be effective in closing the achievement gap and meeting the needs of growing numbers of minority students and families will suffer the budget ax." Kaufman concludes, "Communities will need assistance in understanding the cultural diversity of their growing minority populations, and then meeting those needs."

Public attention is riveted on "average" test scores. However, the "tyranny of the average" means that even when averages go up, some individual students who still need personal help might get lost in the system's general success.

Mandates Straining Efforts to Help Children from Low-Income Homes. Betsy Rogers, 2003 National Teacher of the Year, expresses deep concern about state or federal mandates that are un- or under-funded. "As a classroom teacher, I welcome the accountability but understand the financial strain these mandates are creating," she says. "In order for all children, including those from low-income families, to have safe, healthy, and comfortable school facilities, with well-qualified teachers and high quality curriculum and learning materials, we all must work together. The federal, state, and local governments, along with educators, parents, and citizens, all need to become stakeholders in our schools."

Reduced Emphasis on Certain Subjects. The Council for Basic Education, in a 2004 study, *Academic Atrophy*, noted that "the exclusive focus of the law's (No Child Left Behind) accountability provisions on mathematics, reading, and eventually science is diverting significant time and resources from other academic subjects." The study revealed: decreases in instructional time for social studies, civics, and geography in elementary (K-5) schools; and decreases in instructional time and professional development for the arts and foreign languages, especially in high-minority schools. On the other hand, the study noted increases in instructional time and professional development for reading, writing, mathematics, and science.[203]

In an *Education Week* story, Claus von Zastrow, who wrote the *Academic Atrophy* report, is quoted as saying, "The bad news is we see compelling evidence of a waning commitment to social studies at the elementary level and to the arts and foreign languages. But for us, the most troubling news is that the strongest evidence of curricular erosion appears in schools with high-minority populations."[204]

Time Spent on Testing. In an *Education Week* commentary, standards and testing critic Alfie Kohn noted that, "Our children are tested to an extent that is unprecedented in our history and unparalleled anywhere else in the world." He added that "never have tests been given so frequently, and never have they played such a prominent role in schooling."[205]

Pressure Produces Lock-Step Curriculum. In a February 2002 commentary, Association for Supervision and Curriculum Development (ASCD) Executive Director Gene Carter addressed possible unintended consequences of standards and accountability. He noted, "The pressure to produce results has led many districts to adopt prescribed curricula that dictate precisely what will be taught and when, with little or no room for variation or individualization. To cover this curriculum and produce the desired test scores, educators are often forced to ignore what they know about how students learn. As any teacher will tell you, students are unique individuals with differing talents, interests, and needs. A lock-step curriculum that treats all students the same serves none of our students well."[206]

■ Let's Be Flexible

To freeze is to fail.

In a fast-moving world, any standard and any testing program must be flexible. Neither should, individually or in combination, attempt to freeze the world in place. New programs will be needed and mid-course corrections will be essential. To freeze is to fail.

Supporting this book's predecessor, *Ten Trends . . . Educating Children for a Profoundly Different Future*, former president of the National School Boards Association (NSBA) Mary Maxwell said,

"Parents are demanding high standards, but we must all make sure the infrastructure is there in our schools to support high standards." She added, "We need adequate resources for smaller class sizes, for teacher professional development, and for whatever teachers need to help students reach high standards."[207]

All students, despite their social, economic, or other backgrounds, need to have a chance to succeed. Recognizing and striving to meet the need for personalization could be one of the most powerful forces for improvement in education, and it could pay huge dividends.

■ Implications for Society

Personalization

Obviously, the tendency to balance standards with personalization has a direct impact on the education system. What about society as a whole? The implications are significant.

- As we move into a knowledge/information age, leaders in business and government will need to understand that those communities that are prospering are the ones most able to attract creative, imaginative people, not just those who test well.

- Public officials who impose standards and high-stakes tests will need to be flexible, because the world is moving quickly, and freezing the education system may inhibit rather than enable it to produce the people who will provide leadership in the future.

- Communities will need to constantly ask whether the standards that have been set are appropriate for producing students capable of thriving in a global knowledge/information age.

- Those who aspire to elected or appointed office should be asked in-depth questions about the benefits and potential consequences of the specific policies they recommend.

- The win-lose mindset will need to be replaced with a commitment to considering the interests, talents, abilities, and aspirations of each person. A primary goal should be to give each one the best shot at making a valuable contribution to their families, communities, countries, and world. As part of this approach, we need to move away from the "scoreboard mentality," or the belief that progress in education can be reduced to the reporting of a simple set of numbers, like box scores for baseball, football, soccer, and other sports.

- Communities, states or provinces, and nations that aspire to have students reach legitimately high standards must be expected to provide the resources and other support to make that kind of attainment possible. Commenting on the U.S. federal education law No Child Left Behind, Elizabeth Hale, president of the Institute for Educational Leadership (IEL), comments that the program "is considered by most to be an unfunded federal mandate." She explains, "Districts and states are not being given enough support to deliver all that they are being asked to deliver."

- True leaders in society must stand up for sound education rather than simply making it a political football. George Hollich, retired director of curriculum and summer programs for the Milton Hershey School in Pennsylvania, says, "We have become a nation that wants things done as we say, not as we do. We continue to focus on the extremes. We want standards and accountability for our nation's schools, but don't want the schools to teach values or hold families accountable. We want after school, summer, and enrichment programming, but squabble over how to pay for them. We want well-rounded kids, but demand curriculums that feature depth over breadth."

■ Implications for Education

Personalization

- **Personalizing as a key to reaching standards.** Schools will be challenged to shape education programs that balance the interests, abilities, talents, and aspirations of students with the needs of society. Since students have a world of information and ideas at their fingertips in our fast-emerging global knowledge/information age, they will insist on understanding why what they are expected to learn will be useful to them. We live in an era of mass customization, which constantly puts pressure on standardization.

  In addressing "high stakes consequences," Arnold Fege, president of Public Advocacy for Kids, remarks, "What will be sacrificed is the non-standard student who cannot function in a compliance-based classroom."

  Growing numbers of educators and public officials will need to realize that the only logical way to reach and exceed appropriate standards will be through personalization. "The success of our schools will be measured on how quickly we move toward emphasizing the development and application of each individual's skills and talents, as opposed to being an informational delivery system," George Hollich remarks.

- **Ensuring standards do not limit the curriculum or push students out of school.** Average test scores will likely rise if we teach only a couple of things and forget everything else, but students cannot be considered well educated if the curriculum is narrowed to only those few things that are tested and reported by the news media.

  Another way to raise test scores is to acquiesce as students who are having problems drop out of school. Again, "average" test scores will likely go up as those who are having difficulty leave. Remember, however, that by 2030, only two people will be working for every person drawing benefits from Social Security. Those "people" had better be well educated and make a good living if we hope to have them paying Social Security taxes. Our individual and collective futures are at stake in making sure students stay in school and that their full range of talents is developed.

"While affluent and better educated parents usually provide ample encouragement and support for their progeny, less fortunates do not fare so well," warns futurist Graham Molitor. "Failing to provide every student proper and best opportunities for honing and fully developing their innermost potentials is a tragedy," he remarks.

- **Linking equity and adequacy of funding.** Michael Silver, assistant professor of educational administration at Seattle University, notes, "For the last 50 years, since *Brown v. Board of Education*, the primary focus of schools and school finance has been to provide equal opportunity for students with limited resources." He adds, "With an increasing high needs student population coupled with a set of common standards and assessment measures of quality education, the focus of school funding shifts from equity to adequacy. Simply redirecting existing funding to achieve proficiency standards is inadequate."

- **Clarifying the limits of testing.** Educational institutions may need to launch concerted communication programs aimed at building better community-wide understanding of the benefits and limits of testing. Too often, citizens are confronted with comparisons of apples and oranges when they read stories about test results.

Standardized testing, based on established norms, can provide a snapshot of broad-based performance by students in a school or school system. *College entrance exams* can measure certain aptitudes or knowledge, but the average scores for a school or school system are highly dependent on the percentage of a class that takes them. The lower the percentage of students taking the SAT or ACT, the more likely those taking it will be nearer the top of the class. *Criterion-referenced tests* can be valuable in helping the teacher more clearly understand what a student has learned and where that student needs further help.

The nation needs to be concerned about "an overemphasis on student assessment as a means to improve the education system," remarks Kenneth Bird, superintendent of The Westside Community Schools in Omaha, Neb. "Lack of funding, coupled with a misdirected focus on testing results and expanded expectations . . . can be a recipe for failure," he warns.

- **Developing mutual expectations.** What expectations does a community, state, or country have for its schools? What expectations should the schools have for their communities, their governors and state legislators, their state and federal education agencies, the Congress, and the president? What expectations do we all have for students, and what are the expectations students should have for all of us? While standards often seem imposed, expectations seem closer to home . . . and more personal. We should try to develop a mutual understanding of the expectations we have for each other.

- **Employing more performance-based testing.** Testing should provide students with an opportunity to show what they've learned. On the other hand, tests should provide educators with an indication of what students still need to learn. Performance-based testing often uses portfolios and exhibits of student work. It allows students to demonstrate what they've learned in a number of ways. Teachers are, in many cases, more likely to understand what a student has mastered and where the student needs additional help from this type of performance-focused testing than from a fill-in-the-bubble multiple choice test that is, admittedly, easier to machine score.

- **Developing the individual talents and abilities of all students.** Whatever their social or economic backgrounds, all students should have an equal opportunity . . . and the encouragement . . . to flourish. Educators are generally committed to enhancing the talents and abilities of each student. To get that done, they will need to consciously consider learning styles, strengths, weaknesses, and strategies for releasing each student's genius. Some are concerned this type of personal or individual approach is inhibited by an overemphasis on externally imposed standards. For example, V. Wayne Young, executive director of the Kentucky Association of School Administrators, expresses concern about "the demands of and for assessment and accountability at the expense of other goals."

- **Encouraging educators to prepare students for the future rather than become compliant bureaucrats.** Some educators express concern that they have little time for creating the education system their community needs, because they are too busy managing compliance with mandates.

Whatever programs are mandated, educators need to see it as their duty to build on them to prepare students for life in a new millennium. "Legislators have intervened to overwhelm the authority of educators to set academic standards, but without regard for new ways to organize learning and new ways to make it more productive and successful for more kinds of learning styles," says Rowe, Inc. President Gary Rowe.

Arnold Fege raises concern about what he sometimes sees as "the transformation of education leaders in our country from intellectual icons of their community to bureaucrats who are increasingly just a part of the infrastructure." He calls for educators to "transform education from the industrial model, characterized by efficiency, to the knowledge model, characterized by effectiveness that depends on the quality of educational, political, private sector, and community leadership." That coming together of leadership will be essential, he says, "to begin and sustain the retrofit" . . . that provides "a high level of learning to every child, no matter what that child's zip code happens to be."

■ Questions and Activities

1. Do you believe it will be possible to help students truly achieve without personalizing education in a way that considers their interests, talents, and abilities? Why or why not?

2. If you are an educator, how are you and your school or college currently attempting to personalize education for each student? Identify at least six additional ways you would like to see your education system personalize its services.

3. Briefly, explain how the standards and high-stakes testing movement got under way.

4. React to this statement, "If the education system had regularly focused on the process of creating a future rather than defending the status quo, the standards would not have been imposed in the first place."

5. What questions should we be asking about standards?

6. What are the "multiple intelligences" identified by Howard Gardner?

■ Readings

1. Gardner, H. (1993). *Multiple intelligences: The theory in practice.* NY: Basic Books, Harper Collins.

2. National Governors Association. (2005). *A primer on No Child Left Behind.* Washington, D.C.: Author. Retrieved from http://www.nga.org

3. Council for Basic Education. (2004). *Academic atrophy . . . The condition of the liberal arts in America's public schools.* Washington, D.C.: Author.

4. Kohn, A. (2000). *The case against standardized testing.... Raising the scores, ruining the schools.* Portsmouth, NH: Heinemann.

Trend 7

Assignment—put ideas together!

Release of human ingenuity will become a primary responsibility of education and society.

Information Acquisition → *Knowledge Creation and Breakthrough Thinking*

"In 500 years, we've moved from a world where everything was certain and nothing changed to a world where nothing seems certain and everything changes."

Michael Gelb, How to Think Like Leonardo da Vinci[208]

■ Wanted: Intellectual Entrepreneurs

No kidding! That heading is fast becoming a help wanted ad. Nations are advancing and economies developing not by digging in their nails and hanging on to the status quo but by constantly creating new knowledge.

A fresh generation of intellectual entrepreneurs is putting the pieces together, seeing certain things in a whole new light, dealing with paradox and controversy, developing creative solutions to problems, and conceiving of new knowledge-based industries.[209]

Richard Florida, author of *The Rise of the Creative Class*, calls it "the 'Eureka' step."[210]

As we move at rocket speed into a global knowledge/information age, we are confronted by unprecedented progress, accompanied by a startling number of real and possible side effects, wildcards, and both intended and unintended consequences. It's a time of reinvention. Every institution, including our education system, will be renewed. Either we can take the lead to engage people in that renewal, or others will do the renewing for us.

Why should educators be concerned? The reasons are crystal clear—their job is to prepare students to become good citizens who are employable and well-adjusted people, capable of shaping an even brighter future. Of course, the need for academic knowledge, skills, and behaviors will be as important as ever.

Futurist Joseph Coates sees the purposes of education as "preparation for work, preparation for civic duty, and carrying forward our cultural heritage." Whatever we currently have on our list, educators now face another set of requirements—unleashing the genius of their students, helping them find relationships among what seem to be disparate pieces of information, and encouraging them to become intellectual entrepreneurs. To do that, both the education system and its students will need to be prepared to deal with ambiguity rather than treating each piece of information, each idea, as cut-and-dried, separate, or overly simple.

The ability to explore, to use our ingenuity, and to have the intellectual stamina and courage to overcome apparent adversity will increasingly be seen as 21st-century survival skills. Students—all of us in fact—need to be prepared to move from our lowest common denominators to our highest common possibilities.

Two personal qualities will be major drivers of this earthshaking trend, *curiosity* and *persistence*. Show me a person who is curious and persistent, and I'll show you a person who will be pretty well educated for the rest of her or his life.

Lead Time v. Lag Time

"It is popularly believed that the lead time between new knowledge and its conversion into products and services has recently become much shorter. Not so," said Peter Drucker in his 1980 classic, *Managing in Turbulent Times*. "The lead time today is what it has been for a very long time, about 30 to 40 years," he remarked.[211]

Today, tension is growing not necessarily about lead time, but about lag time. Consider this: Computer speed and capacity are doubling every 18 months. However, today's thoughtful observers note that organizational change can take up to 20 years.

As knowledge creation and breakthrough thinking accelerate, will our organizations be able to keep up with it, no less capitalize on it?

■ Getting It All Together

Teaching, Learning, Thinking, and Making Connections across Disciplines

Education faces substantial challenges in helping students learn and think across disciplines. While educators are committed to teaching their subject, and most organizations are composed of departments that specialize, someone needs to be paying attention to connective tissue. For example, what impact do discoveries in physical or biological sciences have on social science, and vice versa? It is in those white spaces between disciplines—in those connections—that knowledge creation and breakthrough thinking often take place.

Contemporary philosopher Ken Wilber observes, "If we look at various fields of human knowledge—from physics to biology to psychology, sociology, theology, and religion—certain broad, general themes emerge, about which there is actually very little disagreement." What we see as a whole may "simultaneously be a part of some other whole," Wilber reminds us. "The beads of knowledge are already accepted: it is only necessary to string them together into a necklace."[212]

Helping us get it all together has become a mission for Harvard professor and biologist Edward O. Wilson. In *Consilience: The Unity of Knowledge*, he says legitimate human progress is too often brought to a crawl because people don't think or communicate across disciplines and see things in context. "The ongoing fragmentation of knowledge and resulting chaos in philosophy are not reflections of the real world but artifacts of scholarship," Wilson remarks. Many organizations are collections of seemingly disconnected departments. Many education institutions are often seen as collections of disconnected disciplines.

Wilson asks us to link facts and theories across disciplines. Rather than insisting that biology, environmental policy, social science, and ethics are solitary disciplines, we need to see where they intersect and how they relate to others.[213]

Static mindsets that will not yield to the possibilities of an interconnected, multidisciplinary world will increasingly be seen as medieval. "The individual's ability to learn, adapt, and think, independently and creatively, is at a premium," according to Michael Gelb in *How to Think Like Leonardo da Vinci*. "During the Renaissance, individuals with a medieval mind-set were left behind," he points out. "Now, in the information age, medieval- and industrial-era thinkers are threatened with extinction."[214]

Complexity is sometimes clarified when we finally discover the obvious unifying forces that surround us. In recent decades, "string theory" has speculated that "where the quantum effects of gravity are strong, particles (which may seem lonely in their separateness) are actually one-dimensional extended objects," according to Robbert Dijkgraaf, a member of the department of mathematics at the University of Amsterdam. The great thinker Isaac Newton once observed, as he was ponderingly walking the shore looking for small stones, "a great ocean of truth was all around me."

"Creativity is multidimensional and experiential," Richard Florida observes, and it springs from working and thinking across disciplines. He quotes psychologist Dean Keith Simonton, who writes, "creativity is favored by an intellect that has been enriched with diverse experiences and perspectives." It is "associated with a mind that exhibits a variety of interests and knowledge."

In addition to creativity in the arts, culture, and nearly every other field, Florida sees invention as "technological creativity" and entrepreneurship as "economic creativity." He identifies Thomas Edison as a technological creative, for instance, and George Bernard Shaw as a cultural creative.[215] It's a safe bet that, as we move into the future, whole new industries and careers will emerge and people will think and work across disciplines.

Obviously, we also need to be creative and entrepreneurial in the not-for-profit sector, as we work to improve our schools, communities, governments, and general quality of life.

■ Taking the Lid Off Ingenuity

Many of the great geniuses of all time—people like Albert Einstein—had problems in school. Let's face it, geniuses can be a handful. They ask too many questions. They're "incorrigible." In some cases, these complaints might be justified. Yet, the chicken and egg question always emerges: Should the student adjust to the

Avoid "Killer" Comments

Unfortunately, rather than welcoming genius, we often discourage it, find it threatening, or simply don't have time for it.

"Killer" comments too often serve as spoken and sometimes even written roadblocks. They include: "We've tried that before"; "It costs too much"; "It's not practical"; "Let's put that one on the back burner"; "Look, we've always done it this way, and we're not changing now"; "That's not our problem"; "You don't have the authority to do that"; "Let's quit daydreaming and get back to work";[216] and the ever popular, "What nincompoop thought of that idea?"

Instead of reacting to new ideas in a negative way, we should respond with, "Interesting idea! What would you see as next steps?" "Let's add that idea to the list." "Keep thinking. That's what's going to keep us on the leading edge."

school, or should the school adjust to the talents, abilities, and interests of the student? The most enlightened answer likely is both.

Free societies are noted for encouraging the creative genius of people. The searing question is what is the political, economic, social, technological, and environmental mix that encourages persistent researchers, audacious designers, breakthrough entertainers, and so many others who shape a culture?

Consider music and the arts. What was it, in the then-frantic Gilded Age, that sparked Irving Berlin to write "Alexander's Ragtime Band?" What stimulated the creative genius of Aaron Copeland to pen "Appalachian Spring," reflecting what he considered "the direct, plain, optimistic, and energetic" American character? Who would have predicted at the turn of the 20th century that it would become known as the period in history that produced a Louis Armstrong, a Glenn Miller, or a Duke Ellington? How was it, that in the 1950s, in a world of Doris Day and Perry Como, Bill Haley and the Comets changed everything with "Shake, Rattle, and Roll"; Ray Charles produced his "revolutionary hybrid of blues and gospel"; and Elvis Presley burst on the scene with "Heartbreak Hotel"? What stirred the Beatles to concoct a sound that connected with much of humanity beginning in the 1960s? What was the social mix that produced hip-hop and rap?[217]

While we don't know the exact answers to these questions, schools, parents, communities, countries, and our world need to cultivate ingenuity that is waiting to be discovered in each of us. That genius comes in many forms. Indeed, psychologist Howard Gardner helped us identify some of our "multiple intelligences." We need to admit, however, that seeing things in a new light, creating new knowledge, engaging in breakthrough thinking, and using our creativity all take a great deal of discipline. The logical conclusion, then, is that thinking and reasoning skills should be touchstones of modern education.

■ Stirring a New Era of Enlightenment

Are we asking the right questions?

We're moving into a new era of enlightenment, which will likely be propelled by the energy of the Millennial Generation—people born from about 1982 through 2003—who are committed to solving the problems and dealing with the injustices of the world. For the sake of our future, education should help current and succeeding generations of students understand that conventional approaches or habits may not work in improving the quality of life for more people.

In a world intent on quickly coming up with all the answers, our Millennials will very likely be concerned about whether we're

The Arts

Linking creativity, imagination, common ground, and our spirits

The arts challenge our perceptions. They help us see the world in new and creative ways.

Music, dance, musical theater, the visual arts, design, creative writing, and many other art forms stimulate our thinking. Our future might very well depend on our ability to see and think in new ways, across disciplines. The arts help us do just that.

"The future of our nation depends on our ability to create—and to be creative," according to *Performing Together . . . The Arts and Education.* That publication, produced jointly by the John F. Kennedy Center for the Performing Arts and the American Association of School Administrators, notes that the arts: are a basic means of communication, develop creativity and creative talents, help students learn other subjects, lead to a better understanding of human civilization, encourage the development of discipline, prepare students for their adult lives, and develop artistic judgment.[218]

After experiencing the loss of a music program at his old high school, Rod Sims, an advertising executive in Fullerton, Calif., wrote in *Education Week*, "The beauty and power of artistic expression lie in its ability to transport the self beyond present circumstances to imagine what has not yet come to pass. Inspiration, hope, and promise are all part of a complex mix of emotions that can't be placed on a scale and weighed, or burned off as a byproduct in a chemistry lab."[219]

It will take imagination and creativity to conceive of ideas, products, services, performances, and pathways to peace and understanding. The arts can help us find common ground and lift our spirits. Former U.S. President John F. Kennedy said, "I am certain that after the dust of centuries has passed over our cities, we too will be remembered not for victories or defeats in battle or politics, but for our contributions to the human spirit."

asking the right questions. Malcolm Gladwell, in his book, *Blink*, warns, "We have, as human beings, a storytelling problem. We are a bit too quick to come up with explanations for things we don't really have any explanation for." All the more reason that thinking and reasoning should be considered basic skills.[220]

What are the qualities of people who are capable of stimulating and sustaining an enlightenment? In his book, *Culture Shift*, David Henderson suggests they must be confident, aware, optimistic, progressive, reasonable, skeptical, committed to freedom, and always looking to the future. They see politics less as a source of power and more as a process of pursuing moral principles, he says.[221]

Reacting to this trend, Carol Brown, 2004 president of the National School Boards Association, commented, "This is very similar to the concept of a 'liberal' education that 'liberates' human capacity by enabling complex and interrelated thinking."

■ Implications for Society

Knowledge Creation and Breakthrough Thinking

Worldwide, people are affected by the acceleration in knowledge creation and breakthrough thinking. Consider just a few of this trend's implications for society:

- Progressive communities, businesses, governmental and non-governmental organizations, and countries will compete for creative, ingenious people who will conceive of new solutions to problems as well as new generations of ideas, products and services, and whole new industries. Jane Hammond, superintendent in residence for the Stupski Foundation, for example, notes the growing strength of manufacturing in China and its ripple effect around the planet. "Preparation for the U.S. job market will have to change, as there are significantly fewer opportunities in manufacturing," she points out.

- People will become more dismissive of pat answers and arbitrary solutions, preferring instead to consider alternatives or scenarios that result from putting divergent information and ideas together to create new knowledge.

- Those who insist on maintaining the status quo or lack the resources to become part of an accelerating global knowledge/information age may feel left out, lose hope, become angry, and strike out at people and nations that are on a fast track.

- Education systems will increasingly be expected to turn out people who have a broad-based education and who are capable of thinking across and connecting many disciplines and ideas.

- National and multinational organizations, as well as local communities, will be compelled to develop a new social context—a mentality that will accommodate an age of renewal.

- At all levels, attention must be focused on how decisions might lead to unfairness, to progress that is not environmentally sustainable, or possibly even to violence. Creativity must address justice, not just productivity. Growing numbers of people will also realize progress has different meanings in different cultures.

- Because of life experience—some positive and some horrifying—we hope society will learn from history rather than being "condemned" to repeat it.

■ Implications for Education

Knowledge Creation and Breakthrough Thinking

Placing a spotlight on discovering and encouraging human ingenuity, in addition to the longstanding purposes of education, presents opportunities for fresh thinking and can help stimulate renewal of the system. While the numbers of intellectual entrepreneurs and creatives will increase, the education system will be expected to prepare them not only to think well across disciplines but also to ensure they place what they do in an ethical context. Some of the challenges facing education will be:

- **Helping students learn across disciplines.** While the standards movement makes many teachers and administrators cautious about focusing on the white spaces between disciplines, they will need to overcome their apprehension. Look at a person who is truly well educated and wise, and you'll discover a person who sees connections.

- **Applying what we know from cognitive research.** Perhaps more than anything else, the brain makes connections. As educators, we need to give it things to connect.

  Emotion, says Edward O. Wilson, is what "animates and focuses mental activity." He adds, "without the stimulus and guidance of emotion, rational thought slows and disintegrates." Certainly, educators need to apply what they have learned from studies of multiple intelligences, explained earlier in this book.[222]

  Prime questions to ponder: How can we make schools more interesting for all students? How can we help our students develop a broad range of interests, ideas, and skills, and to connect the dots?

- **Making thinking and reasoning basic to education.** Students need to be nurtured in both critical and creative thinking. On the one hand, they need to understand syllogistic logic, inductive and deductive reasoning, and how to use it. On the other hand, educators need to cultivate students' and their own capacities for lateral or creative thinking, flashes of insight, and thinking outside the box.

Research tells us that, when we ask a question, we need to allow more than just a few seconds for a student to answer. Those few extra seconds, that "wait time," will send a message that we really care about what they're thinking.

Zooming out, we encounter metacognition, which involves virtually thinking about thinking. Driving questions might be, What do I know? or What don't I know? Do we understand how to connect new information to knowledge we already have, or to our personal experience? Do we understand and even discuss our thought process and ask others to share theirs? Metacognition is important not only for students but also for educators and other leaders to understand.

One more thing: Let's not lose their imagination. Albert Einstein, in fact, argued, "Imagination is more important than knowledge." Courage will be needed, especially when budgets are tight, to encourage the dreams and rescue the ingenuity of even those we consider, or who consider themselves, unimaginative.

- **Helping students turn data and information into usable knowledge and knowledge into wisdom.** The teacher should celebrate whenever a student has mined the Internet, cracked the books, and discovered new knowledge. In a fast-track, connected world, teachers will, we hope, enjoy using their higher-level skills and their life experience to help students turn raw data and information into usable knowledge. Then, in many cases, teachers will help nudge students toward wisdom, building an understanding of what that knowledge means for us personally, for our school, our community, our country, and the world.

- **Asking if what students have learned has triggered any ideas.** To send a message to students that knowledge doesn't stop with the last version of our lecture notes, try something like this: "Think about what we've studied today—what we've discussed. Does that trigger any ideas for you?" At the end of the class, the world will be smarter than when class got under way. In the process, students will be able to pool what they've learned in class, their life experience, and their insights, as they create new knowledge and engage in breakthrough thinking.

- **Emphasizing the arts as a way to create, express, and think across disciplines.** The arts, in their many forms, are a discipline in themselves. On the other hand, music, dance, musical theater, the visual arts, creative writing, and design appeal to a diversity of people and help to express or capture common ground across all disciplines. The arts can also help us teach other subjects. How about those quarter notes and half notes to make math more interesting, or paintings and mosaics to help us get an historic sense of how the world looked centuries ago?

- **Integrating the curriculum and helping students understand connections.** "Learning across disciplines can help move us from knowledge for its own sake to an understanding of how that knowledge can be used," according to technology leader Willard Daggett.[223]

The late Ernest Boyer, who served as president of the Carnegie Foundation for the Advancement of Teaching, constantly emphasized the importance of connections and how those connections spur further inquiry and learning. His voice still echoes, "Too many children grow up thinking that electricity comes from a plug-in." Boyer suggested relating the plug-in to the power plant, the power plant to the fuel, the fuel to the environment, and the electricity and environment to our quality of life.

Building connections and encouraging growth of that connective tissue has many benefits. Some of those benefits are: building an understanding of relevance and meaning, engaging students through active learning, focusing the program to meet the needs and interests of various learners, and providing an opportunity for educators to build synergy by sharing ideas and techniques across disciplines.

A commitment to integrating the curriculum and building connections can move any organization, but especially a school, from static to dynamic.

- **Moving toward intellectual leadership.** Education institutions are turning a large corner, and it may take us into the future by looking back. History tells us that early leaders in our schools and colleges were statespersons and intellectual leaders in their communities. In too many cases, scientific management has changed all that. Many education leaders were either pushed, or they enthusiastically raced into becoming organizational mechanics. Management was in; leadership was out.

  As we enter the new millennium, we are coming to the stark realization that no matter how well managed an institution might be, it will very likely be lost without visionary leadership. People with vision are able to connect disparate ideas. They are able to explain the implications of a proposal or a decision for numerous groups of real, live people. Courageous and unthreatened visionary leaders are eager to bring people from many disciplines together in the hope of seeing problems or opportunities in a whole new light.

- **Offering gravity-breaking preparation and professional development programs.** As noted, we need to help students turn information into knowledge and knowledge into wisdom. As educators, we need to do the same thing. Both in teaching and in leading, educators need gravity-breaking preparation and professional development programs that go beyond mechanics. Nuts and bolts are important, but we also need to be prepared to apply our thinking and reasoning skills as we plan and work across disciplines, departments, and community, state, national, and international organizations.

Questions that drive this type of thinking include: What are the implications of a certain trend or cluster of trends for how we run our schools and for what students need to know and be able to do? What are the characteristics of the education system we need to become if we hope to prepare our students for the future, not for the past?

What are some of the parts of this preparation and professional development puzzle? Logical items for the agenda are helping students learn across disciplines, putting cognitive research to work in the classroom, teaching thinking and reasoning skills, encouraging teamwork, working with and across departments and community organizations, understanding a multiplicity of cultures, developing communication skills, and triggering ideas.

On the preparation side, Drew Allbritten, former executive director of the Council for Exceptional Children, notes the need to deal with "a major disconnect between what teachers and teacher educators believe is needed in today's classroom." He advocates "respect, relevancy, and reliability as symbols of what needs to change in the American education system."

Singapore's Ministry of Education feels so strongly about helping students become even more creative, innovative, and enterprising that it held a 2004 conference, "The Teacher as Edupreneur: Exploring New Frontiers." The Ministry's director of Training and Development, Angela Ow, in a message to participants, declared, "Taking calculated risks, engaging in experimentation, and working creatively are the essential attributes of the teacher who is at the frontier of knowledge creation."[224]

- **Helping students understand 21st-century interdisciplinary careers.** Students should have a grasp of the opportunities popping up in interdisciplinary industries such as bioinformatics. They also need to know they are the ones who will develop the interdisciplinary industries and careers of the future.

- **Making futures studies an essential part of education.** To excite students' interest, ask them to consider alternative futures and plan backward from the outcomes they'd like to see. Futures studies, as a course, a unit, or simply incorporated into nearly every discipline, stimulates critical and creative thinking skills and encourages students to develop their visions. While students learn and demonstrate their prowess, they are able to educate other students, educators, and the community about the techniques for creating a future. This type of experience could enhance not only their employability but also add value to their role as good citizens.

- **Teaching social responsibility.** In a post-Enron world, all organizations and students need to understand the importance of corporate citizenship and social responsibility. As members of the Millennial Generation move into positions of leadership, they will need to be armed with thinking and reasoning skills and the power to explore connections. As leaders in education,

An Education for the New Millennium

"How should we envision an education for the new millennium? More than any generation before them, today's children need to develop the cognitive skills that allow them to work comfortably with new and evolving technologies. They need to be able to sift through unprecedented amounts of information to figure out what is true, what is trivial, what is worth retaining, and how to synthesize disparate bits into a meaningful whole. They need to learn how to approach issues and problems that cannot be solved within a single discipline, but instead involve a blend of multiple perspectives."

Marcelo Suarez-Orozco and Howard Gardner, Harvard University Graduate School of Education[225] we need to engage broad groups of people inside and outside the system to help us think through our social responsibility, because schools have a massive impact on any community and on our individual and collective futures.

■ Questions and Activities

1. List things that must happen to release the ingenuity of educators and students. Consider the need to move from information acquisition toward knowledge creation and breakthrough thinking.

2. How do we sometimes discourage people from using their ingenuity?

3. What did biologist and philosopher Edward O. Wilson mean when he wrote, "The ongoing fragmentation of knowledge and resulting chaos in philosophy are not reflections of the real world but artifacts of scholarship?"

4. Within the context of your own current position, profession, or situation, what do you see as "unifying forces" that could link disciplines and perhaps bring people together in common purpose?

5. What are the characteristics of intellectual leaders?

6. Develop a list of five principles you consider essential in teaching or learning thinking and reasoning skills.

7. Identify from three to five connections between encouraging creativity and ingenuity . . . and economic growth and development and quality of life in a community or country.

8. Consider development of a "futures studies" course or unit for your school or college. List and briefly discuss things students should learn from this type of course.

9. List and briefly discuss ways the arts help us unleash our creativity and learn across disciplines.

■ Readings

1. Florida, R. (2002). *The rise of the creative class.* New York: Basic Books/ Perseus Books Group.

2. Wilber, K. (2000). *A brief history of everything.* Boston: Shambhala Publications.

3. Wilson, E. (1998). *Consilience . . . The unity of knowledge.* New York: Borzoi Books, Alfred A. Knopf.

4. Gelb, M. (1998). *How to think like Leonardo da Vinci.* New York: Dell Publishing, division of Random House.

5. Suarez-Orozco, M., & Gardner, H. (2003). Educating Billy Wang for the world of tomorrow. *Education Week*, Commentary (October 22, 2003), 34-44.

6. *U.S. News and World Report.* (2003, Spring), Special Collector's Edition, "American Ingenuity . . . The Culture of Creativity That Made a Nation Great."

Trend 8

Every day, in every way, we're getting better and better.[226]

Continuous improvement will replace quick fixes and defense of the status quo.

Quick Fixes/Status Quo → Continuous Improvement

No matter how good we are today, we need to become even better tomorrow.

■ True Story

"How can we tell people that we're going to improve? Isn't that a direct admission that we aren't as good as I've been telling people we are?"

That concern was voiced in response to a proposed theme, "Getting Better for Kids," that reflected some solid goals a local school system developed to elevate student achievement and start building support for a finance election that was less than a year away.

After the theme was adopted and it rang throughout the community, the response was terrific. One businessperson said, "I've lived here all my life, and this is the first time any public institution has admitted it can do even better. I like it!"

On election day, "yes" votes outnumbered the "no."

"Getting Better for Kids" was not just a slogan. Its substance fast became a reality that reflected the culture of the school system and its community.

■ Continuous Improvement

People today expect and demand quality, effectiveness, and service. In the past, an organization might get by with defending the status quo or going for the quick fix—the Band-Aid approach. Now, in an impatient world, people want products and services that work, meet their needs, and are delivered on time.

Continuous improvement should be one of the prime values embedded in the culture of any type of institution, including government, business, and education. In fact, a commitment to becoming even better tomorrow than we are today is a key to survival, maybe even a moral imperative.

How can we move from defining success based on our ability to defend the status quo and keep the world at bay, on the one hand, versus the constant and exciting process of creating a future, on the other? Let's face it. If we were perfect yesterday, we probably aren't perfect today, because the world changed overnight. The question is, "Are we flexible enough to adjust?"

On the topic of continuous improvement, noted leadership consultant Rowan Gibson asks, "How will the 21st century organization develop a sense of foresight about where it needs to be heading? How will it create a meaningful vision and purpose; a goal that is uniquely its own, and that will give it a sustainable competitive advantage; something that it can stand for in a crowded and confusing world?" His answer: leadership.

Gibson adds that these leaders "will be looking forward, scanning the landscape, watching the competition, spotting emerging trends and new opportunities, avoiding impending crises. They will be explorers, adventurers, and trailblazers." He notes the importance of developing a "hierarchy of imagination" and "a democratizing strategy involving a rich mixture of different people from inside and outside the organization in the process of inventing the future." [227]

■ The Quality Movement

W. Edwards Deming, a statistician and consultant, is credited with being the father of the quality movement. His initial claim to fame was the revitalization of Japanese industry following World War II. What emerged from that monumental task was a set of management principles that honed in on improving quality and productivity.

Today, continuous improvement efforts are under way in many organizations, including business, government, and education.

William Ouchi, in his classic work, *Theory Z*, concluded productivity could be enhanced by "managing people in such a way that they can work together more effectively." He described "quality circles" that brought front-line people together to discuss how they could constantly improve both process and product. He contended that people, ranging from managers to manual and clerical workers, should be able to say with conviction, "This is the best place I've ever worked. They know what they're doing here, care about quality, and make me feel part of one big family."[228]

In *A Passion for Excellence . . . The Leadership Difference*, noted leadership consultant Tom Peters stepped into the fray. He declared, "Quality is not a technique, no matter how good." Instead, he said, "quality comes from people who care and are committed." Managers at all levels, he said, need to be "living the quality message, paying attention to quality—spending time on it as evidenced by their calendars."[229]

Deming's Principles

A Short List

W. Edwards Deming carried on an intellectual wrestling match with those who wanted to reduce what was eventually called total quality management (TQM) to a single list. However, in his book, *Out of the Crisis*, he revealed some basic principles that guide the quality movement. They include:

- creating constancy of purpose toward improvement of products and services;

- ceasing dependence on inspection to achieve quality by building quality into the product in the first place;

- improving the system of production and service;

- instituting on-the-job training and a vigorous program of education and self-improvement;

- ensuring that leadership helps people do a better job;

- driving out fear;

- breaking down barriers among departments;

- focusing on zero defects and new levels of productivity rather than on slogans, exhortations, and targets;

- substituting leadership for standards;

- removing barriers that rob a person of his or her pride of workmanship;

- changing the responsibilities of supervisors to reflect quality rather than sheer numbers; and

- putting everyone in the organization to work in accomplishing the transformation.[230]

■ Recognition Programs for Quality

TQM, which is now generally called "the quality movement" or "continuous improvement," captured the imaginations of virtual armies of business leaders and spawned a flurry of thoughtful literature. Major recognition programs for business and education grew around the concept. Perhaps most prominent are the Malcolm Baldrige National Quality Awards, offered under guidance of the National Institute of Standards and Technology (NIST) and the American Society for Quality (ASQ). These awards recognize a variety of organizations for their ongoing improvement efforts.

■ Baldrige Awards in Business

Motorola, a 2002 Baldrige recipient, was cited for productivity that increased 32 percent per employee between 1999 and 2002. The company was cited for overall customer satisfaction and repurchase/recommend satisfaction levels exceeding 88 percent, as well as a 7 percent return on assets versus a negative average for the telecommunications industry. On top of that, the company was recognized for recycling 57 percent of its non-hazardous waste and reducing emissions by 88 percent since 1996.

Among key words and ideas that pop out of the Baldrige Profile on Motorola are: corporate responsibility, uncompromising integrity, customer intimacy, performance expectations, and strong product quality. Performance excellence scorecards have been developed that help communicate values and short- and long-term directions to staff.[231]

■ Baldrige Awards in Education

By the early 1990s, educators became increasingly interested in the quality movement and what it might mean for them. Since most of the movement's history was in business, educators rightfully claimed they were developing people, not manufacturing inanimate

J.D. Power Customer Service Index Study

J.D. Power and Associates has also gained notoriety for its work with a variety of industries aimed at improving product quality and customer satisfaction. Its Customer Service Index Study, for example, measures customer satisfaction during the first three years of ownership of an automobile. The aim is to help car dealers attract maintenance customers beyond a three-year warranty period. Power looks for "hands-on service advisors, honest and courteous customer treatment, and quick, knowledgeable responses to service requests and questions."[232]

objects. If TQM meant simply improving the assembly line, it had no place in the schools.

Education institutions seemed to have spent a good part of their history concentrating on inputs. Critics said schools should pay more attention to outputs or results. Finally, many educators concluded that it was indeed "the process" that connected the inputs and outputs. Maybe a process for continuous improvement *could* make the education process even more effective.

Educators were rankled and fatigued by a mantra that went something like this, *"If Rip Van Winkle had gone to sleep 100 years ago and just woke up this morning, the only thing he'd recognize are the schools."* Thoughtful teachers and administrators were getting the message—*"We'd prefer an organization that is always trying to do better to one that tells us it's as good as it's ever going to be."*

Quality Criteria for Education. With the new millennium, schools were being recognized by the Baldrige National Quality Program. The program's "education criteria for performance excellence goals" include:

- Delivery of ever-improving value to students and stakeholders, contributing to education quality.

- Improvement in overall organizational effectiveness and capabilities.

- Organizational and personal learning.

Those Baldrige criteria are built on a foundation of core values and concepts, which include: visionary leadership; learning-centered education; organizational and personal learning; valuing faculty, staff, and parents; agility; focus on the future; managing for innovation; management by fact; social responsibility; focus on results and creating value; and system perspective. According to Baldrige, these values and concepts "are embedded beliefs and behaviors found in high performing organizations."[233]

Baldrige School Awards

In 2001, the Malcolm Baldrige Quality Award was presented to, among others, two school districts and a university. They included the Pearl River School District in New York, the Chugach School District in Alaska, and the University of Wisconsin-Stout. The following are brief descriptions of the three programs.

Pearl River School District, New York

This 2,500-student school system in Rockland County was recognized for alignment of its mission and goals through a "golden thread" quality structure that runs through all district levels and units. According to the Baldrige Awards Profile, "Carefully devised organizational linkages integrate activities ranging from complying with federal and state requirements to designing curriculum and assessing how individual students are performing. This ensures that efforts to meet mandated standards, for example, or to conform with other requirements do not become ends in themselves, separate from the district's goals."

In 1992, the district "initiated a process to continuously improve performance and deliver value for the entire community, including teachers, families, taxpayers, and businesses." Among other qualities cited by Baldrige were: a strong focus on a core mission, a balanced scorecard of leading and lagging indicators of progress, the removal of structural obstacles to achieving academic goals, a team structure, collaboration in making curriculum improvements, and a deep and wide commitment to continuous improvement in the classroom.[234]

"More important than winning," said Superintendent Richard Maurer, "is the learning and knowledge we've acquired about how to improve our educational delivery system."[235]

Chugach School District, Alaska

Small is relative. While this education system, located in the Prince William Sound area, has only 214 students, it spreads over 22,000 square miles. Many of the students live in remote areas accessible only by aircraft. The district has pioneered "a standards-based system of whole child education that emphasizes real-life learning situations," according to a Baldrige Profile.

In 1994, the district launched an "onward to excellence" process. At the time, student test scores were among the lowest in the state. Only one student went on to college. The district created "a continuum of standards for ten content areas." Minimum levels of mastery were established. Formal and informal assessments were put in place. Students were allowed to work "at their own developmentally appropriate pace."

The Profile notes that "expectations are clear and progress toward meeting them is documented in a running record of assessments completed in all content areas." Teachers, children, and parents regularly consult student assessment binders, "which serve as proof of mastery." In pursuing continuous improvement, the district has developed "a unity of focus among staff and stakeholders."[236]

University of Wisconsin-Stout

Located at Menomonee, the University of Wisconsin-Stout is one of 13 publicly supported universities in the UW System. Highlights of the Baldrige Award Recipient Profile indicate 91 percent of employers surveyed rate UW-Stout graduates as well prepared. Since 1996, the job placement rate for graduates has been at or above 98 percent. About 90 percent of alumni say they would attend the university again.

A special UW-Stout "Mission Driven-Market Smart" focus is characterized by an array of programs leading to professional careers primarily in industry and education. The campus has established a cross-functional mechanism for organizational planning. The integrated approach has enabled the school to respond more quickly and decisively to challenges and opportunities.

A Chancellor's Advisory Group, made up of 19 senior leaders and faculty, staff, and student representatives, is central to that effort. This group aims to foster a unified view of the mission and top priorities of the school, namely student learning and development.[237]

■ Drivers of Continuous Improvement

We live in an age of the end run. If we don't think an institution is meeting our expectations, we're very likely to run around it, through it, or over it. Some basic concepts should serve as drivers for any organization that wants to be considered as earning its place in the future. Each is firmly connected to continuous improvement. These drivers include:

- **Unmet demands for improvement create a market niche for someone else.** Loyalty is earned every day. If constituents perceive that their expectations are consistently not being met, then we are creating a vacuum for someone else to fill. For public or private schools, that might mean other institutions will step in to provide the service. Charter schools,

Reinventing Government

Getting More Responsive to People's Needs

During the 1990s, the White House initiated a campaign called "Reinventing Government." At last, people sighed, someone is trying to help us deal with the bureaucracy and cut through the red tape. The aim was to encourage federal government agencies to consider that their reason for existence was to serve the people. An effort was made to make government more efficient, more accessible, and more thoughtful about and responsive to people's needs.

home schooling, and vouchers gain even greater attention as possible alternatives. While admittedly difficult to document, the U.S. National Center for Education Statistics estimated, based on a 1999 study, that 850,000 children were in home schooling situations, about 1.7 percent of the school population at that time, according to an *Education Week* article.[238]

• **Improvements might be imposed.** If expectations aren't being met, government might step in to impose "improvements," including standards, high-stakes tests, and funding schemes.

• **Maintaining an initiative for renewal.** As we move into a global knowledge/information age, all of our institutions, including our education systems, will be renewed. We face a choice in this process. On the one hand, educators can initiate the process of renewal. On the other hand, if they don't, someone else will, and simply announce to educators how the new system will work—whether it's workable or not. Bottom line: The process of creating a future simply must be ongoing.

■ Taking the Higher Ground

Identify what you want to become.

How we do things makes a big difference. If we take the whole concept of democracy seriously, we will consider the views of those who'll be affected by our decisions. That's our ticket to higher ground, greater respect, and even more substantial ownership for the decisions we make. If an organization's decisions don't make it easier for people to get an even better product or service on time, they'll either turn to the competition or *become* the competition.

We might get the process under way with a series of listening sessions, meetings, and/or questionnaires asking people to describe the characteristics of an education system capable of preparing students for the future. That process of keeping an ear to the ground, of consciously and seriously listening to the wisdom of others, can lead us up the road to continuous improvement, regular enhancements in how we get things done, higher levels of effectiveness, and greater satisfaction. Unless we're willing to make change evolutionary, it might very well become revolutionary.[239]

■ Implications for Society

Continuous Improvement

Continuous improvement should be central to any organization, community, or nation if it hopes to justify its place in society and in the marketplace. The following are some overarching considerations.

• International competition will increasingly drive a demand for products and services that are high quality, safe, useful, and priced so that people in an increasingly global marketplace can afford them.

• Whatever "system" we choose as we consider systems theory, continuous improvement must be an essential part of it. Process improvements will constantly be needed to maintain reasonable costs for goods and services, boost efficiency, and lead to just-in-time delivery in the supply chain. All of these types of improvements are building blocks of a stronger overall economy.

- Public institutions, including government, will be expected to serve their constituencies in a helpful and efficient manner. People, in general, have developed zero tolerance for hassles and inefficiency.

- Members of Generation X and the Millennial Generation will insist on having a voice in how things work. They will want a place at the table and will want their ideas for continuous improvement heard. Support for simply trying to maintain the status quo will disappear.

■ Implications for Education

Continuous Improvement

Continuous improvement can provide a spark for an ongoing process of creating a future. The following are some considerations for education institutions.

- **Putting the status quo to rest.** When confronted with concerns or opportunities, many organizations immediately become defensive, assuming they are doing the best they can. In part, the education system has created its own problem, since people are better educated and their expectations have gone up, even for their schools and colleges.

  As previously stated, it's no secret that people, in general, have less tolerance for institutions that don't respond to their needs. *Preparing Schools and School Systems for the 21st Century*, a study released at the turn of the century by the American Association of School Administrators, said continuous improvement should be "a driving force in every school and school system.... Educators cannot let the system stiffen or become atrophied in our fast-changing world."[240]

Governing boards, administrators, teachers, and the communities they serve will all be key players in making sure the system becomes even better tomorrow than it is today, no matter how great that might be.

- **Developing and adopting a continuous improvement process.** Early attempts at incorporating total quality management may have proven ungainly for many education systems. However, growing numbers of institutions in education, business, and government have been working through the process to make it more user-friendly.

Continuous improvement is a constantly moving bull's-eye. Organizations can readily learn from the experiences of others, select from the volumes of books and articles on the topic, review Baldrige Award materials, seek counsel, and get on with this exciting process.

Randy Johnson, a high school assistant principal in Portales, N.M., warns, however, that continuous improvement is a process, not a philosophy. "It can keep the ship in tip-top shape, floating confidently in a turbulent sea of change. It does this by changing the ship to meet the changing sea. But it won't take the ship anywhere. The process is made just to keep the ship floating."[241]

- **Incorporating quality and continuous improvement into the classroom.** In some classrooms, students are actually schooled on the principles of continuous improvement. It's part of how the learning process works. They enthusiastically point out how their lessons and their personal goals are aligned with the aims of the school system. As they monitor their progress, they confer with other students who may need help with a concept or who might be able to help them. These students, playing a key role as managers of their own learning, work in teams.

Hershey's George Hollich thinks students should know how to gather and use data. "As we enter the 21st century, the explosion of data has achieved nuclear proportions. For students to survive, they will need skills to allow them to distinguish between garbage and information that leads to understanding." He recommends consideration of Mike Schmoker's book, *Results: The Key to Continuous Improvement* (Second Edition). Schmoker writes, in working with students, educators need "to bridge the gap between what they know and what they do."

- **Earning the opportunity to serve.** Organizations take up space. They are there because they've accepted the responsibility for providing what they hope will be an essential cluster of services. They create value. With lightning-speed communication, however, competition has grown. Others may also want to occupy that space. That's why any organization, including an education system, must constantly prove to its constituencies that it is providing value and earning the opportunity to serve.

- **Using continuous improvement as a springboard for constant renewal.** Unless we are committed to a constant process of creating a future, others will create a future for us, and we may or may not like it. The process of continuous improvement will require ongoing attention to political, economic, social, technological, environmental, and other forces buffeting society. After all, we are preparing students for the real world—today *and* tomorrow.

Perhaps one of the greatest values of continuous improvement—the one that constantly pumps new life into an organization—is the belief that we're never finished. "A teacher's real commitment to continuous learning is noticeable when it's present and when it's not," observes Rowe, Inc. President Gary Rowe. "An improving school has teachers who are always talking about new things, new ideas, new concepts in the disciplines they are teaching, and they're actively sharing information with each other," he says.

Rowe, a former longtime corporate education executive for Turner Broadcasting/CNN, says continuous improvement will require "teachers to stay current in their fields through journal subscriptions, conference attendance, departmental dialogue, and the ongoing search for more challenging resources." He adds that "continuous improvement is no substitute for having a leader who will make it happen and continually throw up exciting new challenges."

- **Bringing community and staff on board.** Getting people involved in the pursuit of better education will increase the social and intellectual capital (knowledge and relationships) brought to the endeavor and will increase the sense of ownership exponentially. When people demand high quality, we need to see it as an opportunity to improve, not as a threat.

  Involve staff, board, parents, non-parent taxpayers, and students, as well as representatives of colleges and universities, businesses, and other units of government. Engage non-governmental organizations, consultants, professional and trade associations, and respected community leaders in the process of understanding, conceiving of, and building support for continuous improvement.

- **Offering heads-up professional development.** Organizations are only as effective as their people are. However, those people are increasingly eager to learn. In fact, generational experts remark that the opportunity to learn new things and build skills will be like a magnet for recruiting and keeping talented people who were just moving into education careers. On top of that, a commitment to continuous improvement requires an almost seamless operation, with people working together across disciplines and departments toward common goals.

- **Maintaining flexibility to deal with a fast-changing world.** Opportunities might pop up. Certain needs might grow. Interest in certain topics might virtually explode. Are we flexible enough to deal with what were once called distractions? In a multi-faceted world, we need to find exhilaration in working with at least some level of chaos. No, the world will not stop for us; we need to catch up with it. Better yet, we should do our best to stay ahead of it by making continuous improvement a non-threatening process on the road to creating a future.

■ Questions and Activities

1. What do you think leadership expert and author Rowan Gibson means when he says we should create a "hierarchy of imagination" and "a democratizing strategy involving a rich mixture of different people from inside and outside the organization in the process of inventing the future?"

2. What are W. Edwards Deming's principles that guide the quality movement?

3. Identify three items in the Customer Service Index developed by J.D. Power and Associates.

4. Consider the quality criteria that guide the Baldrige National Quality Program for education. What would you recommend adding to the list, if anything? Why?

5. Develop a five- to 10-minute presentation based on the assumption, "If constituents perceive their expectations are consistently not being met, then we are creating a vacuum for someone else to fill."

6. Prepare a one-page strategy for how education systems might be able to teach the principles of continuous improvement to students.

■ Readings

1. Gibson, R. (2002). Rethinking business. *Rethinking the future.* London: Nicholas Brealey, 10-11.

2. Deming, W. (1991). *Out of crisis* [study]. Cambridge, MA: Massachusetts Institute of Technology, Center for Advanced Engineering.

3. Baldrige National Quality Program. (n.d.). Education criteria for performance excellence. Washington, DC: National Institute of Standards and Technology (NIST), American Society for Quality. Retrieved from http://www.quality.nist.gov and http://www.asq.org

Trend 9

Let's try to do the right thing.

Scientific discoveries and societal realities will force widespread ethical choices.

Pragmatic/Expedient → Ethical

Pragmatic: "Whatever works!" Expedient: "Whatever is easiest!" Ethical: "What's the right thing to do?"

■ Making Ethics a Priority

Our Future Depends on It!

"Almost beyond belief!" That's how virtually millions reacted to a cascade of alleged ethical breaches that left society aghast. Scandals at Enron, Andersen, WorldCom, Tyco, and other corporations sent shocks through the economy. Retirement funds were lost or threatened. Stocks tumbled. The stories blazed across our newspapers and lit up our television screens.

The question loomed, "Can we really believe audited financial statements?"

At the same time, major national newspapers discovered reporters who were lacing fact with fiction. The media took another hit when they were accused of under-reporting a proposal before the Federal Communications Commission (FCC) to allow even broader ownership of media outlets, since their corporations had a great deal to gain from the agency's approval.

Governments have been suspected of withholding information critical to decisions regarding war and killer viruses. People with privileged access to market information have been taken to task for insider or after-hours trading and their attempts to cover up their indiscretions.

Symbolically, *Time* magazine's 2002 Persons of the Year were "The Whistleblowers," Cynthia Cooper of WorldCom, Coleen Rowley of the FBI, and Sherron Watkins of Enron.[242]

As if that weren't enough, a beloved, record-setting baseball home run-hitter was accused of having cork in his bat.

Here's a question every individual and every organization should ask regularly: "Do we have any cork in our bats?"

■ What's the right thing to do?

Few decisions are all right or all wrong. Many involve the lesser of two evils. Constantly trying to do the right thing, however, is basic to a civil society.

If we've seen any positive fallout from the implosion of ethical behavior, it's a renewed interest in ethics. Business schools are introducing or upgrading their ethics courses. More conferences are including an ethics component. Each day, television programs and newspaper and magazine articles point to ethical concerns in every walk of life. Our awareness has been heightened.

Incredible developments in science and technology, coupled with societal realities, are constantly pushing the ethical envelope. As we consider scientific discoveries, for example, we are faced with a virtual explosion of possible benefits that will inevitably be measured against their potential side-effects or unintended consequences.

If we think and care about how our actions will affect our fellow human beings and our environment, we'll be on the road to making better decisions. Albert Schweitzer put it this way, "The first step in the evolution of ethics is a sense of solidarity with other human beings."

■ Ethics! What does it mean?

While ethics may mean different things to different people, we'll let *Webster's New Collegiate Dictionary* be our arbiter. "Ethics," according to *Webster's*, is "the discipline of dealing with what is good and bad and with moral duty and obligation." Let's read further. It's "a theory or system of moral values" that can involve "principles of conduct governing an individual or group, such as a profession."[243]

Some refer to ethics as a set of guidelines, a code of conduct, a basis for professionalism, and a form of behavior. Many agree that ethics often takes over when we reach the limits of the law, since some things might be technically legal but still don't seem appropriate.

Ethics can involve what we say and do, how we say and do it, and what we decide not to say and do. People run into problems because of *commission* (deliberately committing an act), *omission* (deliberately leaving out critical information), *misinformation* (mistakenly providing information that isn't true), and *disinformation* (deliberately spreading information that isn't correct in the hope that people will believe it).

Among the best safeguards in guiding our ethical behavior is a commitment to treating people with respect, rather than imposing our will without consulting them.

Famed Oklahoma comic Will Rogers summed it up when he said, "I'd rather be the one who bought the Brooklyn Bridge than the one who sold it."

Countering Corporate Arrogance

In the spring of 2002, *The Strategist* magazine ran an article addressing corporate arrogance. Writer Rich Long, who is a professor of communication at Brigham Young University, asked a number of public relations leaders about corporate breaches of ethics. He found them "troubled by what seems like a wholesale disregard for decency and a curious ability to self-destruct." Long concluded, "The common denominator seems to be arrogance, pure and simple."

In the same article, John Paluszek, senior counsel for Ketchum Public Relations, observed, "Arrogance in an organization, not unlike that in a person, is often the product of a culture that proclaims it, alone, has the truth. If that was ever the case, it certainly isn't anymore."[244]

■ Markers on the Road to Ethics

Why is ethical behavior so important for people and organizations of all types, especially educational institutions? Three possible answers: reputation, credibility, and ability to get the support we need for educating our students.

Ethics can be examined in numerous ways. One approach might be to test our decisions or our behaviors against some key markers—

the concepts of *integrity* (Are we who we say we are?), *fairness* (How do we treat other people?), *trust* (Are we honest and dependable?), and *character* (What motivates us?). Together, the answers to these questions help define our *reputation*, and we all know the importance of "a good name."

Widely known as a scholar and civic educator, the late R. Freeman Butts identified key values around the U.S. motto, *E Pluribus Unum*. "Unum" values, he said, include the "obligations of citizenship," such as justice, truth, authority, participation, and patriotism. "Pluribus" values, which he identified as "the rights of citizenship," include diversity, privacy, freedom, due process, human rights, and property.[245]

Michael Josephson, president of Character Counts, focuses on the "Six Pillars of Character: trustworthiness, respect, responsibility, fairness, caring, and citizenship."[246]

The Baltimore Public Schools in Maryland developed an expansive list of core values to be considered in driving ethical behavior. Among them are compassion, courtesy, critical inquiry, due process, equality of opportunity, freedom of thought and action, honesty, human worth and dignity, respect for other's rights, responsible citizenship, and tolerance.[247]

A 1996 study, *Preparing Students for the 21st Century*, took a look at the academic knowledge, skills, and behaviors students would need to exhibit to be prepared for life in a global knowledge/information age. A council of leaders in business, education, government, and other fields who contributed to that study concluded students needed to develop a sense of civic virtue, grasp the need for a code of ethics, understand and practice the principles of conflict resolution, and exhibit tolerance and acceptance of people who are unlike themselves. Further, the study suggested students must understand the effects of their actions on others as well as the consequences of their own actions.[248]

■ Teaching Ethics

The teaching of ethics fits naturally into civic education and character education; however, the scope should be broadened. As students discuss issues in social studies, science, or any number of other classes, the teacher might simply ask, "What are the ethical implications of what we discussed today . . . for us as individuals, for our school, for our community, our country, and for the world?" Then, listen to the discussion.

Ethics is often taught through precept and example. In short, we are often most successful at delivering lessons in ethics through building an understanding of ethical principles and reinforcing them with real-life stories and role-playing.

Morley Safer, longtime CBS News *60 Minutes* correspondent, decried the encroachment of new technologies on life in New York City. He said, "Big Brother has been watching us for years and listening as well," referring to ranks of closed circuit television (CCTV) cameras. Safer expressed concern that, in the interest of security, "we are forsaking Athens for Pyongyang." What are the ethical implications of this issue that a prominent journalist felt a need to get off his chest? The situation could spark an insightful discussion.[249]

■ Why do people and organizations use bad judgment?

While the list is by no means complete, here are some of the reasons people walk directly (sometimes indirectly) into an ethical minefield.

- A belief that power means personal entitlement.

- Failure to seek or accept information or feedback that is factual but doesn't support their case.

- Deliberate misinterpretations of information.

- Use of double standards.

- An unwillingness to admit problems.

- Trying to hide information from the media and the public.

- Blaming others or attempting to cover up a problem rather than immediately admitting it and dealing with it.

- *Quid pro quo* (You scratch my back, I'll scratch yours).

- Easy conclusions about complex problems, without consideration of side-effects.

- Arrogance, overconfidence, a sense of immortality, a royalty complex.

Because education is such a vital service and educators are expected to be among the most trustworthy in society, breaches or even suspected breaches of ethics can cause a high level of concern. Problems often surface around issues such as hiring or other personnel decisions, teacher placement, financial concerns, student discipline or placement, class, multicultural sensitivity, the handling of disasters or accusations, attempts to discredit others, privacy and access, and student or staff cheating (sometimes driven by standards and high-stakes tests).

■ Ethical Issues Facing Today's Students

Can we truly say a student is well educated without a firm grasp of ethical behavior? Probably not. As they move into positions of leadership and take on their role as citizens, students who are in our schools and colleges today will be faced with some of the most monumental ethical dilemmas of all time—all the more reason why they will need an understanding of how to consider the ethical dimension. A few of the issues they likely will face include:

- A world population expected to grow from approximately six billion in 2000 to nearly nine billion by 2050. That's about a 50 percent increase in 50 years. Already, about half of all people on Earth live on less than $2 per day, and approximately 1.3 billion people live on less than $1 per day.[250]

- Stewardship of the environment.

- The introduction of life forms that may not currently exist on other planets . . . or actual colonization.

- Crime and corruption.

- Genetically modified foods (GMFs) and genetically modified organisms (GMOs).

- Computer ethics, ranging from using the computer to pirate music and search other people's private files to hacking and implanting viruses, worms, or Trojans.

- Investments that are or are not made in seeking the prevention strategies or cures for major diseases or pandemics.

- Clashes among cultures and civilizations as they vie for dominance.

- Violations of basic human rights.

■ Implications for Society

Ethics

- Competition for the world's resources will lead to growing conflict among the "haves" and the "have-nots."

- Realization will grow that environmental problems cross political boundaries and threaten all life.

Human Rights . . . in Perspective

"The notion of human rights builds on the idea of a shared humanity. Human rights are not derived from citizenship or nationality but are the entitlement of every human being. In this sense, the concept of human rights is a universal and uniting idea."

Mei-Ying Tang, Taipei Municipal Teachers College [251]

- Crime and corruption will be seen as undermining democratic decisions, adding to the cost of goods and services, diverting investments, and demonstrating a lack of maturity and self-control.

- Governments and other organizations will be expected to openly share factual information and their intentions so that citizens can consider them and practice their responsibility as good citizens.

- In general, people will, of necessity, be forced to reflect on the intended and unintended political, economic, social, technological, and environmental consequences of any proposal or intended action.

- New and existing technologies will pose increasing threats to personal, corporate, national, and international security. Some technologies that were developed to enhance the quality of life might also be used for destructive, unethical purposes.

- Battle lines will be drawn over intellectual property rights.

- Ethical concern will grow about practices of the mass media in their choice of programming, their honesty in making a clear distinction between news and commentary, their commitment to appropriately defining journalism, and their corporate interests balanced against their social responsibility.

- Major scientific discoveries and technological developments will stimulate heated discussion about how they might clash with existing values, beliefs, behaviors, habits, and traditions.

- Expectations will grow that families, schools and colleges, religious organizations, and other institutions will help young people and the whole of society understand and exhibit ethical behavior.

- Industries and professions will be expected to have an established code of ethics that is well communicated and reinforced by periodic training.

- Ethical behavior will be considered a key to justifying the existence of business, government, non-governmental, education, and other organizations at all levels, perhaps even nations. Each will be expected to demonstrate its social responsibility and corporate citizenship.

■ Implications for Education

Ethics

- **Modeling ethical leadership.** Educational institutions, by their very nature, are expected to be paragons of ethical behavior, because they play such a central role in modeling that type of behavior for students. As issues are discussed, administrators, board members, and teachers have an opportunity to make the ethical dimension of their pending decisions a part of their discussions.

  For example, education leaders, who are often faced with disparate opinions, are expected to legitimately help their staff and communities find common denominators, to reach some level of consensus. Voices need to be heard, despite social or economic standing or the presence or absence of political influence. Ethically, the bottom line should be drawn at legitimately ensuring equal opportunity for a sound education that will benefit each and every student.

Sometimes, people are reluctant to discuss ethics because of their own perceived shortcomings. It's an unacceptable excuse. No one is perfect. Our imperfections should not stand in the way of helping our students, our organizations, our communities, and even our nations better understand the importance of ethical considerations to our legitimacy, our reputations, and our futures.

- **Including an ethics component in every course.** In any class, daily or weekly, a teacher might present this challenge, "Think about what we've discussed today (or this week). What are the ethical implications for us as individuals, for our school, for our community, for our country, for the world?"

Following corporate scandals of the early 2000s, many colleges and universities—especially business schools—rushed to include or upgrade existing ethics courses. The ethical dimension should be addressed at *all* levels of education. Rosa Smith, president of the Schott Foundation for Public Education in Cambridge, Mass., and a longtime school superintendent, suggests "students will need to be given more responsibility to decide the right thing to do." She sees a need for "volunteer social and civic service learning as a requirement for graduation from high school and college." Smith also believes students should "annually participate in a mock scenario designed to develop moral/ethical challenges and learning opportunities."

- **Clarifying the school's role in teaching about ethics.** Marc Ecker, a past president of the National Middle School

209

Association, foresees "a greater prevalence of ethics courses in the curriculum."

"Teachers need to become advocates for ethical behaviors," agrees Betsy Rogers, 2003 National Teacher of the Year. "Educators need to be retrained and schools restructured to meet the changing needs of a very different population."

The question then becomes, "Whose ethics do you teach?" Some ethical principles are listed in this book. They have a direct bearing on our ability to maintain a free and democratic society, to create a sound learning environment in our school or classroom, and to ensure an understanding of laws that help sustain our domestic tranquility and support fairness.

- **Expanding programs in thinking and reasoning skills as well as civic and character education.** As students develop their critical and creative thinking skills, they will be better prepared to observe the pros and cons as they make choices and solve problems, whether in school, on the job, or as a citizen on the front lines of society.

Civic education provides students with a grounding in how the system works and how they might change it, peacefully and democratically. Students are expected to develop appropriate attitudes, behaviors, and skills, and better understand concepts and principles that undergird democracy such as authority, privacy, responsibility, and justice. Character education might also focus on areas such as trustworthiness, respect, responsibility, fairness, caring, and citizenship.

"I see this as a citizenship issue," says Public Advocacy for Kids President Arnold Fege. "Issues surrounding the implications of science, what ethical issues are involved, what choices are available, what the consequences might be, and who makes the decisions all must be part of the democratization of ethical decision making."

Dilemmas and Moral Questions

James Lukaszewski, a public relations consultant who often addresses the handling of crises, suggests ethical dilemmas will prompt a number of questions. In the February 2002 issue of *Tactics*, he presented a number of "moral questions you can use to assess appropriate ethical behavior." Among them are:

- What did they know and when did they know it?

- Has all the information been presented honestly and correctly?

- What are the relevant facts of the situation?

- What decisions were made?

- Who was involved/affected?

- What alternative actions were available?

- Are our actions open, honest, and truthful?

- What affirmative action is being taken now to remedy the situation?

- How could this have been avoided?

- Are all the critical questions being asked and answered?[252]

- **Offering professional development to build a capacity to teach about ethics.** Not everyone has developed the knowledge and skills to effectively teach an ethics course. Most educators, however, can readily understand how to include a compelling ethics component in their courses, whatever their disciplines. A challenging approach might involve pointing out or helping students discover the ethical balance across disciplines. For example, a scientific decision might lead to both benefits and consequences in the broader society.

- **Making the school system an ethical resource for the community.** Of all institutions, schools and colleges are expected to take the higher ground. With their intellectual integrity, they can become a unifying force in their communities. For example, schools might offer advice and counsel as community and business organizations develop their codes of ethics and deal with ethical dilemmas. Ethical skills are fast becoming survival skills.

■ Questions and Activities

1. List five reactions to this statement, "Arrogance—the sense they can do no wrong and can get by with anything—gets more people and organizations into trouble than nearly anything else."

2. How can schools and colleges teach about ethics using the premise that the subject is best addressed through precept and example?

3. Conceive of and list five ways to add an acceptable ethics component to what educational institutions teach their students. Also, list five "musts" for any organization that hopes to maintain its ethical standing in the broader community.

4. List 10 reasons you believe people and organizations use bad judgment.

5. What do you consider some of the great ethical issues today's students will need to address during their lifetimes?

6. List five reasons students need to understand and adhere to ethical codes.

7. How would you respond to a comment that, "Schools and colleges have no business teaching about ethics" since "that turf is strictly reserved for religious institutions?"

■ Readings

1. Character Counts. (2004.) *Six pillars of character*. Los Angeles: Author. Retrieved from http://www.charactercounts.org

2. Amundson, K.J. (1991). *Teaching values and ethics*. Arlington, VA: American Association of School Administrators.

Trend 10

The Earth is our home. Treat it well.

Common opportunities and threats will intensify a worldwide demand for planetary security.

Personal Security/Self Interest ⟷ Planetary Security

Common Threats ⟷ Common Opportunities

"Only education on a massive and global scale can stand effectively against the array of dangers that confront us."

Douglas Greenberg, president and CEO, Survivors of the Shoah Visual History Foundation

■ Doing the Math

Maybe you've heard something like this: "Don't bother me with these big issues. We have our hands full just teaching math!"

That kind of thinking might keep the wolf from the door for a while. Eventually, however, we're going to have to admit that it will be the students in our schools and colleges today who will develop the ideas, techniques, and technologies to sustain this planet.

Unless those students have some understanding of the issues they confront, they may have difficulty dealing with them. Unless they understand that our personal interest, self-interest, or corporate interest means nothing if we destroy the biosphere in pursuing it, they may miss one of the connections that is fundamental to our very survival.

What about the sense of urgency? In 2005, "the most comprehensive analysis ever conducted of how the world's oceans, dry lands, forests, and species interact and depend on one another" reached a dramatic conclusion. A total of 1,300 authors from 95 countries participated in this Millennial Ecosystem Assessment. One of their conclusions: "Human actions are depleting Earth's natural capital, putting such strain on the environment that the ability of the planet's ecosystems to sustain future generations can no longer be taken for granted."[253]

While we're turning out good citizens for our communities and our nations, we also need to be sure we're producing good citizens of the world, or the world will start closing in on us. The concept isn't that complicated. We just need to "do the math."

■ Maslow . . . and the Hierarchy of Needs

Psychologist Abraham Maslow identified a now-famous list of human needs that are firmly attached to our basic instincts:

- **Physiological:** the need for oxygen, food, water, and a relatively constant body temperature.

- **Safety and security:** the need for security balanced against insecurity, the need to stay out of danger.

- **Belongingness and love:** the need to affiliate with others, overcome feelings of loneliness and alienation, and be accepted.

- **Esteem:** the need to achieve, to be competent, to gain approval or recognition, the need for a stable, firmly based, high level of self-respect and respect from others, a sense of self-confidence.

- **Self-actualization:** the need to be problem-focused, appreciate life, engage in personal growth, develop the ability to have peak experiences, and pursue what we were "born to do." The poet will want to write. The musician will want to make music.

Physiological as well as safety and security needs are a foundation for everything else.

Unless our physical needs are met and we are safe and secure, most of us are basically imprisoned, unable to pursue our other needs and an interesting, satisfying life.[254]

■ Personal and Planetary Security . . . Making the Connection

It has been said, "Why should I be concerned about other people? I've got enough on my plate just handling my own problems."

That attitude has driven the behaviors of people embedded in hundreds of generations over thousands of years. It reflects a level of selfishness, a sense that we have no problem, even if our physical well being, our security, comes at the expense of other people.

However, the population of our planet is growing exponentially. Between 2000 and 2050, for example, the earth's population is expected to grow 50 percent, from six billion to about nine billion people. Each of those nine billion people will be born with a hierarchy of human needs to be satisfied. As competition increases to satisfy self-interest and ensure personal security, the haves will increasingly be pitted against the have-nots. Technologies, devised to improve the quality of life, will also be used for terrorism and to wage wars.

Battles will likely be fought over access to food. Global warming might change the climates of various regions of the world, turning

Spaceship Earth

The Chick and the Egg

Internationally renowned master of science and design, philosopher, and author R. Buckminster Fuller, in his 1969 classic *Operating Manual for Spaceship Earth*, suggested giving greater consideration to the world human beings inherited.

We were blessed with an "abundance of immediately consumable, obviously desirable, or utterly essential resources," he said. Those resources "have allowed us to carry on despite our ignorance. Being eventually exhaustible and spoilable, they have been adequate only up to this critical moment."

Fuller compared those resources to what a bird has available when it's still inside the egg; they only last for a certain length of time. "The nutriment is exhausted at just the time when the chick is large enough to be able to locomote on its own legs," he wrote. "And so as the chick pecks at the shell seeking more nutriment, it inadvertently breaks the shell." Then, "[s]tepping forth from its initial sanctuary, the young bird must now forage on its own legs and wings to discover the next phase of its regenerative sustenance."[255]

Fuller warned that we must prepare for that day when our sustaining nutriment is exhausted. We will likely come to the stark realization that much of what we thought was infinite—such as clean air and water—are finite, unless we intervene to protect them. The myth of our traditional definition of "infinite supply" might very well be shattered.

rich farmland into desert. Glaciers and ice caps are reported to be softening. "War of the Worlds" will likely be replaced by wars over fresh water. Some fear that, through our behavior, we may create the symptoms of our own planetary "nuclear winter," even without exploding a nuclear device.

Certain threats involve intensifying polarization that leads to fanaticism and could trigger actual use of chemical, biological, radiological, or nuclear weapons, often referred to as weapons of mass destruction. From asteroids to microbes, threats seem to multiply. SARS, bird flu, the West Nile virus, and concerns about the spread of Ebola and anthrax have captured worldwide attention.

While consequences of these dilemmas seem bleak, many are likely avoidable. Everyone on earth has one thing in common. They live on the same small planet, rotating at about 1,000 miles per hour, circling the sun every 365 days. The fact is that we are the first generations of people who have the capability to destroy the world, and we may be the last generations that can save it. Much depends on how we educate our people.

Contemporary philosopher Ken Wilber, in his book *A Brief History of Everything*, puts the pieces together. "If you destroy the biosphere—that is, if you destroy all life forms—then the cosmos or physiosphere could and would still exist. But if you destroy the physiosphere, the biosphere is instantly destroyed as well."[256] In short, destroy what supports life on the planet, and we destroy ourselves. Wilber's alarming reminder should put us into a quickstep in a search for common ground.

Perhaps our greatest dilemmas, however, are much more mundane, generated by an unwillingness to understand what motivates the values, opinions, attitudes, customs, beliefs, and perceived needs of people who are different from ourselves.

The unavoidable conclusion is that our personal security depends on the security of our planet. We are past the point that any one group, wherever it is, can survive only at the expense of others. At some point, "United We Stand" may become a rallying cry to preserve life on Earth. What happens to one of us happens to all of us. We're all in this together. We have nowhere else to go. Optimistically, our common threats may be well-disguised common opportunities.

■ An Interconnected World

Pick up a balloon. Press it at one spot. It will expand somewhere else. To some extent, that same principle applies to the growing interconnectedness of our planet.

The world was struck in 1997 when Thailand devalued its currency, the Baht. Within moments, Hong Kong's stock market, the Hang Seng, dropped like a rock. Seeing the possible consequences of an Asian economic crisis, the U.S. stock market plunged 554 points in a single day.[257]

In April of 1999, when two students went on a rampage at Columbine High School in Colorado, the world watched in real time as SWAT teams approached the building and students came streaming out. When New York's World Trade Center and the U.S. Pentagon were attacked on September 11, 2001, people in every part of the world watched the events unfold live. People around the globe felt a kinship with suffering families as if they were part of those communities.

■ Common Threats

Nothing galvanizes us more than common threats or common opportunities. Unfortunately, it has too often taken natural or human-caused disasters to rally our attention in a fast-moving world. Opportunities never seem as compelling as threats.

Perhaps that is why we are constantly threatened—because we fail to recognize and pursue the opportunities that surround us. Damage control has become the new norm, but will there come a time when we ultimately do damage that is beyond repair?

Natural Disasters

Massive changes in the ecology of our planet have likely been caused by natural disasters, such as volcanic activity or direct hits by meteorites, according to scientific consensus. The rise and fall of dinosaurs is credited to these types of events.

At Capital Science 2004, a March conference organized by the Washington Academy of Sciences, Martin Schwab of the Home-planet Defense Institute presented scenarios for possible threats from wayward asteroids. He placed them in three categories: kilometer-sized "Yucatan Class," which he described as "earth killers"; 200- to 800-meter "Eros Class," the most common threat; and 50-plus meter "Tunguska Class" asteroids, which he described as "city killers."

While scientists track many asteroids, there are so many of these bodies that they are almost too numerous to follow. Solid plans and technologies to meet the threat of an asteroid or comet colliding with the planet are generally not in place and would be astronomi-cally expensive. However, Schwab suggests that, given a plan and sufficient warning, possible safety measures might include inspec-tion missions, blowing up the object (which he does not necessarily consider a good option), or redirecting its course. Schwab recom-mends the use of space-based telescopes, such as Hubble, and ground-based telescopes, located on the Earth, moon, and Mars, as part of an early warning system.[258]

Natural disasters, such as those caused by floods, tornadoes, hurri-canes, typhoons, droughts, heat waves and extreme cold, volcanoes, earthquakes, and tsunamis have largely been thought to be some-what predictable, minimally controllable, and largely unpreventable. They often cause death, injuries, displacement of people, and heavy economic consequences, as we've witnessed time and again in events such as Hurricane Katrina's utter devastation of New Orleans and surrounding parts of Louisiana and the Gulf Coast in 2005.

Whether we like it or not, many scientists credit human activity, including possibly global warming, with the increase in intensity and frequency of severe and shifting weather events.[259]

Human-Caused Threats

Instability can lead to threats, which often have worldwide implications. Just a few of those threats include:

- **Terrorism.** The same technologies designed to improve our lives have been used to disable and destroy. Growing numbers of incidents girdle the globe. Weapons of mass destruction, while possessed by growing numbers of countries, have slipped from national control into the hands of sub-national groups with a reach that ranges from local to international. Those weapons, coupled with a variety of tactics, are used to intimidate; to cause death, injury, and destruction; and to make a case for the group's particular point of view. While substantial attention is focused on biological, chemical, radiological, and nuclear weapons, other concerns include suicide bombers and pulse bombs, meant to disable or destroy computer systems.

- **The Economic Divide.** Between 1960 and 1995, the disparity in per capita income between the world's 20 richest and 20 poorest nations more than doubled, from 18 to 1 to 37 to 1, according to the World Bank. The disparity has caused suffering and unrest that has led to misunderstanding, disagreements, and attacks.[260]

- **Refugees and Genocide.** The world has seen the killing, rape, and plunder of masses of people who were caught in tribal, racial, or ethnic wars or genocidal "cleansings." These and other types of disasters have steadily increased the numbers of refugees. According to Human Rights Watch, "a refugee is someone with a well-founded fear of persecution on the basis of his or her race, religion, nationality, membership in a particular social group, or political opinion, who is outside of his or her country of nationality and unable or unwilling to return.[261] At the beginning of 2002, the U.N. High Commissioner for Refugees (UNHCR) estimated that one of every 300 people on Earth—19.8 million people in all—were "people of concern." Of that total, 12 million were officially designated as refugees.[262]

- **Carbon Emissions.** Measurements taken at the Mauna Loa Observatory in Hawaii indicated an 18 percent increase in carbon dioxide levels between 1960 and 2002. Scientists estimate that those levels have risen 31 percent since the beginning of the industrial revolution in about 1750. The present concentration has not been exceeded in at least 420,000 years, and likely in 20 million years, according to scientists. Global temperatures have been generally rising since 1880. From 1950 to 2002, for instance, average temperatures climbed from 13.87 to 14.52 degrees Celsius or approximately 56.8 to 58 degrees Fahrenheit.[263]

- **Disease.** AIDS, SARS, and other diseases have threatened the lives of people worldwide. By 2003, only 4 percent of people living with AIDS in low- and middle-income nations could afford the $350 per person needed for antiretroviral drugs to help reduce suffering and death from that disease.[264] The monetary price tag can be expected to fluctuate over time. We should not forget that we share the planet with microbes that can help us or hurt us, and they certainly outnumber us. *(A case can be made that disease falls into the category of either natural or human-caused events. Much depends on conditions that might have been encouraged or avoided to prevent, treat, or bolster the spread of the viruses, bacteria, and other agents. We might have more control over root causes than we realize or are willing to admit.)*

- **Poverty and Armed Conflict.** Wars have continued to deepen poverty, ruin economies, destroy private and public infrastructure, and displace millions. As noted earlier, refugees are often trapped in camps, subjected to the will of warlords, and made susceptible to disease or exploitation. Some crowd the borders of other countries, their land or other property destroyed or peppered with mines, and their productivity put on indefinite hold. Wars and the spread of arms reduce investments that could strengthen economic growth for individual people and nations.

The Stockholm International Peace Research Institute reported that world military expenditures amounted to approximately $839 billion in 2001. The United States accounted for approximately 36 percent of that total, other NATO nations for 24 percent, U.S. Asia-Pacific Allies for 7 percent, Russia for 6 percent, China for 4 percent, and states considered hostile by the United States for 3 percent.[265]

• **Natural Resources to Support Combat and Suppression.** Warlords and organizations specializing in terror have captured the resources of some countries to support their efforts. Those resources include but are not limited to diamonds, lapis Lazuli, emeralds, timber, oil, opium, and cocaine.[266]

This list, drawn largely from *Vital Signs 2003*, published by The Worldwatch Institute, in cooperation with the United Nations Environment Program, just skims the surface of the numerous issues that are heightening global threats.

Ervin Laszlo is founder and head of the Club of Budapest International, an independent organization dedicated to the idea of creating and implementing "holistic solutions to problems that face the entire human family."[267] Each year, the Club presents a Change the World—Best Practice Award for "projects that foster sustainable development and a planetary consciousness." In a foreword to Laszlo's book, *You Can Change the World: The Global Citizen's Handbook for Living on Planet Earth*, Mikhail Gorbachev urges readers to "understand the current situation of our planet and to find the path we must take. The relationship between man and

Meeting the Challenge of Global Threats

"Rapid population growth in the developing world and unsustainable consumption patterns in industrialized nations are the root of both present and potentially even greater forms of environmental degradation and resource depletion. Even when making the most generous allowances for advances in science and technology, one cannot help but conclude that population growth and environmental pressures will feed into immense unrest and make the world substantially more vulnerable to serious international frictions."

A National Security Strategy of Engagement and Enlargement, The White House, 1995[268]

[Note: Events since 1995 attest to the unrest and vulnerability reflected in the statement.]

nature has become more and more complex and strained; the air has become poisoned; the rivers polluted; and the forests decimated." He then, hopefully, urges readers to "determine what we must do and how we must do it to ensure our common well-being." Laszlo himself frequently reminds us that, depending on what we do, we're either headed for breakthroughs or breakdowns.

■ Mixing Oil and Water

Liquids that Power the Economy and Sustain Life as We Know It

Two of the most powerful liquids on earth are oil and water. Whether they mix or not may be less a problem than whether we have fresh supplies. Fortunately or unfortunately, both have become heated political issues. Whatever our politics, we need to realize that what comes from the gas pump or the water tap may be at high risk.

Oil. For hundreds of millions of years, animal, vegetable, and mineral matter settled to the bottoms of ancient seas. In some cases, it sank deep enough and the temperature became hot enough to turn it into oil. Today, it powers our planes, trains, and automobiles; heats our homes; yields hundreds of derivative products; and lubricates the wheels of industry. Oil has become the catalytic agent for the world economy. Yet, until about 200 years ago we hardly knew it existed.

In about 1956, long before most people even considered a future shortage of oil, geophysicist Marion King Hubbert developed what we now call Hubbert's Peak. As an employee of Shell Oil Co., he conceived of a graph to help anticipate when total usage of fossil fuels would outstrip the amount of fossil fuels stored in the earth. While we might want to believe that the flow of oil will continue unabated, at a price we can afford, it will not. Running short or running out could lead to wars and even worldwide economic meltdown.

David Goodstein, in his 2004 book, *Out of Gas*, says he believes we should develop new sources of energy and propulsion with the same level of energy that we devoted to making our first trip to the moon. "There were formidable technological obstacles to overcome, but we are very, very good at overcoming that kind of obstacle when we put our minds to it," he says. "The energy problem is exactly of that nature."[269]

Water. "It is the essence of life. Yet despite the seemingly limitless supply—it covers over two-thirds of the planet—there is never enough of it to safely quench the world's thirst or to reliably irrigate all its crops. The stuff of countless conflicts throughout history, nature's elixir, will become more precious still," according to *U.S. News and World Report*.[270]

In its 2004 special issue devoted to "The Future of Earth . . . A Planet Challenged from the Arctic to the Amazon," *U.S. News* reported, "In a nation where abundant, clear, and cheap drinking water has been taken for granted, it is hard to imagine residents of a major city adjusting to life without it."

Gary Wolff, an economist for Oakland's Pacific Institute for Studies in Development, Environment, and Security, observes, "The idea of water as an economic and social good, and who controls this water, and whether it is clean enough to drink, are going to be major issues in the country."[271]

Among the numerous issues surrounding water are: contaminants such as dirt, debris, bacteria, and even lead, as water mains age and spring leaks; diversion of water for irrigation or to supply cities, leaving behind a parched landscape; the need for desalinization plants and waste from those plants that could "poison" land; oil spills, emissions, and the dumping of garbage and waste into rivers, oceans, and other bodies of water;[272] privatization of water treatment and distribution facilities; and over-fishing of the oceans. When it comes to water, "testing," "filters," and "bottles" have become household words.

Still another issue is climate change and concern about whether a "megadrought" could come calling. Add to that the increasing population of the planet and the growing demand and competition for water. When the water goes, crops fail, and land blows away, the businesses in town also pay the price, according to the *Pueblo Chieftain* newspaper in Colorado.

A water gap could soon get even more notoriety than the digital gap.

"The drought is a warning signal," said U.S. Secretary of the Interior Gail Norton, referring to the state of the weather in summer 2004. "Water shortages," she predicted, "will be repeated even in average rainfall years because there's simply not enough supply to satisfy the growing demands."[273] Former Environmental Protection Agency Administrator Christine Todd Whitman has called water quantity and quality "the biggest environmental issue that we face in the 21st century."[274]

The Silver Lining. If every problem presents an opportunity, then oil and water should move toward the top of the list. Today's students, if they wish to devote their talents to dealing with the growing number of issues that surround these two "natural" commodities, could become tomorrow's heroes.

■ Common Opportunities

Now, we'll don our opportunities hat. Let's face it. We are surrounded by exciting possibilities for dealing with many of the threats the world is facing. Necessity should be the mother of invention. The profit will come through not only economic growth but a possible reduction in the rate of decline, sometimes called "the cost of neglect."

Do we have a choice? One thing we know with some certainty. The earth's species have been adapting to life on this planet for millions of years. We do not have evidence of a nearby planet that could readily sustain us. In short, we have nowhere else to go. That should be incentive enough to see problems as opportunities in disguise.

Here are just a few of the economic and civic opportunities that should get the nerve endings tingling for students in our schools and all the rest of us. Think, for example, of the employment opportunities that could be created by seriously pursuing any or all of these possibilities.

- **New sources of energy and propulsion.** The door is wide open for the further development of new generations of vehicles, propelled by hybrid engines (part electricity/part gasoline or other fuel), or hydrogen fusion, to name a few. Renewable sources, such as wind, solar, biomass, and others, coupled with conservation and efficiency and the likely development of efficient synthetic fuels, will likely supplement our energy supply. These technologies would likely reduce carbon emissions and spin off products and services that would stimulate the economy.

- **Treatments, cures, and prevention strategies for diseases.** The mapping of the human genome has opened new areas for medical research and development. The bioinformatics industry has linked high-powered computers with our growing knowledge of biology. That could lead to medications tailored to our genetic makeup and vaccinations against now hard-to-treat-or-cure diseases or infections triggered by bacteria, viruses, and other anomalies.

- **Development of technologies and treaties that will guarantee adequate fresh water.** As noted earlier, future wars may be waged over access to adequate fresh water. Millions are taken ill or die every year from waterborne diseases. While treaties and protocols will be needed, so will more economical approaches to desalinization and tapping water sources that are closer to people's homes. In many parts of the world, hours of productive time are spent each day walking to and from a well or river to bring home what is too often contaminated water.

- **Preparation of growing numbers of people for careers in diplomacy.** The gaps separating people often become chasms. To avoid escalation in the frequency of armed conflict and its accompanying destruction, death, and displacement, we need more people who can communicate effectively, who can attempt to build understanding across cultures and political boundaries.

- **Development of scientists who will be needed to probe the depths of the atom and the outer reaches of the universe.** These are ventures that should involve and benefit all of humanity.

- **Preparation of new generations of economists** capable of further developing economic theories, policies, and strategies to fit the needs of a world moving forward at warp speed.

- **Promotion and support for even better education.** Education brings hope, which has become scarce in too much of the world. Some see hopelessness and the vulnerability of people who are un- or under-educated and unemployed as a root cause of terrorism.

Why is education listed last? Because education is the bottom line. It will be our schools and colleges, whether they meet in a fancy building or under a tree in some remote part of the world, that will spell the difference between opportunity and disaster. Yes, education is that serious.

■ Implications for Education and the Whole of Society

Personal/Planetary Security

The following implications have repercussions for both education and the whole of society as they work together to address our individual and planetary security.

- **Balancing economic development and environmental sustainability.** As we make progress in our communities, in our nation, and globally, we need to measure what we do against its impact on our environment and the legacy we leave for future generations. Let's put it this way: In the short-run, an unsustainable activity might make a few people much richer. In the long-run, it might make all of us much poorer.

"Our grandchildren and their children will be left trying to clean up the environmental mess we are leaving behind," observes Ted Blaesing, superintendent of the White Bear Lake Area Schools in Minnesota. "All ages of schooling will have an increased focus on the science and ethics of environmental issues," he predicts. Blaesing also sees "environmentally friendly" school buildings. "Green schools—located to minimize transportation of students to the building —will be the norm."

- **Considering the impact of globalization.** "Globalization has the paradoxical effect of simultaneously increasing human interconnection and decreasing human physical security," observes the Shoah Foundation's Douglas Greenberg. "Every great revolution in transportation and communications has had this perverse effect." Greenberg suggests we "think about the human consequences of Europeans figuring out how to navigate the Atlantic. It led to an epidemiological catastrophe in the form of smallpox epidemics and other diseases among the natives of the Americas, and it also made the slave trade possible." Greenberg submits, "Only education on a massive and global scale can stand effectively against the array of dangers that confront us."

- **Offering futures courses.** As students study futures, they will develop techniques for better understanding the social, political, economic, technological, and environmental forces that drive us today and the potential impact our decisions will have on those forces tomorrow. Futurist Joseph Coates suggests development of "a curriculum around threats and remedies from the immediate to those we might face in 1,000 years or more." Coates envisions students getting involved in national and community service projects and "making a film or doing interactive presentations for school television or cable." Through futures studies, students will become even more interested in learning about natural and human forces affecting their communities and the planet. Many will discover or even develop careers for dealing with those challenges.

- **Stimulating creativity.** Faced with gigantic issues and often skepticism or outright resistance to addressing them, students will need to develop their creativity. "Creativity needs to be more central to the learning process," according to Frank Method, an international relations veteran who is director of education policy for the Research Triangle Institute, International. "Learners have immense potential for reframing issues and for finding ways to imagine the world as plastic and responsive to action, not just threatening and predetermined." Method suggests "simulations, modeling, exploratory learning that can help open new possibilities, and the arts to help articulate feelings and visions not yet demonstrated in the reality that we've already faced."

- **Building media literacy skills.** "Media awareness and critical thinking skills need to be prominent in the preparation of learners," Method recommends. Students, he says, "need to understand the tendency of news media to conflate events and images and to extrapolate patterns from anecdotal data drawn from a large world. At the same time, they will need critical thinking skills to help them sort things that they can do something about from those that only tangentially affect their lives." Method adds that students will also need, "values of resiliency, tolerance, and openness to change . . . balanced with strength and courage in the face of challenges."

- **Building an understanding of basic human needs.** In our schools and communities, we need to better understand ourselves and others. We need a better grasp of what motivates people, whether they live next door or on the other side of the planet.

- **Developing a philosophy of possibility.** We've all heard the comment, "It's no use. It'll never work anyway." In totalitarian regimes, one of the more frequent responses when people are presented with a suggestion is, "It is not possible." In more democratic societies, we are more likely to encounter the philosophy that "anything is possible." How we feel about possibility will play a huge role in charting our future. At its best, education and community leaders should instill a sense of possibility.

Our Legacy

We are the first generations of people who have the capacity to destroy the world . . . and we may be the last generations that are capable of saving it. What happens will depend largely on how well we educate our people.

■ Questions and Activities

1. How does Abraham Maslow's "Hierarchy of Needs" support the need for us to pay more attention to planetary security?

2. What was the approximate population of Earth in 2000? Foregoing some cataclysmic event, approximately what will the planet's population be in 2050? What is the estimated percentage increase in those 50 years?

3. Do some further research on "Hubbert's Peak." What implications does it have for our energy future?

4. What should schools and colleges teach students about common opportunities and common threats facing people across all political boundaries?

5. Prepare a paper or presentation indicating how our personal security is connected to planetary security. Conclude the work with at least five to 10 ways we can teach students about those connections.

■ Readings

1. Fuller, R.B. (1969). *Operating manual for spaceship earth.* New York: South Illinois University Press, Touchstone Book by Simon and Schuster.

2. Wilber, K. (2000). *A brief history of everything.* Boston: Shambhala Publications.

3. Goodstein, D. (2004). *Out of gas . . . The end of the age of oil.* New York: W.W. Norton.

4. Lavelle, M., & Kurlantzick, J. (2004). Water, tapped out, the coming water crisis, *U.S. News and World Report,* Special Edition, The Future of Earth. (Summer 2004), 58-63.

5. Hayden, T. (2004). Trashing the seas, *U.S. News and World Report*, Special Edition, The Future of Earth. (Summer 2004), 66-67.

Trend 11

I want it my way!

Polarization and narrowness will bend toward reasoned discussion, evidence, and consideration of varying points of view.

Narrowness ⟷ Open-Mindedness

Polarization—the grouping of opinions around two extremes. In politics: "As the debate continued, the . . . members were polarized into warring factions."

The Dictionary of Cultural Literacy[275]

■ Civility

A major driver of education is a commitment to prepare students to become engaged, contributing members of civil society. That should mean they understand the importance of reasoned discussion; they know how to gather, consider, and present evidence; and they have some commitment to comprehending, not necessarily accepting, a variety of points of view. This chapter traces the reasons a truly free and open society needs to be based on open-mindedness, not on an isolating form of narrowness. Students need to understand how they can most constructively function in that kind of intellectually rich environment.

■ What's at stake?

Futurist, philosopher, educator, and diplomat Harlan Cleveland, based on his experience, estimates there are, on average, 5.3 sides to most issues.[276] That's between two and three times, maybe even 5.3 times, the number some leaders are willing to acknowledge—despite the fact that any free society should be a crucible for consideration of divergent or even conflicting ideas. Throughout history, factions have provided the fuel that keeps the flame of liberty burning.

Nonetheless, we have what seem to be a growing number of people whose righteousness has hardened their attitudes and limited their view. For some, everything is straightforward black or white. Shades of gray have disappeared. Rather than considering an idea or an opinion on its merits, many of us rush to reject the idea and discredit its source. "I'm right, and you're wrong. It's as simple as that." No discussion.

Factions are a normal part of any society, including democratic ones. As much as they might have irritated even those who wrote the U.S. Constitution, factions were seen as stimulating, as extending the conversation about issues and directions. The hope of our nation's founders was that those conversations would help us constantly reach for an elevated purpose or higher ground.

Yet, even with all of our sophisticated communication technology, we are moving from talking *with* each other to talking *past* each other. Listening to the reasoning for another case seems to have gotten lost in the shuffle, replaced by preconceived conclusions, biases, and unbending ideologies. Unfortunately, many have forgotten that by constantly insisting on having everything their own way, without regard for others, they may end up with nothing.

Polarization and narrowness play out inside families, friendships, and communities, and both within and among nations. Talk shows on radio and television are more often shouting matches than civil discussions. Web sites proliferate to justify a single, often narrow, point of view. Conspiracy theories abound.

Political candidates, and many who already hold elected or appointed office, confront the opposition rather than learn from it. Partisanship reigns, too often crushing bipartisanship and even principle, when the principle might possibly be the common good. People declare themselves liberal or conservative and vow against all reason to justify the moniker they've adopted.

People come down on "one side or the other" of issues, rather than considering the merits of numerous arguments. Groups "not like us" are often labeled and set apart, causing some of them to demand, protest, demonstrate, shout to gain attention, and revolt. Extremists provoke tensions and conflict. Fundamentalism and extremism can easily tip toward fanaticism. Even labels such as these tend to isolate, stereotype, and discount any legitimacy of concern. Reason disintegrates in the face of bias-driven emotion.

What's at stake with this way of thinking? The very future of civil society.

■ The Missing Ingredient

Civil Discourse

What's missing in this scenario? Absent is the civil discourse that is urgently needed to continuously chart our course for the future. Seemingly discarded is the search for common ground—the quest to, when possible, turn "my" into "our." *Multiplication* of the common good is subverted by a commitment to *division*. The purely emotional overcomes reason.

The Cold War did not quench our worldwide thirst for common enemies. Often unnoticed or ignored is a stark reality—the stakes of rancorous conflict are becoming exponentially higher. Perhaps the greatest casualty of an over-polarized society and world is that it keeps us from putting divergent ideas and information together to create new knowledge that could enrich economies and civil societies. Sometimes we forget that a democracy is intended to accommodate the divergent views and voices of many people, often in the search for a policy or set of values to guide us in what should be a constant seeking for truth.

■ Looking at scenarios

Choices on a Macro Scale

At a recent conference, a consultant to the U.S. military described the planning process for strategies to meet global threats. He started by noting that everything must rest on a foundation view of the country's role in the world, and offered three scenarios. They included:

- **The country as the sole superpower.** This role involves worldwide engagement and serving as planetary police officer.

- **The country as part of a bipolar world.** The Cold War provided our most dramatic recent example, with the U.S. block facing off against the Soviet block, with some nations either remaining neutral (non-aligned) or falling into one camp or the other. The concept of a Third World emerged from this conflict.

- **The country as a member of the international family of nations.** While maintaining its national security, cultivating alliances and partnerships, and remaining concerned about issues such as trade, the nation works closely with the international community to take on the multitude of challenges and opportunities facing the planet.

The Federalist on Factions

When the U.S. Constitution was set for ratification by the states, some of the nation's more eloquent leaders addressed various concerns raised during their discussions and by citizens. Among them was James Madison, who later became president. The following is a segment from a piece on factions that Madison wrote for the November 23, 1787, *New York Packet*. It became part of what we know today as *The Federalist Papers*.

By a faction, I understand a number of citizens, whether amounting to a majority or minority of the whole, who are united and actuated by some common impulse of passion, or of interest, adverse to the rights of other citizens, or to the permanent and aggregate interests of the community.

There are two methods of curing the mischiefs of faction: one by removing its causes; the other, by controlling its effects.

There are again two methods of removing the causes of faction: the one, by destroying the liberty, which is essential to its existence; the other, by giving to every citizen the same opinions, the same passions, and the same interests.

It could never be more truly said that of the first remedy, that it was worse than the disease. Liberty is to faction what air is to fire, an ailment without which it instantly expires. But it could not be less folly to abolish liberty, which is essential to political life, because it nourishes faction, than it would be to wish the annihilation of air, which is essential to animal life, because it imparts to fire its destructive agency.

The second expedient is as impracticable as the first would be unwise. As long as the reason of man continues fallible, and he is at liberty to exercise it, different opinions will be formed.[277]

■ Pulling the Problem into Focus

Much of what happens in world affairs and how we're organized in a national and international context has been focused on what divides us. Those divisions might include political boundaries; continents; regional or self-selected economic alliances; economic systems; ideologies; racial, ethnic, social, economic, gender, tribal, and religious differences; or interpretations of environmental science, coupled with personal philosophy.

In his controversial 1987 work, *The Closing of the American Mind*, professor, author, and political philosopher Allan Bloom wrote, "A man needs a place and opinions by which to orient himself. The problem of getting along with outsiders is secondary to, and sometimes in conflict with, having an inside, a people, a culture, a way of life." Bloom went on to observe, "A very great narrowness is not incompatible with the health of an individual or a people, whereas with great openness, it is hard to avoid decomposition."[278]

Quite another view was posed by political scientist, economist, author, and lecturer Barbara Ward in her 1966 classic, *Spaceship Earth*. She states, "I can think of only one way of expressing the degree to which interdependence and community have become the destiny of modern man." She draws from professor and philosopher Buckminster Fuller, "who," she says, "more clearly than most scientists and innovators, has grasped the implications of our revolutionary technology."

Ward relates Fuller's suggestion that we see "the whole human race as the ship's crew of a single spaceship on which all of us, with remarkable combination of security and vulnerability, are making our pilgrimage through infinity." She concludes, "Our planet is not much more than a capsule within which we have to live as human beings if we are to survive the vast space voyage upon which we have been engaged for hundreds of millennia—but without yet noticing our condition."[279]

If topics are considered taboo, they can become stumbling blocks to civil discourse and barricades on the road to opportunity. This occurs when someone has declared, either directly or through innuendo, that certain topics or points of view should simply not be discussed. "Don't bring that up! Don't you know he's a conservative/liberal/Democrat/Republican/Social Democrat/Unionist/Independent/Green/you name it?" The room is eventually filled with a tension no one dares acknowledge, all in the interest of not offending someone's narrow view. The problem for leaders who limit the agenda is that they themselves are eventually blindsided and left out of the loop. Problems that could have been easily solved become crises and sometime escalate into catastrophes.

Let's go back to the concept of polarity. If you've bought a pair of sunglasses lately, are they "polarized?" That means the shades are designed to block glare on a sunny day while letting other light filter through. In finding perspective in a highly divided world, we need to be careful not to simply polarize or wear only rose-colored glasses.[280]

■ Managing our Diversity

Education Is Our Hope!

The management of our diversity is critical to our future. If we manage it well, it will enrich us. If we don't manage it well, it will divide us. That realization goes beyond race, ethnicity, gender, and other factors, to our attitudes, beliefs, and biases.

Democracy was designed to bring factions together in common purpose. There are, however, those who preach democracy but still want everything on their own narrow terms.

While democracy depends on people who feel strongly and have competing opinions about certain issues, and who will "stand up for what they believe in," it also relies on some degree of acquiescence, or the willingness to compromise in the interest of the

Red States v. Blue States? Conservatives v. Liberals? Right v. Left?

"Ideological and theological divisions running deep. Opposing factions so far apart they no longer seem to respect one another. A breakdown in communication. The elites of each side, neither able to appeal to the other, posed like opposing armies ready to do battle."

That's how Joel Kotkin, a senior policy fellow at the Davenport Institute for Public Policy at Pepperdine University, writing for *The Washington Post*, described the state of affairs in mid-17th century England. That fractious time led to a seven-year war between the royalist Cavaliers, under Charles I, and the Puritan Roundheads, under Oliver Cromwell.

"They grew to hate each other so much that they could no longer accommodate a common national vision," Kotkin reveals. "This is not," he says, "merely the age-old split between income groups, but something even more fundamental—a struggle between contrasting and utterly incompatible worldviews. Demographic trends suggest that Republicans and Democrats are less likely to live next door to each other, attend the same churches, or subscribe to the same media."[281]

While political division is natural in a democratic society, and the discussion it generates is beneficial, extreme polarization may ultimately be damaging to the body politic. If we are so intent on the battle between red states v. blue states as we watch election results, conservatives v. liberals, and Right v. Left that we can no longer engage in civil discourse, any chances of maintaining a national vision in a fast-changing world might be dim.

Communicators in a Group Setting

In any group, there are at least four types of communicators:

- **Controlling.** This is a person whose mind is made up, who doesn't want to be confused by the facts. A primary role in life is to impose his or her will on others.

- **Withdrawn.** These are people who have little to say. Their heads move back and forth, as if they were at a tennis match. To their credit, some are good listeners.

- **Relinquishing.** This type of communicator generally spends little time considering facts surrounding the issue at hand. Generally, this person will say something like, "I have a lot of respect for Joe/my political party/etc., and I'll just go along with what they decide."

- **Developmental.** A developmental communicator listens intently to the views of others and constantly tries to move the group toward some level of consensus, combining what he or she considers the best thinking of many, if not all, members of the group.

It's okay to function in any of these categories, depending on the issue, and all of us eventually reach a limit of our willingness to compromise on certain issues. However, the most constructive communicator is the developmental one, the person who listens, considers possibilities, and helps move people away from unbending confrontation and toward consensus.

common good. At the end of the day, some are generally willing to accept that they haven't achieved total victory in the marketplace of products or ideas.

Taken to extremes, when diversity of any kind is not seen as the norm, conflict is likely to follow. That conflict will probably involve:

- Tribal divisions

- Racial and ethnic divisions

- Religious differences

- Ideological divisions

- Other social and economic divides

Without some level of democracy, people in each of these types of groups will either feel in power or out of power.

Samuel Huntington predicts that future clashes will take place not necessarily along political boundaries, but along cultural and civilizational boundaries.[282] The minute we abandon "The Golden Rule—Do unto others as you would have them do unto you," we move immediately to "An eye for an eye and a tooth for a tooth."

The challenge seems overwhelming. For some, being at each other's throats is almost a sport, often a cover for an unwillingness to think beyond their narrow point of view. Again, education is our great hope. Students, and citizens in general, must be prepared to civilly engage in reasoned discussion . . . to consider evidence and varying points of view.

■ Implications for Education and the Whole of Society

Polarization

- **Prepare people to engage in reasoned discussion.** Whether in the classroom, a community organization, or in conversation with colleagues, friends, and fellow citizens, we need to practice civil discussion. Thoughtful people know that it is important to seek other opinions rather than simply filtering out any point of view other than our own. Of course, that doesn't stand in the way of having strong feelings or a point of view. How far anyone can move toward consensus will depend on how far they are willing to go, to compromise, after considering the common good. We're not talking about "going along to get along" or "caving in." Instead, we're making a case for civil discourse.

- **Offer courses that encourage thinking and reasoning and communication skills.** Any organization worth its salt has frequent or at least occasional discussions about its vision and the values that drive it.

  In a fast-changing world, especially in a democratic society, students should be prepared to do objective research. They should be media literate, capable of separating wheat from chaff, truth from fiction. Students need experience in engaging others in civil discussion and the communication skills they'll need to coherently present their case. All of the above are grounded in a belief that thinking and reasoning are basic skills.

  "There are six or seven clearly delineated values systems at work in our society," observes Jane Hammond, superintendent in residence at the Stupski Foundation. "We need to find common ground upon which we base public discourse. Those value systems, while appearing to be more and more diverse, can at the same time form the foundation for establishing our common values," she remarks. "Kids in schools need to be having discussions about those common values."

- **Individuals, governments and institutions at all levels, and students need to develop an attitude and belief that polarization and narrowness can be overcome.** We have become so accustomed to escalating conflict that we sometimes don't realize how far it can escalate and how destructive it can be.

Throughout history, wars have been fought over the conflict of ideas. More will likely follow, based on clashes along cultural and civilizational boundaries. However, as weapons have become more lethal, we're coming to realize that life on Earth may be the stakes we've placed on the table.

Not convinced that the balance has shifted in favor of this trend, Drew Allbritten, former executive director of the Council for Exceptional Children, senses that "the driving forces continue to be power and control," which he describes as "the next manifestation of the 'cold war' mentality." He points out that "we are now reckoning with various subcultures that do not value an 'open-minded' society." Allbritten concludes, "[S]ociety as a whole should not let the 'tail wag the dog' and proceed from narrowness."

- **Students and other citizens will need to master the art of making change peacefully and democratically.** Constitutional democracies generally create a marketplace of ideas where a broad range of issues can be discussed. The First Amendment to the U.S. Constitution declares "Congress shall make no law respecting an establishment of religion, or prohibiting the free exercise thereof; or abridging the freedom of speech, or of the press, or the right of the people peaceably to assemble, and to petition the Government for a redress of grievances." A challenge for schools, colleges, and society at large will be to build a greater understanding of the implications of this amendment as we civilly deal with controversy.

As George Mason said in 1783, "Happiness and prosperity are now within our reach, but to attain and preserve them depends on our own wisdom and virtue."

■ Questions and Activities

1. What can educational institutions do to help current and future citizens become more adept at civil discourse in dealing with disputes rather than becoming increasingly polarized?

2. How can treating certain subjects as taboo sometimes keep us from having a free, full, and open discussion of problems, issues, trends, and opportunities?

3. Do you believe civil discourse, coupled with thinking and reasoning, is essential to maintaining a society based on the principles of democracy? If yes, why? If no, why not?

4. What are the four types of communicators in a group setting?

■ Readings

1. Cleveland, H. (2002). *Nobody in charge . . . Essays on the future of leadership.* San Francisco: Jossey-Bass, A Wiley Co.

2. Any edition of *The Federalist Papers*, with particular emphasis on James Madison's paper on factions. For example, see *The Federalist . . . A Commentary on the Constitution of the United States*, Bicentennial Edition. (1976). Washington, DC: Robert B. Luce, Inc.

3. Kotkin, J. (2004, March 28), Red, blue and . . . So 17th century," *The Washington Post*, Outlook Section, B-1.

Trend 12

We're all in this together.

As nations vie for understanding and respect in an interdependent world, international learning, including diplomatic skills, will become basic.

<u>Sub-trend</u>: To earn respect in an interdependent world, nations will be expected to demonstrate their reliability and tolerance.

Isolationist Independence ↔ Interdependence

"All these are global problems. Each country has to muster its own resources to deal with them, but they concern all of us—and many countries do not have sufficient resources, whether financial or institutional, to confront them on their own."

United Nations Secretary General Kofi Annan[283]

■ National Reputations . . .

They depend on each of us and all of us.

Aristotle had it right. When he said that our individual reputations—the personalities we project—are based on our competence, good character, and good will, he opened a Pandora's Box that will not stay closed. Today, we realize we judge not only individuals by those criteria, but we also judge nations.

Former U.S. Attorney General Elliot Richardson once noted, "The human beings who make up every ethnic group and every political entity share common bonds with all other human beings on this planet. All of us want a safer, more orderly, and more humane world, not simply because such a world is better for ourselves, but because we recognize our kinship—however distant—with those of others."[284]

The behaviors of governmental and non-governmental organizations, businesses, and individuals help shape national reputations. How people feel about a country depends on more than glowing words in a travel brochure. Policies and actions speak more loudly than words. Over time, national reputations become directly tied to the level of respect any country enjoys as a member of the community of nations. That level of respect could ultimately be a key to a country's success, even its survival.

Let's take a quick look at some of the most basic of those international relationships.

- **Relationships among governments** are often a reflection of foreign policy, the handling of expected and sometimes unexpected issues or events, and longstanding friendships or rivalries. Issues might range from war and peace to trade agreements, environmental concerns, and human rights. The stage is often bilateral, between two nations, and increasingly multilateral, involving several nations. Sometimes, these relationships take on an added dimension, directly affecting regional alliances and world organizations. Examples include the European Union, NAFTA, World Trade Organization, and the United Nations.

- **Business relationships** bring people together to tap natural and human resources; develop, sell, or purchase products or services;

and make a profit, sometimes called trade. Communities, states, and countries often send delegations to another country in an attempt to attract investments in business or infrastructure.

- **Educational, scientific, and other non-governmental relationships** often involve international organizations and individuals who share information, conduct research, and rally communities of interest around projects or ideas.

- **Personal relationships** are often stimulated by study, correspondence, and travel across international boundaries.

An exponential growth in satellite and online conferences and courses, as well as rapid transportation, has caused these types of relationship building and idea sharing to blossom. It has also exponentially multiplied the pace of change and has led to nearly instant international response to national or even local decisions.

■ National Respect and International Education

Many people, including some educators, might dismiss the idea that national respect is related to education, believing that international relations is the government's business. While most people in nations around the globe do depend on their governments to handle macro-diplomatic issues, we can't escape individual responsibility. We are, after all, the ones who elect and/or tolerate the behavior of our governments.

In a world grown small, countries earn their respect by regularly demonstrating that they are connected to their own citizens and considerate of their neighbors. That simple but stark fact has significant implications for schools and colleges and for international education. For one, it means all students should have at least basic diplomatic qualities, skills, and knowledge. That means they need open minds, natural curiosity, patience, courtesy and good manners, a sense of tolerance, and the ability to empathize with others.

All students should have some understanding of economics, history, law, political science, government, civic responsibility, and human rights. Add to that list the need for thinking and reasoning skills, language proficiency, technical and information management skills, the ability to negotiate, and an understanding of the intellectual and social skills that serve as a foundation for diplomatic behavior and protocol. International, global, civic, law-related education, and character education are fast becoming basics in an interdependent world.[285]

Think about the body of knowledge and skills we've just shared. Consider it a checklist. To some extent, we might already be covering a number of those bases, but how well? Are there some items that should command further attention? Which would require a student, or educators for that matter, to develop new knowledge? How about skills? Behaviors? Our future might very well depend on our thoughtful answers to these questions.

Here is a stark reality. Growing numbers of people will live and work outside their home country, hold a job with a multinational organization, have their lives affected by social or economic conditions in another part of the world, or realize they can only be successful by working with people who hail from many different cultures and are different from themselves.

It's time we realized that, wherever we are, whatever our line of work, we are affected by nearly everything else that's happening in the world. Students who leave school without some grounding in international education may turn out to be the new disadvantaged.

■ Competence, Good Character, and Good Will

Most of us have the reputations we've earned.

Let's briefly get back to Aristotle's premise that people view who we are largely based on how we demonstrate our competence, good character, and good will. All have a direct impact in international relationships and implications for international education.

- **Competence.** How legitimately and astutely do individuals and nations handle political, legal, economic, social, technological, environmental, educational, demographic, and other issues, problems, and opportunities? In short, do they have some understanding of what should be done to help ensure the common good? Do they demonstrate the ability to do it well, or do they project an impression of incompetence or highly confident ineptitude?

- **Good Character.** Inevitably, people will ask, "Why are they doing that?" Responses are often a measure of our character. Answers can range from "They're doing it because it's the right thing to do" to "They're doing it out of self interest, and they don't care who gets hurt in the process." People tend to measure our character based on what they perceive as motivating us. Are we committed to the ethical, or will we simply settle for the "easiest" or "most practical" solution, whatever its ethical consequences?

- **Good Will.** In essence, good will can be reduced to how we treat other people. Do we listen? Are we engaging? Do we care about other points of view? Do we try to understand the consequences of our own actions? Do we have a grasp of the impact our actions could have on others?

We earn our reputations by demonstrating our levels of competence, good character, and good will.

■ How would people describe us?

Totalitarian? Democratic? A Hybrid?

Let's cut to the chase. Based on these criteria, we might define some nations as totalitarian or authoritarian and their people as submissive—willing, by choice or by force, to tolerate an iron fist. Others might be seen as democratic, with citizens who are demanding and have high expectations for those elected to serve them. Of course, some are hybrids.

Any of these types of nations, depending on their behaviors, might be described as: committed to taking the higher ground, aggressive, havens for terrorists, reliable, tolerant, fair, tribal, self-centered or self-serving, to list a few possibilities. Apart from individual nations, economic, military, and other alliances and power blocks develop similar reputations based on their policies and actions and their impact on others.

Let's say a country wants to develop a reputation more compatible with the 21st century. Here are some questions its political leaders would need to consider. "How do people currently describe us as a nation?" "How would we like to have them describe us?" "How can we get from where we are to where we'd like to be?" The answer to the last question is fairly clear—the nation will need to adjust its behavior to earn that reputation. That might be tough without an understanding of the people, histories, and cultures of both its own nation and others in the world.

■ The Road to Interdependence

The idea of interdependence is stirring. Imagine the benefits of collaborating across political boundaries to launch a globe-circling network of weather satellites. Think about nations working together to construct and maintain an International Space Station. Consider people coming together from various parts of the world to stanch a possible outbreak of a disease that threatens to become a pandemic. Think of regional alliances that have joined forces to deal with everything from economic to human rights issues. It has all happened.

Realization is growing that some things can only be effectively accomplished together, whether we're pursuing advancements or dealing with dilemmas. Perhaps one of the greatest dilemmas we face is the prospect of not working together to advance scientific discoveries, or consider environmental issues that have an impact on the future of life on the planet. Other areas ripe for collaboration include the sharing of educational knowledge and expertise, the promotion of corporate citizenship and social responsibility within and across national boundaries, and dealing with security concerns that know no borders.

Yet, the word "interdependence" upsets many people who consider it a threat to nationhood. Some equate it with "globalization" and the loss of national and cultural identities. A prime example is the debate that raged throughout many European nations as the region contemplated the move to a common currency and a central bank located within one of the many participating nations. They offer cautions that must be considered even as our shrinking globe brings us closer together.

Many problems and opportunities that could once be contained to a single country or even a neighborhood are now a matter of concern for everyone. One example might be, "That dam helps you control floods, generate power, and irrigate crops upstream, in your country, but it's depriving us of the water we need for our rice crop downstream, in ours."

Some challenges cascade around the globe, such as the problems of religious or environmental terrorism. Interdependence is a new paradigm for our venerable world. Those nations that earn respect as we move into a new millennium will be those that are not only considerate of their own citizens but who also seriously consider the implications of what they do for their neighbors.

In today's world, everyone is becoming "our neighbor." We are connected by a web that is woven by communication and transportation technologies. In open societies, information is so freely available that we almost have to deliberately choose not to pay attention. We have fewer excuses for not knowing the benefits and the consequences of our policies and our actions, both as individual citizens and as nations. Let's hope this interconnected explosion of information means, for all of us, that we will eventually strive to use the word "familiar" more—and the word "foreign" less.

While some countries will demonstrate little concern about earning international respect, others will find it essential. Reliability and tolerance of diversity will be among the keys to earning that respect. Reliability equates to being dependable. For example, can we rely on a country's commitment to abide by treaties and trade agreements and to pursue the common good?

Just as a company is expected to demonstrate its social responsibility and corporate citizenship and an individual is expected to engage in ethical behavior, the future of independent nations may also depend on their reputations as interdependent world citizens.

■ Expectations of Nations

Fundamental Questions

What should we expect of nations? Let's give that question some thought.

Unless a nation considers the needs of its citizens, it might not truly represent them. Not listening, not staying in touch, can lead to instability, as conflict overcomes consensus. Lack of appreciation for diversity can also lead to an "us and them" society, which might become divided against itself. A lack of stability internally raises questions about reliability externally, and could cause breakdowns in relationships with other countries. We're not talking about stability that's imposed by a forceful leader. Instead, we're talking about the stability that comes with inclusive leadership that is directly connected to the common good.

As baseball legend Yogi Berra once said, "You can observe a lot just by watching." In getting a snapshot of nations as citizens of the planet, some questions seem obvious. Are citizens captives in their own land or are they free to cross boundaries and explore other parts of their communities, countries, continents, or the world? Can we depend on a country to devote its resources, no matter how abundant or scarce, to improving life for those who live there and to becoming a reliable member of the family of nations?

Still other fundamental questions that have a bearing on a country's place as a respected member of the world community might include the following:

- Does the government operate with the consent of the governed?

- Does the government exist for the people, or do the people exist for the government?

- Are crime and corruption under control, or do they divert investments, add cost, undermine democratic decisions, and demonstrate a lack of maturity or self-control?

- Are basic human rights guaranteed?

- Is freedom of the press, speech, and religion encouraged?

- Are citizens generally well informed about issues that affect them?

- Does the country practice equal justice under law?

- Does economic growth benefit a vast array of citizens or just a scarce few?

- Is civic education for students a basic part of the curriculum?

- Are exchange programs with other countries encouraged?

- Does the society cultivate and can it tolerate inclusive, democratic leadership?

These questions are fundamental to an understanding of any nation. The answers will reflect any work yet needed for improvement.

Facing Overwhelming Challenges . . .

with Steadfastness and Responsibility

Most nations face some combination of political, economic, social, technological, environmental, or other problems. Some carry burgeoning national debts. They are burdened with un- or under-developed economies, limited education opportunities, drought, rampant disease, or war. Some have "a debt overhang that deters foreign investments and drags down the economy, as governments fail to meet people's basic health and education needs," according to Jeffrey Sachs, in the Worldwatch Institute's *Vital Signs 2003*.[286]

The problems are real. To prove their intentions, nations facing these overwhelming challenges are expected to demonstrate, as best they can, a sense of responsibility and steadfastness in addressing them. They may not be able to do it alone. In an interdependent world, we need to consider the role others should play in lending a hand.

■ A Measuring Stick for Members of the Global Community

Four Factors[287]

Do thoughtful and legitimate leaders worldwide consider the performance and reputations of countries? Absolutely. In fact, some of their approaches provide an excellent framework for stirring discussions among students and citizens. Let's take a look at one prime example.

The fourth annual A.T. Kearney/Foreign Policy Globalization Index, published in the March/April 2004 issue of *Foreign Policy* magazine, took a snapshot of 62 countries, based on 2002 data, ranking them according to four factors:

- **Economic Integration**—trade, foreign direct investment, portfolio capital flows, and investment income.

- **Technological Connectivity**—Internet users, Internet hosts, and secure servers.

- **Personal Contact**: international travel and tourism, international telephone traffic, and remittances and personal transfers.

- **Political Engagement**—memberships in international organizations, personnel and financial contributions to U.N. Security Council missions, international treaties ratified, and governmental transfers.

The study indicated that the world economy grew at an average rate of 1.9 percent in 2002, compared with 1.3 percent in 2001 and 4.8 percent per year during the 1990s. Even with a slowing in the global economy, Internet growth increased in poor countries, and cross-border travel helped forge linkages. On the other hand, free trade issues and armed conflict took their toll on both international and regional alliances, ranging from the United Nations to the World Trade Organization, Free Trade Area of the Americas, and the European Union, the report contended.

Within certain categories, the United States ranked first on Internet hosts and secure servers and fifth on Internet users. On the other hand, of the 62 nations, the United States ranked 33rd on travel, 60th on treaties, and 61st on trade, according to the study.

Countries such as Ireland, Singapore, Switzerland, The Netherlands, and Finland led the list of countries ranked in the globalization index. In

2004, the United States, for the first time, broke into the top 10, ranking number 7. Simply to illustrate the concept, we'll share the rankings of 14 countries: Ireland (1), Singapore (2), Finland (5), Canada (6), the United States (7), the United Kingdom (12), Italy (25), Poland (31), Argentina (34), Nigeria (42), Mexico (45), China (57), India (61), and Iran (62).

Figure T12.1
A.T. Kearney/Foreign Policy Globalization Index
Ranking of 62 Nations
Rank by Category

2004 Ranking (Overall)	Country	Economic Integration	Technological Connectivity	Personal Contact	Political Engagement
1	Ireland	1	14	2	11
2	Singapore	2	10	3	40
5	Finland	7	4	15	12
6	Canada	18	3	5	20
7	United States	56	1	35	28
12	United Kingdom	20	11	13	7
25	Italy	34	23	25	6
31	Poland	42	32	26	32
34	Argentina	33	33	56	9
42	Nigeria	22	61	42	27
45	Mexico	48	39	40	43
57	China	37	49	59	56
61	India	61	55	53	57
62	Iran	59	48	62	61

Foreign Policy magazine, March/April 2004

What's important in reviewing these rankings is the opportunity they give us to understand how countries are viewed in a variety of contexts. Anyone is free to agree or disagree with the categories or the rankings. If the analysis stirs discussion, then we are all richer for having paid attention to conditions outside our home country, wherever we happen to live in the world.

Soft Power

Walter Russell Mead, Henry A. Kissinger senior fellow in U.S. foreign policy at the Council on Foreign Relations, credits "soft power" as being highly influential in reflecting a country's ideals and culture. He recalls that, during its history, the United States used soft power by espousing anti-imperialism, actively encouraging empires to grant independence to their colonies, championing political democracy and human rights, and promoting inclusion in a global community. Mead notes that millions encountered those "values" through business people, government representatives, educators, entertainers, and others traveling, working, and/or living abroad. Humanitarian and developmental assistance from both the public and private sectors and personal contributions directed at people in need secured what became, but wasn't necessarily intended to be, "soft power."[288]

■ Implications for Education and the Whole of Society

Interdependence

Earning international understanding and respect isn't easy. It's earned over time. One thing is certain. You don't have to be rich to be respectable. Perhaps our greatest admiration should go to those who struggle with limited resources, drought, hunger, and disease but demonstrate their resolve and dignity as they rally the world to the plight of their people.

The ideas and challenges posed in this chapter should stir our thinking about the implications of this trend for how we handle international education; how we can engage students in conceiving of legitimate measuring sticks for respectable nations; what we can do as communities and education systems to build relationships with other countries; and how we can stimulate discussion of benefits and concerns raised by globalization.

- **International education will become basic.** The stakes are high and the possible benefits so great that schools and colleges will be expected to strengthen their international education programs.

The United States and several other nations benefit from having students and educators in their schools from many parts of the world. Relationships that grow from international study and exchange programs foster understanding and an opportunity to develop appreciation, even admiration, for others.

Educators and students will want to explore programs in diplomacy, international relations, global issues, conflict resolution, languages other than their own, and the histories and cultures of other parts of the world. International studies is also enhanced by a grounding in civics; economics; law; geography; history; political, arts, and character education; and an introduction to cultural anthropology. Social studies can help us develop a deeper understanding of issues close to home and an even more expansive view of the world.

As many as "18 U.S. states have initiated policies that encourage or require greater attention to instruction in world history and cultures, foreign languages, and the interactions between the United States and other countries," according to a March 2, 2005, article in *Education Week*. "The reality is that there are six billion people in the world, and 95 percent of them don't live here," educator and publisher Catherine Scherer told participants at an International Studies Schools Association (ISSA) conference. The ISSA, a network of K-12 schools, is housed at the University of Denver and is one of a number of groups that seriously call attention to the need for a less myopic view of the world around us. Some at the conference expressed concern about existing standards and high-stakes tests that put a squeeze on international studies. Others considered how to take steps, in addition to highlighting "food, flags, and festivals," to add a global dimension to "social studies, science, math, business education, physical education, language arts, and service learning."

Futurist Joseph Coates, considering solvency, tolerance, and reliability as possible measures for national respect, notes, "Beginning in high school, kids need courses in economics." He adds, "solvency is not equal to fiscal responsibility." Coates also observes that some societies are, by their nature, intolerant. Cautioning against the tendency for Western middle class bias, he points out "reliability has many meanings that must be clarified" and expresses concern about U.S. reliability in the world, in terms of "its standing by international agreements."

International relations expert Frank Method predicts "open information systems and networked learning will increasingly lead to dialogue and exchanges across political, economic, and social boundaries." He cautions, "These exchanges will not necessarily lead to agreement or comity. Young learners will need help managing these exchanges. Listening skills in framing/reframing questions and issues will be as important as debating and advocacy skills." Method notes that students will also need skills in developing and respecting standards and values, and in defending ideals. He adds, "Balancing these skills will be a delicate task for educators, who will need both to nurture the ideals and support the principles of learning to live together in a shared world."

On the agenda for learning and discussion, Method suggests, might be principles underlying the development of international agreements, the resolution of disputes, setting international standards for acceptable practices, criminality, business law, accounting standards, food safety, environmental stewardship, human rights, and myriad other topics.

• **Society should be prepared to communicate and do business across international boundaries.** Growing numbers of companies have multinational owners. Today's students likely will work for and even lead many of these business organizations. To be successful—even to survive—some products and services need to appeal to people in many parts of the world, agricultural products among them. Cities and towns will link, through programs such as Sister Cities, to exchange people and ideas and to share information about how to deal with problems or opportunities they have in common.

Of course, national governments are expected to be among a family of nations in exploring issues ranging from trade and economics to environmental protocols, world health, and peacekeeping. Since pronouncements, decisions, and actions are immediately beamed around the world and have a nearly instant impact on a nation's reputation, greater concern will be focused on public diplomacy. Lee Hamilton, a co-chair of the 9-11 Commission, former member of the U.S. Congress, and now director of the Center on Congress at Indiana University, calls for more U.S. exchanges with the Arab world, for example. "We should aim for a constant flow of people between the U.S. and the Arab world: students, scholars, performers, artists, athletes, farmers, and tourists," he recommends.[289]

The Fulbright Commission and the Civitas International Civic Education Exchange Program are among the many vital programs that bring together educators and other leaders whose homes may be halfway around the globe. The Peace Corps stands out as a leader in providing ongoing assistance while building relationships. Examples of international exchange programs for students include but are by no means limited to Youth for Understanding and the American Field Service. Numerous opportunities exist for study abroad, participation in international seminars and conferences, seasonal or permanent work abroad, attracting people from other nations to work in a local community, internships, volunteering abroad, and participating in international online programs.

Education systems will be expected to turn out new generations of professional diplomats, but that might not be enough. Each of us, in a shrinking and fast-moving world, will very likely need a strong set of diplomatic skills.

• **Students could engage in discussions that result in what they consider a legitimate measuring stick, or criteria, for any country that hopes to become a respected member of the family of nations.** Taking the process a step further, students and communities could expand their conversation to consider the impact of those criteria on future national or even local goals.

White Bear Lake (Minn.) Superintendent Ted Blaesing looks ahead to "students of all ages increasingly traveling as part of their normal course of study and certainly connecting with each other via the latest technology." He expresses concern about working an international curriculum into an already crowded school day, largely focused on state and federal requirements.

Blaesing also sees international implications for school policy. "I can foresee a school district policy that might read in part, 'all products will be purchased by the school district from manufacturers and companies that offer economic justice to workers,'" he said.

• **Professional development programs will provide educators with a grounding in international education.** Some educators travel and try to understand and appreciate the histories,

The Universal Declaration of Human Rights

The Universal Declaration of Human Rights is part of the foundation for any nation that hopes to secure respect among its worldwide neighbors. A dedication to these basic rights can also build confidence that all voices are being heard and that progress is built on a sound foundation.

First adopted by the United Nations General Assembly in 1948, the declaration notes that all human beings are born free and equal in dignity and rights; that everyone is entitled to the rights, despite their differences; that everyone has the right to life, liberty, and security; that no one should be held in slavery; that no one should be subjected to torture, or to cruel, inhuman, or degrading treatment or punishment; and that everyone has a right to be recognized as a person before the law. In 30 articles, the declaration describes these and other rights that are bestowed at birth.[290]

This document and others can be used to spark discussions about a measuring stick for a respected nation. Without a concerted effort to deal with expanding inequities within and among nations, the world risks sustained conflict that could bring unprecedented human suffering and death.

cultures, and peoples of the world. Nonetheless, few have been able to explore the range of possibilities for incorporating an international perspective into courses ranging from math to social studies and the arts.

- **Demand will grow for continuing education programs that focus on international issues and opportunities.** Students will increasingly understand that they will need to be able to live, work, and thrive in a multitude of cultures and locations worldwide. People of all ages and walks of life are likely to demand expanded opportunities to learn about other people and nations through college, university, online, and adult education courses. As members of the Baby Boom Generation retire, those who can afford it are spending time visiting other countries, and even tours are sometimes billed as educational events.

- **Community, business, and civic leaders increasingly will build relationships with counterparts in other nations.** While students pursue internationally oriented projects, communities might develop relationships through programs such as Sister Cities; host festivals celebrating the richness of the many cultures that comprise their areas; encourage participation in programs such as the Peace Corps; sponsor student, educator, and other community exchange programs; and pursue business relationships with people in other nations. Both students and their communities should consider the international benefits and consequences, both intended and unintended, that could result from various proposals for economic and other types of development.

- **Coherent discussions will be needed to address benefits and concerns raised about globalization.** In the view of Douglas Greenberg of the Shoah Foundation, globalization "may actually threaten reliability, solvency, and tolerance." He warns of "concentrating capital and power in very small communities, establishing a system of rich nations and poor nations more invidious than any in history, underemploying the poor in wealthy nations, underpaying labor in poor nations, and controlling the flow of information in order to advance political and economic goals that undercut reliability and solvency." On the other hand, Greenberg submits that, in some communities, tolerance may be seen as a danger and may present what some consider "a real threat to traditional values."

Comments such as these, coupled with a variety of other views, can help spur discussions that trigger ideas for even greater understanding of the interconnected nature of international issues.

■ Questions and Activities

1. Identify from three to five projects that have required the collaboration of several countries to accomplish.

2. What do you consider as five of the most important skills and/or bodies of knowledge students (and others) need to work effectively with people from other nations or cultures different from their own?

3. What are the downsides if students are not prepared to work effectively with people from a variety of nations and cultures?

4. Consider this statement: "Countries earn their respect by regularly demonstrating that they are connected to their own citizens and considerate of their neighbors." Prepare a paper or PowerPoint presentation that addresses this premise. Provide actual examples.

5. Prepare a one-page paper or PowerPoint presentation on why our independence may depend on understanding and practicing some degree of interdependence.

6. If you were assigned to determine whether a society is democratic, what questions would you ask?

7. Study the four factors in the Globalization Index briefly described in this chapter. What additional factors would you include, if any? How could discussions of these factors be useful in preparing students for life in a global knowledge/information age?

■ Readings

1. Fuller, R.B. (1969). *Operating manual for spaceship Earth.* New York: Simon and Schuster.

2. Several publications from the Center for Civic Education, Calabasas, CA: *National standards for civics and government; Civitas: A framework for civic education; Project citizen; Comparative lessons for democracy;* Civitas International Exchange Program materials; and other materials. Available from htttp://www.civiced.org

3. Materials and programs developed and/or offered by StreetLaw, which provides "practical, participatory education about law, democracy and human rights," Silver Spring, MD. Available from http://www.streetlaw.org

4. Materials and programs developed and/or offered by the International Youth Foundation, Baltimore, MD. Available from http://www.iyfnet.org

5. Materials and programs developed and/or offered by the Constitutional Rights Foundation, Los Angeles, CA. Available from http://www.crf-usa.org

6. Materials and programs developed and/or offered by the National Council on Economic Education, Washington, DC. Available from http://www.ncee.net

7. "Measuring Globalization, Economic Reversals, Forward Momentum," study conducted and copyrighted by A.T. Kearney, Inc., and the Carnegie Endowment for International Peace, *Foreign Policy* magazine, March-April 2004 (or the most recent report on this periodic study).

8. "Universal Declaration of Human Rights," United Nations; adopted by the General Assembly as Resolution 217 (AIII) of December 10, 1948. Available from http://www.un.org/Overview/rights/html.

Trend 13

Give me a break!

Greater numbers of people will seek personal meaning in their lives in response to an intense, high-tech, always-on, fast-moving society.

Personal Accomplishment ↔ Personal Meaning

"Simplify your life. Enough of the frenzy. How you can step back a little—or set a new course."

Coverlines, Kiplinger's Personal Finance *magazine*[291]

■ Easy Street, Treadmill, or Lonesome Highway?

In July and August of 2001, two major business magazines, *Fortune* and *Kiplinger's*, carried cover stories on the need people were feeling to step back from the frenzy and seek spiritual renewal.[292] Those stories reflect what many identify as a growing frustration with being wired, accessible at all hours of day and night, working 24/7, and seeing the consequences for their families and their own personal interests.

"Most people are in a rut, doing what they are expected to rather than what they want to do," Kirstin Davis and Mary Beth Franklin noted in their *Kiplinger's* article. They kick off their timeless piece with this statement, "You've heard it all your life: Time is money. But a growing number of Americans are deciding that the relentless pursuit of money is leaving them too little time to enjoy it. They are stepping back from their fast-paced, workaholic lifestyles and making changes to bring more balance into their lives, carving out more time for their families and passions—even when it means making do with less."[293]

Marc Gunther, in his *Fortune* article, "God and Business," described a group of "middle-aged rebels in business suits" who get together for lunch "in a conference room on the top floor of the LaSalle Bank building in Chicago." Gunther explains, "They have come for sandwiches, and for spiritual sustenance, and before long they are floating radical ideas: Work less. Slow down. Stop multitasking. Listen to your heart."[294]

We can expect that, in addition to looking outward, even more people will be looking inward to personal relationships—as the physical and emotional foundation that supports them. Rather than being satisfied with lowest common denominators, they'll aspire to highest common possibilities.

■ How fast do we want to go?

While two articles don't necessarily form a trend, and we all know how important productivity is to our economy, growing numbers of people seem ready for some kind of renewal, and they're not always sure what that means.

It's inescapable. Wherever we go, if we are the least bit sensitive to those around us, we find legions of people working two or more jobs, just to make a go of it. Others have a hard time separating their sense of personal value from what they do for a living or how much money they make. Here are samples of recent comments that illustrate the conflict. **The Boss:** "I go to the office every weekend.

It's tough on my family, but I want everybody to know that I give the job more than 100 percent." **The Employee:** "I go to the office every weekend, because the boss is there, and I don't want her to think I'm a slacker. I missed my son's Little League game last weekend, and I'm not sure I should take a few days to visit my parents. They're getting older, and I feel guilty about not seeing them more than once a year."

"Polls show that Americans increasingly want to find time for family and friends first, even if it means earning less money," *The Washington Times* reported in a June 24, 2002, article by Patricia Hill. "The all-consuming dream jobs of the 1990s came with stock options that promised to make even clerical workers millionaires, but workers today are putting greater emphasis on achieving emotional gratification and social improvement," she reported. The article suggests that the September 11, 2001, terrorist attacks, the Enron scandal, and a slowed economy might, at least in part, have stimulated this transformation.[295]

American Demographics magazine confirms this trend, noting that 77 percent of Americans wanted to spend more time with their families, while only 19 percent thought making a lot of money was important.[296]

"Half of Americans are searching for meaning and purpose in life," according to Barna Research, based in Ventura, Calif. The American Heart Association's *Scientific Study 2000* was among the first to document that "laughter and an active sense of humor may influence heart and artery disease." "The old axiom that 'laughter is the best medicine' appears to hold true when it comes to protecting your heart," says Michael Miller, M.D., director of the Center for Preventive Cardiology at the University of Maryland Medical Center in Baltimore.[297]

Speaking of laughter, comedian George Carlin, who is known for pressing the limits, is quoted as saying, "The paradox of our time in history is that we have taller buildings, but shorter tempers; wider freeways, but narrower viewpoints. We spend more, but have less. We buy more, but enjoy less."[298]

We build bigger, faster, more comfortable cars, filled with gadgets and safety devices. They're generally air conditioned and more dependable that anything we might have dreamed possible in the 1950s or 60s. These vehicles are capable of getting us where we want to go, whether it's a job, restaurant, gym, school, soccer practice, or store in record time. As a result, we frustrate ourselves by deciding the car will allow us to do even more and in many more places. We become harried. Traffic jams, parking (or the lack of it), and road rage become major complaints.

"Most men and women in the Western nations have attained the conditions of which previous generations dreamed," says Gregg Easterbrook in *The Progress Paradox*, "and although this is excellent news, the attainment makes it possible for society to verify, beyond doubt, that personal liberty and material security do not in themselves bring contentment." He adds, "That must come from elsewhere, making it time to awaken from the American dream."

The United States has enshrined "life, liberty, and the pursuit of happiness" in its founding documents. In the early years of the 21st century, growing numbers of people have luxuries that were not even a gleam in their ancestors' eyes, such as advanced medical treatment, longer lifespans, automobiles, centrally heated and air conditioned homes, air travel, television, and the Internet. Yet, happiness can seem elusive. Easterbrook points out "society is undergoing a fundamental shift from 'material want' to 'meaning want,' with ever larger numbers of people reasonably secure in terms of living standards, but feeling they lack significance in their lives." He adds, "Meaning is much more difficult to acquire than material possessions."[299]

In a 2005 international survey of futurists, academics, and business people, the Global Futures Forum found significant agreement that "work-life balancing," especially for women in top management positions, is likely to become a fairly high-impact scenario during the first decade of the 21st century. That group similarly agreed, but by a lesser margin, with the scenario that "people will prioritize 'life experiences' over job security."[300]

Health is another life-quality issue. While obesity and other health concerns raise alarms, many people are getting involved in wellness programs, often sponsored by their workplace or local community. Personal and family nutrition has become a significant topic for both casual and serious conversations. Personal trainers, psychologists, and massage therapists are helping thousands of people work through stress- or fatigue-related dilemmas and consider how they can more fully develop their own potentials. Health tourism, along with eco-tourism and adventure tourism, is growing in popularity. With the aging of the population, grandparents are now finding fulfillment in not only helping care for their grandchildren but also in taking them on trips or tours. The quest for renewal may lead some people to want to impose their particular formula on everyone, however, which could create ongoing challenges for education and other institutions.

Perhaps among the most satisfying ways of finding inspiration and confirming self-worth is helping others as a volunteer or working in a profession or industry that improves the lives of others. Many find meaning, as well as opportunities to serve others, through communities of faith or religious institutions.

Some of us pick up a brush or musical instrument and create our own version of a work of art. Others find satisfaction in being a consumer of the arts, buying a CD, DVD, photo, sculpture, or a painting. In the late 1990s, the National Endowment for the Arts surveyed more than 12,000 people in the United States. They found that half of U.S. adults, 18 and older, had attended at least one of seven arts activities (jazz, classical music, opera, musical plays, non-musical plays, ballet, or art museums) during the previous 12 months. "That," according to the report, "would translate into 97 million different people who attended one or more of these events during the year."[301] Sporting events, sightseeing, dining, shopping, nightlife, and visits to historic sites also provide diversion.

This is reminiscent of the Broadway musical, *Stop the World, I Want to Get Off*. Rather than continue to burn the candle at both ends, the time has come to admit one of the limits of our new technologies— they can actually work us into a frenzy or even work us to death.

Are we prepared to deal with this conundrum? Let the discussion begin as we consider that growing tug between personal accomplishment and personal meaning in our lives.

Treadmill to Oblivion

In 1954, famed radio, television, and standup comic Fred Allen wrote a book aptly titled *Treadmill to Oblivion*. He was expressing his frustration as a comedian who had to compete with what he called, "the machine age."

"We are living in the machine age," Allen said. "For the first time in history the comedian has been compelled to supply himself with jokes and comedy material to compete with the machine. Whether he knows it or not, the comedian is on a treadmill to oblivion. When a radio comedian's program is finally finished, it slinks down Memory Lane into the limbo of yester-year's happy hours. All that the comedian has to show for his years of work and aggravation is the echo of forgotten laughter."

A fitting reminder that even those who entertain us, who provide us with comic relief, are also looking for meaning and a legacy that they feel counts.[302]

■ Implications for Schools and the Whole of Society

Personal Meaning

- **Considering how business, government, education, and other institutions can contribute to work-life balance.** Many institutions can play a role. Some will find perspective in religion or their community of faith. Some might seek renewal of the spirit by simply spending a bit more time with their families and friends. Others might want to create a work of art or commune with nature—watching birds, walking through a park or forest, listening to the wind in the trees, or tracking Saturn as it drifts across an evening sky.

There are at least two rubs. First, we need to understand that it's OK to do those things, to unwire long enough to unwind and refresh. Second, we need to know how. Some people have been so busy for so long that they either feel guilty or have no idea what to do when they are presented with leisure time.

At the risk of compromising productivity, the need is urgent. Unless people recharge their batteries, they're going to burn out way too early. That burnout happens with teachers in the classroom, business people pursuing and fulfilling contracts, aid workers delivering services to people in need, and even families pursuing the income they need to make payments on the house and car and save for the kids' college tuition.

Michael Silver, assistant professor of education administration at Seattle University and a veteran superintendent, foresees an expansion of school curriculum to provide students with a greater number of humanities and arts courses of study, helping students learn how to build relationships and reach out to others for friendship and collaboration, and making a search for identity an interdisciplinary theme for middle and high school courses. "A sustainable world cannot be built without full engagement of the human spirit," says Gary Gardner, director of research for the Worldwatch Institute.[303] The quest is on for purposeful lives and meaningful legacies.

- **Attracting more young people and seasoned workers into public service careers, including education.** The good news is that many people seeking greater meaning in their lives have considered making a move into education, health services, social services, local government, and various creative careers.

"The high tech collapse of the early 2000s led to a realization that high times can end swiftly," observes Carol Peck, president and CEO of the Rodel Charitable Foundation. "Young people were drawn back into service careers where there was a generally more stable source of demand." She adds, "… loyalty wears thin when money is the only source of fulfillment—as seen when employees hop from firm to firm, seeking the best compensation."

Peck, a longtime educator who was named a National Superintendent of the Year, points out that "after experiencing the increased intensity, competition, and depersonalization of the job market, people are coming to place a higher value on loyalty and engagement in work environments—like teaching—that value relationships and the opportunity to change lives."

- **Paying more attention to emotional health.** For decades, educators have recognized the need to help people deal with their leisure time and pursue a broad range of interests, talents, and abilities. Schools and colleges play a key educational role in building an understanding of these skills.

With limited life experience, students need skills to cope with situations that may seem overwhelming—a bad grade, the loss of a boyfriend or girlfriend, or being bullied. Gangs are identity groups, often providing a home-base for people who feel they have been excluded or marginalized. A thoughtful array of essential life and leadership skills could help students find perspective and give them a framework for dealing with emotional trauma that might otherwise lead to self-destructive behavior. Psychologist Daniel Goleman's 1995 book, *Emotional Intelligence: Why It Can Matter More Than IQ*, serves as a milestone on the road toward helping people reasonably recapture their sense of personal identity. Let's face it. In a world of exponential change, people need skills just to cope.

Organizations can support emotional health among their employees, and maybe even among their customers and suppliers, by developing supportive policies and practices. Among the benefits are heightened personal effectiveness; better relationships; the confidence to communicate positively and effectively; enhanced ability to manage personal emotions and help others deal with theirs; and increased flexibility to deal with conflict, change, and growth. Even greater levels of creativity and productivity flow from empowered people, who feel more confident working in teams, and who have greater respect for their organization or community. Obviously, emotional health has significant implications for personal relationships that range from being a good citizen of the world to being a balanced and positive force in a family.[304]

Individually, or in groups, we can give more thought to our legacies. The driving question might be, "How do I want to be remembered?"

■ Questions and Activities

1. Develop a list of five to 10 reasons spelling out how abandoning our personal lives in favor of even greater productivity can eventually become damaging to productivity.

2. How can organizations give people a greater opportunity to pursue a balance between their work and their personal lives?

3. What, if anything, should we be teaching students about "emotional intelligence?"

■ Readings

1. Easterbrook, G. (2004). *The progress paradox, How life gets better while people feel worse.* (Trade Paperbacks Edition.) New York: Random House.

2. Goleman, D. (1997). *Emotional intelligence . . . Why it can matter more than IQ.* New York: Bantam Books.

Trend 14

Poverty makes us all poor.

Understanding will grow that sustained poverty is expensive, debilitating, and unsettling.

Sustained Poverty ←→ Opportunity and Hope

"For every talent that poverty has stimulated, it has blighted a hundred."

John Gardner, former U.S. Secretary of Health, Education and Welfare[305]

A Discussion Starter

As with other trends, a brief section in this book cannot contain more than a very small part of what we need to know about poverty. The purpose of the commentary that follows is to stimulate reflection and further study. At the very heart of any discussion should be serious consideration of not only the implications of this trend for education and the whole of society, but also how it might be more constructively addressed.

■ Poverty . . . What are we talking about?

To be poor. The meaning is all too clear for nearly half the people on planet Earth, who live on the equivalent of less than two dollars a day. Approximately 1.3 billion people live on less than one dollar a day.[306]

The definitions of *poverty* seem too clinical—"the state of one who lacks a usual or socially acceptable amount of money or material possessions" or "debility due to malnutrition." *Destitution*—"the state of a person who has insufficient resources." *Indigence*— "seriously strained circumstances." *Penury*—"a cramping or oppressive lack of money."[307]

Some people are born into poverty. Others are limited by discrimination or a lack of educational opportunity. Still others might have been marginalized by downsizing. Whatever the reason, the frustration people feel is universal when the golden ring is always slightly out of reach.

Pulitzer Prize-winning author David Shipler writes in *The Working Poor . . . Invisible in America* about those who labor every day but simply can't break the bonds of poverty. His examples include: "The man who washes cars but doesn't own one. The clerk who files cancelled checks at the bank has $2.02 in her account. The woman who copy-edits medical textbooks has not been to a dentist in a decade." Shipler notes that the working poor are "shaped by invisible hardships." He describes people who are "climbing out of welfare, drug addiction, or homelessness" or "trapped for life in a perilous zone of low wage work." Some of their children suffer from asthma, made worse by their crumbling housing, or can't see the chalkboard at school because they need eyeglasses that they can't afford," Shipler says.[308]

In a fast-moving world, the distinction between haves and have-nots is broadening and becoming even clearer. Perhaps the most worrisome concern is the growth in "sustained poverty." We find it in our individual communities, in our nations, and worldwide. It's a situation that almost seems to be inherited. From generation to generation, it increases exponentially. For too many, hope is a long forgotten dream.

■ Poverty and Education

Socioeconomic Gaps Too Often Equal Achievement Gaps

Achievement gaps rear their heads in many ways: standardized test scores, student grades, dropout rates, and both college entrance and completion. When a student is lost because of poverty, we all lose. The cost of neglect is expensive.

Poverty among children is not spread evenly. According to the U.S. Census Bureau, about 13 percent of White children younger than 18 live in poverty, compared with 27 percent of Hispanic and 30 percent of Black children.

That child who comes to school after being raised in poverty very likely did not benefit from the quality of health care and nutrition available to other children. Other disadvantages, right from the start, likely include fewer learning resources at home, negative stereotyping, placement in lower tracks or ability groups, retention, an anti-school attitude and value system, and test bias, according to 2000 information from the U.S. Department of Education. In some cases, these children might have less qualified teachers in their classrooms, or their highly dedicated teachers might be frustrated by a lack of respect or parental involvement.[309] While students who suffer from poverty may get good grades, some studies have shown that those marks are based too often on lower expectations.[310]

"An extensive body of research has shown that youngsters from lower socioeconomic strata are less likely to succeed in school," according to *Teaching and Learning*. "This does not mean that poor or disadvantaged children cannot learn. However, social class and economic condition are important factors related to success and cannot be ignored." A 1994 Rand Corporation study found that parents' level of education was the most important factor affecting student achievement. Income, family size, and the mother's age when the child was born were modestly related to achievement.[311]

Ensuring equal educational opportunity for all, despite socioeconomic and other factors, is an ongoing quest. Attention to this critical issue heats up and then wanes. At the federal level, the historic Elementary and Secondary Education Act focuses on the needs of disadvantaged students. No Child Left Behind is intended to be an extension of that effort.

Programs and models have been developed at the local, state, national, and even worldwide levels. "Success for All" is a program created by Robert Slavin, co-director of the Center for Research on Education for Students Placed at Risk at Johns Hopkins University in Baltimore, Md. The "Comer School Development Program," employing the wisdom of education professor and researcher James Comer, has emerged from Yale University. Its purpose is to close the learning gap between low- and high-poverty schools.[312]

The future of our nation and world depend on addressing the impact of poverty on education as well as the impact of education on poverty. (Readers can find more information on this issue in the earlier discussion of the minorities trend.)

■ What do we have to lose?

"Why should we be concerned about sustained poverty?" "The poor will always be with us. What do we have to lose because some people are poor?" As facetious as they sometimes are, they are questions that deserve our thoughtful response.

The answers are glaring: lost talent and productivity, human frustration, increased welfare and other subsidies; more gang activity, vio-

True Story

(Quotes are from a local newspaper article. Names of the school and school system are not included in this text.)

It happened right after a couple of "high-profile fights in which students and teachers were pummeled." The school is "all-Black, almost-all-poor . . . in a supposedly integrated and equalized society." In a visit to the high school, the superintendent asked "what went wrong and how to fix it." He promised specific help.

Meeting in the library, "teachers rattled off a 30-point list in two minutes. Discipline. Class cutting. Vulgarity. Security. Attendance. State takeover. Books. Supplies. Facilities. Accountability. Vocational Education. Business partners. Unity."

A reporter summarized the concerns of a number of teachers. Some, he reported, made the point that, "Many students struggle every day against formidable obstacles to get an education. They feel the sting not only of that struggle, but of the public perception of (their school) as little more than a holding tank for thugs."

One teacher described the student brawls as "a predictable revolt." Another said, ". . . there's only so much a human being can take. We have students here who just get up and walk out of class. What do you do with a high school diploma (from the system)? You open doors, you clean toilets, make up beds, and fix things. That's all. You don't think they (the students) know that?"[313]

These are just a few of the struggles some schools, their students, and their teachers face in dealing with the impact of sustained poverty.

lence, and self-destructive behaviors; fuller jails; expansion of physical and mental health concerns; compromised performance in school; and a demonstrated lack of civility toward those in need. Too often, those who have felt unjustifiably deprived and who may, for various reasons, be un- or under-educated and unemployed, could pose threats to their communities, their countries, and the world. The anger that often accompanies poverty can lead to everything from crowded homeless shelters and soup kitchens to civil unrest, street protests, and terrorism.

In 2002, Canada's National Council of Welfare issued a report on the cost of poverty. The document drew on studies in the areas of health, justice, human rights and human development, work and productive capacity, and child development. In a news release, the Council noted that "bringing people at the very bottom of the scale up has positive effects. It can help a society better manage health care costs, reduce crime, develop a productive labor force, advance human well-being, and foster social cohesion and public confidence in governments and in the economy." In addition, the Council pointed out that "programs designed to achieve these goals would actually pay for themselves and generate substantial returns on investment."[314]

In communities worldwide, people should gather to thoughtfully build on this list as they form their rationale for helping those in poverty develop bootstraps and increase their chances for a better life.

The cost of sustained poverty is high. What more is at stake? Hope and human dignity.

■ War Declared

"Separate but equal," enforced under an 1896 U.S. Supreme Court ruling, *Plessy v. Ferguson*,[315] kept legions of Black Americans from pursuing a full range of personal goals and economic opportunities. In 1954, the Court started tearing down the walls. *Brown v. Board of Education* ordered the desegregation of schools and colleges. The Civil Rights Act of 1964 took equal rights and opportunity a step further.

Also in 1964, U.S. President Lyndon Johnson declared a war on poverty, "because it is right, because it is wise, and because, for the first time in history, it is possible to conquer poverty." Fast forward to 1973. Robert McNamara, then president of the World Bank, announced a major escalation in the battle by calling for extreme poverty to be eradicated worldwide by the end of the 20th century.

Later, former World Bank President James Wolfensohn would declare that a famous speech McNamara delivered in Nairobi, also in 1973, proposing the term *absolute poverty*, "still rings in our ears." It is, he said, a condition of deprivation that "falls below any rational definition of human decency."[316]

Actually, "reducing poverty around the globe—and particularly in the developed countries—has been a goal of governments and the international community at least since the Second World War," according to the December 2003 issue of *Finance and Development*.

How goes the war? According to the World Bank, by 2015, the global incidence of *extreme poverty*, characterized by the percentage of the world population with incomes of less than one dollar a day, will be under 15 percent. That would be half the percentage reported in 1990. As the world population grows, however, the absolute numbers of those who are poor is expected to be about the same in 2015 as it was in 1973, approximately 800 million.[317]

"The U.S. declared war on poverty, and poverty won," said Ronald Reagan, commenting on progress in the War on Poverty.[318]

■ The Unfinished War

The war on poverty in the United States provides a case in point for how frustration and anger can lead to crisis and, eventually, to some level of political resolve. In 1954, *Brown v. Board of Education* reflected not only a growing response to unrest but also a realization that education was a major key to dealing with poverty that was too often built on racism. People's frustrations boiled over, and they took to the streets.

A "Poor People's March on Washington" stepped off in 1963 as parts of the nation erupted in civil strife. Martin Luther King Jr.'s "I Have a Dream" speech became almost a spoken anthem for those who were committed to solving what had become a sustained/endemic problem for society. Watts in Los Angeles and other big city ghettos were hit by riots beginning in 1965, putting domestic tranquility at risk unless equal opportunity became a reality for many more people.[319]

Through that historic and traumatic time, growing numbers of people who were living somewhat comfortably discovered the face of poverty. They started to get it—sustained poverty is expensive, debilitating, and unsettling, and the solution has to include opportunity and hope. The war continues.

■ A Vast Array of Situations

Terms such as "the poor" or "those in poverty" are perhaps too generic. There are, after all, the "urban poor" and "rural poor." Some, who by most standards are considered rich, consider themselves "house poor." Often, people either complain about being "on welfare" or about "those receiving welfare," not understanding that most people, at least in the United States, benefit from an array of entitlements.

During the Great Depression of the 1930s, innovative programs were developed to put people to work. The Works Progress Administration (WPA), Public Works Administration (PWA), and Civilian Conservation Corps (CCC) employed millions who were victims of an economy that had fallen on hard times. Later, programs such as the Job Corps and summer employment opportunities for youth attempted to address poverty. In part, they were also

Figure T14.1
Poverty Background and Statistics

- **Poverty Threshold.** In 1960, the poverty threshold for nonfarm families in the United States was $1,490 for individuals, $1,894 for a family of two, and $3,022 for a family of four. In 2001, the figures moved to $9,039 for individuals, $11,569 for a family of two, and $18,104 for a family of four.

- **Percentage of Poor in the United States.** In 1959, 22.4 percent of people of all ages lived in poverty, including 26.9 percent of children under 18, 16.5 percent of people from 18-54, 21.5 percent of people from 55-64, and 35.2 percent of those 65 and older. In 2000, 11.3 percent of all U.S. residents lived in poverty, including 15.7 percent of children under 18, 9.6 percent of people from 18-54, 9.4 percent of those from 55-64, and 10.2 percent of people 65 and older.

- **Money Income of Those 65 and Older, 2000.** In 2000, the primary sources of income for individuals who were 65 or older, living alone or with nonrelatives, in the United States included: *earnings*, 14 percent; *public programs* such as Social Security or Supplemental Security Income, 44 percent; *employment-related pensions, alimony, or annuities*, 19 percent; and *other sources*, such as dividends, interest, or rent, 20 percent. In 2000, the median income for people 65 or older was $13,767, which placed many older citizens in a precarious position, especially in areas where the cost of living is high.[320]

- **Consumer Spending Compared with Population, by Region of the World, 2000.** In 2000, using World Bank data, the Worldwatch Institute calculated that while the U.S. and Canada constituted only 5.2 percent of the world population, they accounted for 31.5 percent of the world's expenditures for private consumption. South Asia, with 22.4 percent of the world population, accounted for 2.0 percent of those expenditures, while the Middle East and North Africa, with 4.1 percent of the world population, accounted for 1.4 percent of those expenditures. The numbers provide insight into conversations about economic haves and have-nots worldwide.[321]

- **Household Expenditures for Food.** The United Nations Statistical Division reports that, in 1998, people in the United States, on average, allocated 13 percent of their household expenditures for food, while in Tanzania, people allocated 67 percent of those expenditures for food.[322]

addressing longer-term economic health and concerns about domestic tranquility.

In 2003-04, approximately 95 percent of public schools participated in the National School Lunch Program. During 2002-03, more than 27.8 million children in more than 97,000 schools and residential child care institutions directly participated. This historic program, which offers free or reduced-price lunches for those who qualify, helps address nutrition and its impact on health and student achievement.[323]

Worldwide Concerns. Around the globe, people are often forced into poverty by natural disasters such as drought, authoritarian regimes, and a gross lack of educational or economic opportunity. Worldwide, immigrants often go through periods of poverty and sacrifice while they get a foothold on the ladder to accomplishment

A Global Campaign for Education

Worldwide, the United Nations reported that, in 2003, 104 million children between the ages of six and 11 were out of school, 60 percent of them girls. Nearly 40 percent of those children lived in Sub-Saharan Africa, and 35 percent lived in south Asia. Still another 150 million children were at risk of dropping out of school.

Where educational opportunity is scarce, poverty runs high and productivity runs low. The byproduct of a lack of education is poverty in its many forms, and poverty breeds frustration, anger, and an unstable world.

A coalition, "Global Campaign for Education," brings together civil society groups such as advocacy organizations, charities, teachers' unions, and citizen groups, working to promote education opportunity for all.[325]

and reward. Consider also the estimated 13 million refugees who often have little more than the clothes on their backs, some living in camps for years on end.[324]

What happens when vast numbers of young people, generally in their "coming of age" years of 16 to 24, are un- or under-educated and unemployed? We know from our own experience that many lose hope, become frustrated, and then get extremely angry. If they can garner the strength and support, they may take to the streets.

In 2004, the five countries with the highest gross domestic product per capita were: Luxemborg ($36,400), the United States ($36,200), Bermuda ($33,000), San Marino ($32,000), and Switzerland ($28,600), according to an aneki.com listing of the richest countries in the world. Those with the lowest GDP per capita, listed as the poorest countries in the world, were: Sierra Leone ($500), Tanzania ($550), Ethiopia ($560), Somalia ($600), and Cambodia ($710).[326]

As the world population expands, poverty will multiply geometrically unless it is effectively addressed, within communities and nations and among nations. For many, crisis has already become catastrophe. The problems posed by sustained poverty will have profound implications for our individual and collective futures. Poverty is everyone's problem.

■ Implications for Education and the Whole of Society

Poverty

- **Understanding the history and consequences of sustained poverty.** Schools and communities need a heightened understanding of the role poverty has played throughout history and the challenges it poses for the future. If we choose not to learn from history, then we may, indeed, be forced to relive it.

Arnold Fege, president of Public Advocacy for Kids, calls for "living wage programs." He remarks, "Cost cutting as a result of cheap labor both in the U.S. and overseas will actually move us toward an economy similar to those in developing countries—and in some areas of our nation, we are already there economically." Fege adds, "If this trend persists, the quality of one's education will be determined, if not de jure, then de facto, by a student's zip code. A two-tier system of education, based on race and income, will then be imminent—one school system for the rich and the other for the poor."

- **Offering education programs that prepare people to avoid or overcome poverty.** Unless students understand issues posed by poverty, they are probably not well educated. Rosa Smith, president of the Schott Foundation for Public Education and a veteran superintendent, speculates, "Schools need to produce students capable of quickly mastering our ever changing technology, with high levels of analysis and judgment skills." She also points out that, unless the problems posed by poverty are effectively addressed, students may have to realize that the future could hold less in resources for the middle class.

"The school must be the great equalizer while it is assuring high achievement for its students," Fege submits, noting that "this has never before been accomplished." He comments on the importance of "an investment in education, from birth to, in some cases, adulthood." Programs offered before and after school, tutoring, Head Start and other opportunities for early education, free and reduced-price lunches and other meals, counseling, and many other programs, at least in part, attempt to address many of the challenges that accompany poverty.

Marc Ecker, a school superintendent in California and former president of the National Middle School Association, believes the need is growing for "increased incentives for teaching professionals to choose urban and other inner city assignments."

Betsy Rogers, the 2003 National Teacher of the Year, advocates "using incentives to recruit master teachers for our most needy schools, early intervention through preschool programs, and quality career tech programs at the high school level to help close the achievement gap between the affluent and the poverty stricken."

■ Questions and Activities

1. Identify five to 10 ways poverty interferes with student achievement.

2. If the "war on poverty" is an unfinished agenda, what items do you believe should be added to that agenda to further reduce poverty in the nation? In the world?

3. Prepare a paper or PowerPoint presentation on the topic, "What education needs to do now to help students overcome sustained poverty."

■ Readings

1. Shipler, D.K. (2004). *The working poor . . . Invisible in America.* New York: Alfred A. Knopf.

2. Wolfensohn, J. (2000). Speech given at a White House Conference on the New Economy, April 4, 2000. Available from http://www.worldbank.org by searching on James Wolfensohn, 2000 White House Conference on the New Economy.

3. Worldwatch Institute. (2004). *State of the world 2004.* Washington, DC: Author. (Also see other annual editions, including *Vital Signs.*) Available from http://worldwatch.org or http://www.wwnorton.com

4. Current world almanacs.

Trend 15

What am I gonna do?

Pressure will grow for society to prepare people for jobs and careers that may not currently exist.

Career Preparation ↔ Career Adaptability

"Who am I anyway? Am I my resume?"

Broadway musical, A Chorus Line[327]

"I owe my soul to the company store."

Popular song, "Sixteen Tons"[328]

■ What are we doing tomorrow?

That's a question traditionally reserved for Fridays as we look forward to the weekend. Confident that our jobs will be there on Monday morning, we can focus on other things. The world is changing, however, and we'd better be prepared to change with it or even lead the change.

Imagine that you had spent most of your life traveling by horse and buggy and occasionally used a canal boat. An innovation might be a better buggy whip or a wider canal with more efficient locks. But, what to our wondering eyes should appear? The railroad. Your first reaction might be, "The railroads will never amount to anything."

"By 2015, more than half (some argue 80 percent) of us will be working at jobs that don't exist yet," says internationally respected forecaster Faith Popcorn, founder of Faith Popcorn's BrainReserve, a future-oriented marketing consultancy. Some predictions, she admits, "might seem overly dramatic" but they "project the current rate of change." Popcorn ventures, "Jobs that are commonplace today will become museum pieces, along with buggy whip manufacturers, typewriter repair people, and those who own money-changing kiosks seen all over Europe that will be rendered obsolete by the Euro, sooner rather than later."

All of this is important to us, as individuals, businesses, professions, educational institutions, and as countries concerned about our economic futures. Fast-changing careers hit close to home, because we tend to identify ourselves, at least in part, by what we do for a living. Popcorn puts it this way: "Job descriptions are the subtitles of the culture."[329]

> *"You and me, we sweat and strain, bodies all achin' and racked with pain ... but old man river, he just keeps rollin' along."*
>
> **"Old Man River," from the Broadway musical, *Showboat* (written by Oscar Hammerstein II and Jerome Kern).**

■ Today's Career Clusters

Turning out students who are employable—that's one of several expectations we have for our education system, along with creating good citizens who are relatively well adjusted, curious, persistent, and ethical.

While career, vocational, and technical education, at all levels, have always been important, they have very likely never been facing such exponential change. We are moving, head first, into a global knowledge/information age. To add perspective, Marvin Cetron, president of Forecasting International, reveals, "Half of what engineering students learn as freshmen in college is outdated by the time they're seniors."

Take a look at this fairly typical list of *today's career clusters*, developed by the Pennsylvania Department of Education:[330]

- Agriculture, food, and natural resources

- Architecture and construction

- Arts, audiovisual technology, and communication

- Business management and administration

- Education and training

- Finance

- Government and public administration

- Health science

- Hospitality and tourism

- Human services

- Information technology

- Legal, public safety, and security

- Manufacturing

- Marketing, sales, and service

- Science, technology, engineering, and mathematics

- Transportation, distribution, and logistics

■ New Industries Developing across Disciplines

Get educators into a room for 20 minutes, and the conversation will likely include how to effectively help students learn across disciplines. It is a multidisciplinary world after all.

The issue is bigger than just what happens in the classroom. Whole new industries and occupations are emerging from our cross-disciplinary, convoluted, and chaotic world. Whatever we do might have a significant impact on something else. That means we could find ourselves doing things today that just yesterday "were not part of the job description." Industries and careers are changing and combining.

Let's look at some cases in point:

- **Bioinformatics.** This combination of high-powered computing and biology is revolutionizing medicine. Driven in part by the Human Genome Project, it will likely lead to pharmaceuticals tailored to our individual genetic make-ups. We are seeing industries form to map the genome and coax cells into replacing those destroyed by accident, disease, or some predestined trigger pulled by our genes.

  Take a look at the spin-offs: biologists who need deep grounding in computers and mathematics, careers in genomics, venture capitalists willing to invest in this emerging field, drug discovery companies, biotech divisions within computer firms, ethicists, and intellectual property and patent attorneys, to name a few.[331]

- **The Internet and World Wide Web.** Their parents were telecommunications and computers. Their offspring have literally changed the world and dramatically accelerated the pace of change. We have email, Web sites filled with information (some reliable and some not), demands for media literacy courses, choruses of concerns about pop-up ads and spam, and a cavalcade of emerging occupations. For instance, consider these: computer scientist, database administrator, network and computer systems administrator, software engineer, computer systems analyst, computer engineer, computer science teacher, Web security specialist, wireless developer, Wi-Fi specialist, Web cataloger, computer linguist, smart-home technician, tech support, and again, ethicist and intellectual property attorney.[332]

- **Telematics.** This revolutionary marriage of telecommunications, computer science, and car design is about to change the menu of things we look for or even demand when we buy a new set of wheels.

For starters, there are global positioning systems (GPS). Then, there are miniature electronic metering systems/micro electro mechanical systems (MEMS) that can constantly monitor engine performance and air pressure in your tires, instantly keeping you and your mechanic (telematics technician) apprised of how things are running and what corrective actions might be needed. To top off everything, you have the MP3 player, satellite radio, and other communication and entertainment technologies.

John Meagher of the International Center for Environmental Technology (INTERCET Ltd.) is building scenarios for smart cars and smart highways. Think about it: Robotic cars could possibly reduce the number of accidents and injuries, help save energy, improve the environment, reduce the need for at least some road construction, ensure insurability for older and younger drivers, and allow us to do other things while technology takes us to our programmed destination.[333]

Career spin-offs? Your mechanic may already be your auto technologist. Consider also that *robotic technology*, similar to the guidance system you'll have in your car, may lead to a new cluster of careers in deep mining and security, as well as excavation and construction on the moon and other planets. On the medical side, your friendly household robot may be able to take your temperature and blood pressure when you're not feeling well and send that information instantly to your physician. Another micro-robot or nanobot might zip through your blood vessels, sending back digital pictures of any blockages or other problems.

Forecaster Marvin Cetron believes the world needs "a new kind of vocational education, suited for tomorrow's medical technicians, computer programmers and repair people, and other technology specialists." He expresses concern that this form of "high-tech vocational education is another crucial educational resource that is blocked or endangered by today's draconian budget cuts."

■ The New Realities

Career education is poised to take an even more central role in preparing students for the future. Career awareness, attitude development, career exploration, career preparation, and internships, among other things, will continue to be important.

Reality 1—Career educators help form connections. Career education is not about just getting a good job and making a lot of money. In fact, we will depend on career educators to help us see the connection between what we're learning in our regular classes and how it might be useful to us in any number of fields or lines of work.

Reality 2—We are our office. Today, people can carry their office with them in a small bag or even in their pocket or purse. Some of us can be at work whether we're sitting on a park bench or ensconced at a traditional desk.

More of today's students will, after a few years as a regular with a large or small organization, become consultants and freelancers. They will likely take on projects in collaboration with talented

Energy to Propel Us . . . The New Employment Frontier

As petroleum supplies dwindle and prices escalate, demand will grow for new sources of energy. That situation opens a multitude of possibilities for scientists and engineers as well as creative designers of vehicles ranging from aircraft and spacecraft to automobiles and "smart" highways. Developing, building, and maintaining new forms of transportation, less reliant on foreign or domestic petroleum supplies, is likely to drive a series of occupations in the immediate future.

There will be service providers, including technologists who will maintain these new vehicles and run filling or charging stations for topping off hydrogen or batteries. The energy frontier, of course, is even broader, since it spreads to involve heating and cooling, lighting, and powering the information highway.[334]

colleagues who they only see in a small box in the corner of their computer screens. Many will not necessarily go to an office but instead will orbit many companies or other institutions, selling their expertise and wisdom. Their stock in trade will be social and intellectual capital. (See trend devoted to social and intellectual capital.)

Reality 3—New generations reshape the workplace. During the first two decades of the 21st century, the work force will increasingly be composed of Generation Xers and the Millennial Generation. They will be seeking "life-friendly organizations," according to Barbara Moses in her book, *The Good News about Careers . . . How You'll be Working in the Next Decade.*

Moses adds, "Organizations continue to slash overhead costs and associated payroll and obsessively monitor the bottom line; parents continue to be spooked about the prospect of their kids not making it in the new workplace; organizations continue to be puzzled about how best to manage under the new deal at work; boomer bosses are perplexed by their 20-something staff, who seem to have a different attitude toward work; and everyone is grappling with the competing demands of managing very complicated work and personal lives."[335]

Not only will students need to be prepared for employment, but the people in charge are also likely to need guidance in how to shape the workplace of the future to meet the expectations of a new work force.

Reality 4—Knowledge workers will be in high demand to power an economy increasingly based on social and intellectual capital. Intellectual and social capital will become economic drivers, intensifying competition for well-educated people. That trend, discussed in greater depth in an earlier chapter, will lead communities toward knowledge industries. It will also stir creative juices as entrepreneurs conceive of entirely new industries and careers that will meet the needs of a changing marketplace. As we noted earlier, knowledge workers made up about 30 percent of the U.S. work force at the turn of the 21st century but commanded 50 percent of all wages and salaries.

Hot knowledge-based professions include: educators; computer scientists; cardiology technicians; public relations, marketing, and communication professionals; civil engineers; biological scientists and technicians; security and commodity brokers; architects; surveyors; cartographers; civil engineers; interior and exterior designers; and many others.

Reality 5—The aging of the population will create a new generation of students, workers, and jobs. As Baby Boomers retire in droves, many will want to pursue their intellectual curiosities or further develop their skills. Some will want to get ready for "a retirement job."

Retirees are already becoming an expanding source of students for schools and colleges and a goldmine of expertise. Most will have a lifetime of experience to share with younger colleagues who are getting ready to seriously enter the work force for the first time. It won't stop there. With the aging of the population, demand will surely grow for residential care, social services, physical therapy, and a host of other specialties to affordably meet their needs.

People who've "taken time out to raise the kids" may want to wedge back into a personally and economically fulfilling position. Then there are those who have been in the work force for years, who either want to upgrade their knowledge and skills or move through another of the three or four career changes each of us realistically might expect during our lifetimes. The training may be more than technical. We may also want to polish up our skills in understanding and appreciating generational differences and in working side-by-side with people who have substantial life experience, perhaps even exceeding our own, or, in some cases, less.

The clientele for career education will grow, and it will have profound implications for schools, colleges and universities, corporate training institutions, and society as a whole.

■ The Nanotech Future

"Nano. It's Greek to me!" You're right. Nano is a Greek prefix that means "billionth of a specific unit." That, of course, means something very small.

Today, we are able to move atoms around within a molecule. That means we'll be able to develop superconductors that will have a quantum impact on computer speed and capacity. On the way are stronger, lighter weight materials, based on nanotube based components, that will allow airplanes and spacecraft to fly higher, farther, and faster while using less fuel.

Look for nanotech research and development to produce improved bioterrorism detection, slow-release drug therapies, improved MRI and other medical imaging, solar and fuel cells, computers using light instead of electricity, implants to enhance treatment for paralysis and blindness, and thermal or chemical energy conversion. While the United States has been a leader in developing these technologies, Europe and Asia "show evidence of gaining," according to a 2005 article in *The Washington Post*.[336]

Because of its implications for biotechnology, electronics, data storage, semiconductors, optical components, materials science, chemicals, films, plastics, aerospace, energy, the military, and other fields, nanotechnology "means jobs," according to Karen Breslau with Joanna Chung in a *Newsweek* article, "Big Future in Tiny Spaces." Nano is "rapidly moving from the laboratory to the marketplace," the authors point out. In fact, they note the National Science Foundation's estimate that the United States alone will need 800,000 to one million nanotech workers to take this emerging technology from the laboratory into the marketplace. The economic opportunities and social benefits could be huge.

Breslau and Chung add, "To attract a new generation of scientists, the NSF requires each of its nanotechnology centers to develop K-12 outreach programs."[337] (See a fuller description of nanotechnology in the chapter devoted to technology.)

■ Titles, Titles, Titles

Consider the emerging occupations and titles asssociated with nanotechnology. Where do they fit into the career clusters we shared earlier? Are we ready for any new clusters?

Fastest and Slowest Growing Occupations[338]

The U.S. Department of Labor has identified what it believes will be some of the fastest and slowest growing occupations between 2002 and 2012. Figure T15.1 is a sampling from those lists, showing the percentage increase or decrease.

Figure T15.1
Fastest and Slowest Growing Occupations, 2002-2012
U.S. Bureau of Labor Statistics

Fastest Growing Occupations (A Sampling)	Percentage Increase 2002-2012
Medical Assistants	59
Network Systems and Communication Analysts	57
Physician's Assistants	49
Social and Human Service Assistants	49
Home Health Aides	48
Medical Records and Health Information Technicians	47
Physical Therapist Aides	46
Computer Software Engineers, Applications	46
Computer Software Engineers, Systems Software	45
Fitness Trainers and Aerobics Instructors	44
Database Administrators	44
Veterinary Technologists and Technicians	44
Hazardous Materials Removal Workers	43
Dental Hygienists	43
Preschool Teachers, Except Special Education	36
Slowest Growing Occupations (A Sampling)	**Percentage Decrease 2002-2012**
Farmers and Ranchers	-21
Sewing Machine Operators	-31
Word Processors and Typists	-39
Electrical and Electronic Equipment Assemblers	-18
Computer Operators	-17
Telephone Operators	-56
Textile Knitting and Weaving Machine Setters, Operators, and Tenders	-39
Door-to-Door Sales Workers, News and Street Vendors, and Related Workers	-12
Fishers and Related Fishing Workers	-27
Meter Readers, Utilities	-14

The Need for Teachers

As Boomers retire and enrollments rise, the U.S. Department of Education estimates the nation will need more than two million new teachers during the first decade of the 2000s. Among these millions will be a new generation of technology teachers. (See fuller explanation of the demand for teachers in the next chapter.)

New Wrinkles

Some new occupations are also coming on line. Consider these:

- **Cybrarians.** These librarians of the Internet will try to get this fountain of information even better organized as it expands at more than a million pages a day.

- **Web Gardeners.** These busy people, much like cybrarians, will "keep web sites planted, weeded, inviting, and perfectly maintained," according to Faith Popcorn. The Web gardeners and cybrarians might even attend the same cyber-convention.[339]

- **Robotic Engineers.** If you choose this occupation, expect to design, build, and maintain robots that transport people, go deep into mines, explore planets and satellites, probe the wreckage of destroyed buildings, defuse explosive devices, and even care for aging people or individuals with disabilities.[340]

- **Astrogeologists, Astrophysiologists, Astrobiologists.** People who hold these positions will study geology, people, and other organisms in space. On a longer journey, perhaps a trip of several years, expect a demand for astropsychologists.

- **Terrorism Analysts.** Many types of struggles, as we know, can trigger acts of terrorism. These analysts might be capable of studying everything from the sociological triggers for terrorism to the origins of materials used in the act.[341]

- **Automotive Fuel Cell Battery Technicians and Hybrid Technicians.** Someone will need to maintain these new cars, which are powered by a combination of gasoline or some other type of fuel and batteries. As hydrogen becomes more practical as a fuel of choice, we can expect more hydrogen fueling and electrical charging stations.[342]

- **Programming Artists.** These are people who develop virtual media and Hollywood animation, among other things. According to *Newsweek*, "the U.S. Labor Department projects employment for commercial artists to rise 25 percent by 2008, spurred by an increased demand for digital talent."[343]

- **A few more for consideration:** Fusion engineer, cryonics technician, tissue engineer, supply-chain manager, and leisure consultant.

■ Implications for Education and Society

Careers

- **Schools and colleges will become centers for continuing education, training, and retraining.** "Schools will be natural centers for training for all ages, year-round, and for extended hours," predicts George Hollich, retired director of curriculum and summer programs for the Milton Hershey School in Pennsylvania. He speculates this trend may reveal an increased need for "day care, elder care, and neighborhood training programs." Many of these service providers "could be brought under one roof."

Michael Silver of Seattle University agrees. "Students will need to develop a disposition for continuous lifelong learning and take responsibility for their own career management," he says. To keep pace with changing employment needs, "students will need to reinvent themselves and redirect their skills," and they will need "to have the willingness and ability to respond quickly and flexibly to changing work force needs."

- **Fresh approaches will be needed to teach career and entrepreneurial skills.** "Entrepreneurism can be taught as a simulation, using models that help students develop strategies to gauge economic demand, and then create and deliver products and services to meet changing circumstances," points out Carol Peck, president and CEO of the Rodel Charitable Foundation. "Every effort should be made to expose students to the many possibilities for career choices and the necessary flexibility it will take to adapt to changing economies and technologies."

"Attitude is also important," Peck remarks. "Curriculum and content should be designed to allow students opportunities to experience different roles and responsibilities as individuals in groups." Students will also need "practice assessing their own skills and creating positive profiles in the form of resumes and proposals for productive engagement in the economy," Peck suggests.

- **Education systems will need to understand changes in industries and careers, and be able and willing to adapt.** Emphasizing the importance of understanding history, Gary Rowe, president of Rowe, Inc., in Atlanta, Ga., points out "entire railroads disappeared, heavy industries turned to rust, and new technologies transformed workplaces." For high school students, "the expectation of change must be a part of their view of the world," he emphasizes.

Rowe points out how a teacher in Fulton County, Ga., "is leading her students to create visual representations of the school's diversity as a way of making this a virtue to celebrate and an asset for wider learning." In the process, students not only are learning how to use new technologies but also learning the richness that comes with diversity in the workplace.

"Seat time in the classroom is no guarantor of the skills needed for modern vocations and careers," Rowe adds. "The best way for students to absorb how to be entrepreneurial, how to manage, and how to be flexible comes with 'up out-of-the-seat' experiential learning." Those careers that capture the interest of students might turn out to be in either the for-profit or nonprofit sectors.

- **Communities will need to fully understand that their economic future may depend on their ability to understand rapid changes in technology and to maintain a work force that will help them adapt in the future.** A community, or an industry for that matter, can no longer be content with simply doing one thing well and doing it forever. Those who thrive and survive will be the communities that encourage research and development, who support their educational institutions, and who pay particular attention to their mix of profession als'/workers' skills and attitudes. Whether they are competitive will also depend on the quality of life, the ethos or personality of their communities, and the ability to attract and keep knowledge workers.

Communities should engage in serious discussions focused on how they can develop knowledge industries and attract the well-educated knowledge workers who will cause them to thrive. While rethinking and even redefining will be essential for the economic advancement of cities, it will also be a source of hope to smaller communities that might be losing population. Too often, in towns and villages, children go off to school and then go to live somewhere else where they find greater opportunity. Quality of life in some smaller communities may be a significant attraction for people who want to practice as connected professionals while avoiding the hassle of metro life.

■ Questions and Activities

1. What qualities and skills do people need to be employable, whatever jobs they hold?

2. What can educators do to prepare students for careers that do not currently exist?

3. How would you suggest your education system become even better connected to the economic infrastructure of your community, so that it can suggest possible new industries and become more aware of work force needs?

4. What are the five new realities for career educators highlighted in this chapter? What should be added to the list?

5. Prepare a paper or a PowerPoint presentation devoted to "The Nanotech and Energy Revolutions . . . How Our Education System Can Get Students Ready for the Opportunities."

6. Identify two additional multidisciplinary industries or careers not mentioned in this book. The possible industries or careers you identify do not have to currently exist. Examples would be biotechnology and astrogeologist. Feel free to use your imagination.

■ Readings

1. Popcorn, F. (2001). *Dictionary of the future*. New York: Hyperion.

2. U.S. Department of Labor, Bureau of Labor Statistics. (n.d.) "Fastest Growing Occupations, 2002-2012" and "Occupations with the Largest Job Declines." Washington, DC: Author. Available from http://www.bls.gov

3. Breslau, K., & Chung, J. (2002). Big future in tiny spaces. *Newsweek* magazine, September 23, 2002, 56.

4. Regular issues of *The Futurist* magazine, World Future Society, Bethesda, MD. Available from http://www.wfs.org

5. Annual issues of world almanacs.

Trend 16

Educators . . . apply here!

Competition will increase to attract and keep qualified educators.

Demand ↔ Higher Demand

"Next in importance to freedom and justice is popular education, without which neither freedom nor justice can be permanently maintained."

James A. Garfield, on accepting his party's nomination for the presidency, July 1880[344]

■ Help Wanted:

Two Million Teachers

Recruiting New Teachers, an organization committed to attracting even more talented people for the nation's classrooms, estimated a need for 2.2 to 2.4 million teachers during the first decade of the new millennium.[345]

That fresh crop of teachers will have to replace a generation of veterans who will be retiring during the first few decades of the

2000s. The *Detroit News* added that "the demand will increase dramatically because of a law (No Child Left Behind) that requires a highly qualified teacher in every classroom."[346] For the education system, competition is getting intense.

As the nation and world move from an industrial age into a global knowledge/information age, demand is shifting from manufacturing to knowledge workers. That's what educators are, and that's why schools are facing more competition than ever for talented people. That competition is coming not just from the school district or college next door but from other public- and private-sector institutions.

■ Handwriting on the Wall

Demand, Shortages, Enrollments, and Requirements

Because the ability of schools and colleges to attract outstanding educators is crucial to our individual and collective futures, let's explore some of the factors driving this escalating need. While the following items cover only a few of the issues, they should be sufficient to spur heated discussion and further research.

Demand for Teachers. It bears repeating. The United States is faced with attracting around two million-plus teachers during the first decade of the 21st century. Not surprisingly, the U.S. Bureau of Labor Statistics (BLS) has said the demand for teachers will be "very high." Because of escalating enrollments and lower class sizes, BLS estimates that, by 2012, the actual numbers of elementary school teachers who will be needed will go up 15.2 percent, secondary school teachers up 18.2 percent, secondary vocational educators up 9.0 percent, preschool teachers up 36 percent, and postsecondary teachers up 38.1 percent.[347]

Looking globally, *cnn.com* reported in 2002 that "some 35 million more (teachers) are needed throughout the world" to be on track for meeting an 'Education for All' goal set for 2015 by 83 countries.[348] Education is increasingly seen as the key factor in securing a brighter future. That's why leaders in growing numbers of countries are busy trying to interest even more people in education careers.

Demand for Administrators. Between 2002 and 2012, BLS predicts a 20.7 percent increase in the total number of administrators needed in elementary and secondary schools.[349] In a 2000 report, *Career Crisis in the Superintendency*, Bruce Cooper of Fordham University in New York City reported that 80 percent of respondents to a survey he had conducted were at retirement or retirement-eligible age. The average age of superintendents at that time was 57, he reported.[350]

A 1998 study conducted by Educational Research Service for the National Association of Elementary School Principals (NAESP) and National Association of Secondary School Principals (NASSP) concluded that about 55 percent of rural, 45 percent of suburban, and 47 percent of urban school districts were experiencing shortages of qualified candidates for principalships.[351]

The American Association for Employment in Education (AAEE) also points to a need for superintendents and principals, citing shortages at all levels—elementary, middle school, and high school. "As more of the individuals filling these positions reach retirement age, the shortage can be anticipated to increase," AAEE reported in 2000.[352]

Demand and Earnings Compared with All Other Occupations. Expected increases in the number of teachers (overall approximately 25 percent) and administrators (20.7 percent) compares with a projected total rise for all occupations of 14.8 percent during the period of 2002-2012.[353]

While salaries within education vary substantially from one state or community to another, they generally are not competitive with other professions that require fairly rigorous academic preparation.

The gap was dramatic among people ages 44 to 50 who held master's degrees. During 1998, teachers in that category earned approximately 44 percent less than non-teachers with master's degrees. At that time, the difference was $32,511 a year.[354]

Specific Shortages. Among the teaching fields particularly affected by competition, increased enrollments, and retirements are math, science (particularly chemistry and physics), technology, and foreign languages. Shortages have also hit areas such as early childhood, bilingual, and special education.

In its 2000 research report, reflecting responses from numerous teacher preparation institutions in the United States, AAEE noted additional shortfalls in specific areas that include: English as a second language, vocal and instrumental music, audiology, speech pathology, school psychology, and counseling.[355]

Recruiting New Teachers (RNT) also points out a need to attract additional "teachers of color" as schools and communities become more multiethnic. RNT emphasizes a growing need for male teachers, noting "just over 80 percent of the largest urban school districts reported an immediate demand for male teachers at the elementary level."

Some districts have extended their searches for qualified candidates overseas. *Education Week* reported in 1998 that New York City, for example, "hired 25 Austrians via teleconference over the summer to teach math and science." The district also "imported seven teachers from Spain to teach middle school Spanish."[356]

Enrollments. According to the National Center for Educational Statistics (NCES), kindergarten through 12th-grade enrollments were expected to grow from 53.16 million in 2000 to 53.69 million in 2012.[357]

Pupil/Teacher Ratios. RNT focuses on the relationship between lower pupil/teacher ratios and the increasing demand for teachers.

Quoting NCES "Common Core of Data" surveys, RNT points out the average pupil/teacher ratio in public and private elementary and secondary schools during 1988 was 17 students per teacher. That ratio dropped to 15.9 per teacher in 2001 and was projected to reach 15.8 in 2013.[358]

Stopgap Measures. Concern has grown about the hiring of noncertified teachers to fill certain openings where fully qualified people can't be found. Other approaches have included alternative certification, the employment of long-term substitutes, and the assignment of teachers to subjects outside their field of preparation and expertise. Districts have also used certification waivers and internship programs to fill the gaps.[359]

Requirements and Expectations. As stated earlier, the 2002 No Child Left Behind Act mandated "highly qualified teachers" for the nation's schools. While few, if any, would question the desirability of this noble goal, it came at a time when increasing numbers of teachers were about to leave the profession. Many would be retiring. Some would be moving into other occupations.

On top of all that, the economy had softened. State and local school budgets were tight. In many parts of the nation, education salaries were not competitive with other fields.

That meant the education system faced a dichotomy. At the same time opportunities were multiplying, competition was intensifying for the people education systems wanted to hire.

■ The Race Is On

Recruitment and Retention . . . Running Neck and Neck

The starting gun has been fired. Education systems are in a race to attract and keep highly qualified teachers.

Education . . . An Investment that Pays Off

In 2002, median earnings for employees in all fields with master's degrees came to approximately $56,600 (unemployment rate 2.8 percent), for bachelor's degrees $47,000, for associate's degrees $36,400, for those with some college/no degree $34,300, for high school graduates $29,200, and for some high school but no diploma, $22,400 (unemployment rate 9.2 percent), according to the U.S. Bureau of Labor Statistics.[360]

While the actual numbers will vary over time, they make clear that education is an investment, and it pays off. The more education, the greater the likelihood that people will be employed and they'll make more money. When they spend it, they'll help strengthen the economy. When they pay their taxes, they'll be contributing to what we hope will be an even better quality of life.

■ Recruitment

How are we going to get them?

Education systems have generally intensified their efforts to attract teachers. Incentives vary. For example, some have offered signing bonuses, moving expenses, salary advances, and, to the extent possible, improvements in benefits. Job fairs and classified ads, while essential, may not cut it. The same kind of aggressive recruiting may be needed that is used to land top executives.

Las Vegas, where enrollment more than doubled in a decade to 230,000 students, was facing growth of about a thousand students a month at the turn of the century. The district was doing some of its recruitment using videophones and cell phones. A sign at the Las

Vegas Airport during 2000 read, "Elvis has left the building. We now have a vacancy at our school. Las Vegas is looking for teachers."[361]

In addition to Recruiting New Teachers, another organization, Teach for America, headquartered in New York City, recruits graduates of colleges for at least a two-year commitment to teaching in low-income rural and urban communities.[362]

"The nation must make a concerted effort to attract more and more highly qualified teachers to urban classrooms if we are to provide opportunity for the one-fourth of our students who attend urban schools," says Michael Casserly, executive director of the Council of the Great City Schools.[363]

On the other end of the spectrum, rural schools are confronting the vacuum. Some are now touting spirit-lifting benefits of living in a smaller community. Several school systems thrive by attracting husband-and-wife teams.

■ Retention

How are we going to keep them?

Say a school has been lucky enough to land some great teachers. How will it convince them to stay?

"The number of teachers entering the schools increased steadily during the 1990s. The problem is that teacher attrition was increasing even faster," according to the National Commission on Teaching and America's Future in its 2003 report, *No Dream Denied . . . A Pledge to America's Children.* "It's as if we were pouring teachers into a bucket with a fist-sized hole in the bottom," the report points out.

Approximately a third of the nation's new teachers "leave teaching sometime during their first three years; almost half may leave during the first five years." Turnover rates are high, but "attrition rates are even more troubling," the report observes, noting that during the 1999-2000 school year, 534,861 teachers started in the profession, while in 2000-01, 539,778 left. The total teaching force that year was approximately 3,451,316.

In an issue brief, "Attracting and Keeping Quality Teachers," the National Education Association (NEA) reports, "Too little attention has been paid to holding onto the quality teachers already hired—both the beginning teachers as well as the more seasoned ones."[364]

Recruitment and retention have become public issues. Here are just a few examples of issues and concerns raised in interviews and articles that have focused on the challenge of keeping motivated people in classrooms.

- New teachers need mentors to help them over the unexpected hurdles they'll inevitably encounter during their first few years on the job.[365] Some may feel overwhelmed by the expectations and scope of the job, feel unsupported in their classrooms, or sense that expectations for them are unclear.[366]

- Many teachers are highly sensitive to issues involving school climate and the quality of school leadership, preferring "strong leadership and collegial, professional faculty relations," according to Victoria Van Cleef, vice president of The New Teacher Project.[367]

- Even though controversial, salary programs might allow for incentives based on achievement and types of services.[368]

- Given other factors, the culture of the school and system—the sense of belonging and being a part of something great—will serve as a magnet for people who could likely make a lot more money doing something else.

Another dramatic realization for education systems is that teachers and administrators are no longer as place-bound as they once might have been. Talented people are less reluctant than at some times in the past to accept that offer, even if it takes them hundreds of miles from their hometown.

■ Implications for Education and Society

Attracting and Keeping Educators

- **Providing the community with its number-one attraction.** What is the first question many people ask when considering where to live? "How are the schools?" Communities that invest in education and are determined to attract and keep the very best educators are making an investment not only in their children's future, but also in their future property values. They understand the interlocking connection between education and a community's economy, quality of life, and reputation.

- **Ensuring a qualified work force.** Education is the key to developing a work force that will attract business and industry and stimulate economic growth. Some communities have not only discovered that truth, but they are committed to building an infrastructure capable of producing creative, well-educated people. At the same time, they are recruiting knowledge workers who will then, in turn, insist on and support 21st-century education for their children.

- **Setting up programs for recruiting and retaining outstanding educators.** For communities large and small, whether they are rural, suburban, or urban, recruitment and retention have become bottom-line issues in the quest to ensure "highly qualified" educators to prepare students for the future.

Just putting an ad in the paper and waiting for people to break down the door may not work anymore. Competition is stiff, and that competition is coming from both inside and outside education. Other industries have discovered that people who are outstanding teachers and administrators also perform well outside schools and colleges, particularly in positions using similar skill sets, such as corporate trainers, staff development coaches, or executives.

Some experienced educators who qualify for retirement might be willing to stay on if schedules could be a bit more flexible. Schools lose many retirement-eligible people who would like to continue their service, but not full time. Also, keep this in

What Some Urban School Districts Are Doing

Some of the largest school systems in the nation are employing a variety of special recruitment and retention techniques. Examples include:

- Nearly two-thirds of urban school districts that were surveyed now offer induction and support programs (67.5 percent) to keep talented new teachers in the classroom.

- Nearly as many offer alternative routes to teacher certification (65 percent) to bring professionals with backgrounds in shortage subject areas into the classroom.

- Almost as many districts offer on-the-spot contracts to hire teachers without the waiting or red tape that in the past often resulted in teachers not taking jobs in urban schools.

- Virtually all urban districts (95 percent) are recruiting at historically Black/Hispanic colleges to address minority teacher shortages.

- Districts also are offering financial incentives for teaching in high-need subject areas.[369]

mind: While the country strains to attract nearly 2-1/2 million teachers, another knowledge occupation—nursing—will be trying to lure more than a million new registered nurses (RNs) to replace those who retire and to fill fresh slots expected to develop by 2012.[370]

- **Exercising caution in stretching the supply to meet the demand.** Gene Carter, executive director of the Association for Supervision and Curriculum Development (ASCD), has expressed concern about setting people up as teachers when they don't understand pedagogy. In a column titled, "Content Knowledge Without Pedagogy Shortchanges Students," he quotes a Hart/Teeter opinion poll commissioned by the Educational Testing Service. A majority of those responding said that "having skills to design learning experiences that inspire and interest children" is the most important attribute of a quality teacher.[371]

  Carter's concern is reinforced by R. M. Ingersoll of the University of Pennsylvania, who has studied teacher shortages and notes that principals, when faced with insufficient numbers of qualified job candidates, "most commonly do three things: hire less-qualified teachers, assign teachers trained in another field or grade level to teach in the understaffed area, and make extensive use of substitute teachers."[372] Alternative or temporary certification is sometimes used to open classroom doors for many people who promise they will then take needed education courses.

- **Assigning excellent teachers to schools where needs are greatest.** Complaints have been raised that go something like this, "You're assigning first-year teachers and teachers who are having problems somewhere else to schools where kids have the greatest needs and the parents are least demanding." In 2004, in fact, the U.S. Department of Education issued a complaint against a large urban school system stating that, "Qualified and skilled teachers—the most crucial 'input' in the district's instructional program—are inequitably distributed within the system, with more-qualified, more-experienced teachers going to the city's lower-minority, lower-poverty schools." In response, the district noted that it was strengthening its recruitment and professional development efforts and negotiating a new contract that could bring changes in the way teaching talent is distributed among schools.[373]

- **Improving preparation and professional development programs.** First, teachers and administrators need to be well prepared to ensure a sound education for their students. Second, unless they are well prepared for the realities they will face in teaching children or providing executive leadership for the institution, they may simply give up and do something else.

  Preparation programs at colleges and universities need constant upgrades to ensure they are equipping educators to prepare students for the future. Professional development programs should perhaps range from individual mentorships as a new teacher first sets foot in the classroom to ongoing knowledge, skill, and behavior-building activities.

  Becoming and then staying well prepared is especially important for members of Generation X, who may be highly motivated to teach but will also want to learn as much as possible on the job. Similar challenges are true for members of the Millennial Generation, who want to be prepared to make the world an even better place.

- **Making teaching an international profession.** Many U.S. teachers currently work in international or military dependents schools around the world. According to the NEA, "As many as 10,000 foreign teachers work in the U.S. public school systems on 'nonimmigrant' or cultural exchange visits." In some cases, these temporary employees are "helping to address perceived teacher shortages, particularly in math, science, foreign languages, and special education, as well as in . . . poor urban and rural school districts."

Increasingly, teaching will become an international profession, especially for those with a combination of subject matter expertise, a missionary spirit, an innate curiosity, and language skills.

- **Collaborating with the competition.** In the competition for talent, schools and colleges may not always win. The same businesses and other institutions that depend on the education system to turn out good citizens who are employable are generally quite comfortable hiring outstanding candidates who originally prepared to be teachers. In some cases, education systems may need to collaborate with the competition so that each can benefit from the talent that might otherwise be diverted from the classroom.

■ Questions and Activities

1. Develop a one-page outline for a recruitment plan to attract qualified candidates for positions as teachers and administrators in your education system.

2. List 10 things you believe should be done during the next year to retain qualified professionals in your education system.

3. What are the primary reasons many school systems are experiencing shortages of highly qualified candidates for educator positions?

■ Readings

1. Publications produced by the National Teacher Recruitment Clearinghouse, Recruiting New Teachers, Washington, DC. Available from http://www.rnt.org

2. American Association for Employment in Education. (2000). *Educator supply and demand in the United States, 2000 research report.* Columbus, OH: Author. Available from http://www.aaee.org

3. National Center for Education Statistics, U.S. Department of Education. (n.d.). *Projections of education statistics*. Washington, DC: Author. Available from http://www.nces.gov

4. Web sites of the National Education Association (http://www.nea.org) and American Federation of Teachers (http://www.aft.org)

5. Voke, H. (2002). Understanding and responding to the teacher shortage. *Infobrief: Attracting and retaining quality teachers* (May 2002), Issue 29. Alexandria, VA: Association for Supervision and Curriculum Development. Available from http://www.ascd.org

6. Glass, T.E., Byork, L., & Brunner, C.C. (2000). *The study of the American superintendency, 2000*. Arlington, VA: American Association of School Administrators. Available from http://www.aasa.org

7. The Education Trust. (n.d.). The real value of teachers. *Thinking K-16*. Washington, DC: Author. Available from http://www.edtrust.org

Conclusion

Dealing with the Trends

Shaping a Future for Our Education Systems and the Whole of Society

Too often, we have good intentions, but we're so caught up in meetings, appointments, emails, and the countless stuff that keeps drifting into our lives, that the idea of actually creating the future we need gets lost in the shuffle. But as the world seems to spin faster and faster, problems pile up.

Every day, we give hundreds of answers, but we have little time to think about whether we're asking the right questions. Things that worked two years ago aren't now. We defend the old ways, because we haven't taken the time to consider that accelerating trends are creating new expectations.

How can we get a handle on the future? How can we demonstrate our intellectual leadership and breakthrough thinking? How can we energize our education system and our community? How can we take those exciting steps toward creating a new agenda for a new millennium?

Archimedes said it: "Give me a lever and a fulcrum and a place whereon to stand, and I'll move the world." He was making a point that using the right levers and pulleys can make it possible for us to move objects that are greater than our own weight.[374] If we think creatively, the trends we've discussed in this book could provide us with not only a place to stand but also with a lever and a fulcrum.

■ A New Plan of Attack

Let's explore some of the ways we can turn words and ideas on the pages of this book into positive action that will help us shape the future. We'll address a number of possibilities, such as planning, turning our plan into a living strategy, generative thinking, futures councils, agenda time, professional development, college and university courses, futures studies, and futures processes and tools for scanning the environment and forming a vision, among others.

Whatever we do, we should try to be sure that the action we take is not just a one-shot deal. In a world moving at rocket speed, the quest to redefine an organization and refresh our thinking is an ongoing proposition.

■ Futures Processes

Identifying, monitoring, and considering the implications of trends is one of the most basic processes for creating a future. There are other ways to scan the environment and develop a vision, of course; all fit comfortably under the umbrella of trends. They either help us identify and deal with them or discover what we might have to do to become trendsetters. Here are a few of those futuring processes:

- **Trends Analysis.** This book obviously is devoted to identifying and dealing with trends. Our challenge is to identify trends that do or soon will have an impact on society. In some cases, we first spot trends through our intuition. Things we hear and read about start adding up. Evidence becomes clearer, as similar ideas or concerns show up in our reading, listening, or conversations. We might identify trends through content analysis—by systematically considering the frequency that a topic is mentioned in the media—or through a number of other systematic processes for scanning the environment, such as the ones that follow. Once we think we've spotted a trend, we do further research, then pull thoughtful people together to consider its implications for us.

- **Issue Management.** This process starts by identifying issues facing an organization, industry, profession, government, or nation. Next, individual issues are first sorted based on the *probability* that each will become a major force and second on its potential *impact*—high, medium, or low. We'd better pay attention to issues that rank high in probability and high in impact. Even issues that rank low in probability and high in impact could become significant wildcards. The process can spur a discussion of side-effects, including intended and unintended consequences. Figure C.1 provides a hint of how to sort issues using a probability/impact matrix. Using this matrix, it is also possible to classify each of the issues by type. Some are

Figure C.1
Probability/Impact Matrix

Issue Type				Issues Identification and Sorting	Impact			
Critical	Ongoing	Emerging	Priority	Issue Statement	Probability (%)	High Impact	Medium Impact	Low Impact
X			1	Student writing skills are inadequate for a global knowledge/information age.	90	X		
	X		2	Parents are expecting immediate responses to email and voicemail messages they leave for teachers.	30		X	

critical, some ongoing, and some just emerging. Based on that analysis, we can then decide what priority to assign each of the issues.

- **PEST, STEEPV, STEEPED.** For the PEST process, consider political, economic, social, and technological forces that will likely affect the organization and the whole of society. For STEEPV,[375] add environmental forces and values. For STEEPED, further add educational and demographic forces.

- **Gap Analysis.** Here, we engage a thoughtful and diverse group in developing a number of statements describing the organization we want to become. Then, we might ask an even more inclusive group to use a scale—perhaps 1 to 10—to rate us on how well each statement currently describes us. The process helps us discover the gaps between where we are and where we'd like to be. Then, we can figure out how to fill those gaps.

- **Flexibility/Innovation Analysis.**[376] This involves having a diverse group develop a series of five to 10 statements describing a flexible organization. Then, again on a scale of perhaps 1 to 10, ask knowledgeable groups of people to rank how accurately each statement describes the organization. An example of one of those statements might be, "The organization can readily introduce new programs and services."

- **Demographics.** Constant research is necessary to study the demographic factors that define students and community, ranging from race and ethnicity to age, socioeconomic data, marital status, and even home ownership.

- **Psychographics.** Demographics may not be enough. People within certain demographic groups don't necessarily have the same opinions or sets of values. Psychographics will help us identify people by their interests, their views on certain issues, and what motivates them.

The following processes are among the many that can help us establish a vision for our organization or program.

- **Characteristics.** Ask a diverse and thoughtful council of people to develop a list of characteristics describing the organization they would like to see in five or 10 years.

- **Scenarios.** Based on sets of assumptions, develop a series of three or four scenarios describing alternative futures. Scenarios have been described as "a coherent picture of a plausible future."[377]

Our companion book, *Future-Focused Leadership: Preparing Schools, Students, and Communities for Tomorrow's Realities,* published by the Association for Supervision and Curriculum Development, focuses on these processes and provides greater detail on how they work.[378]

■ Generative Thinking

Things often go haywire when we don't stick to an agenda. They also come apart when the agenda is so cut and dried that it excludes agenda-setting.

To keep the agenda and our organization fresh, we should regularly engage people in generative thinking.[379] Put simply, this means ensuring significant groups of people are identifying, studying, and considering the implications of trends, as well as critical, ongoing, and emerging issues that will likely affect our organization and its mission. These groups can provide ideas that will help us keep our decisions connected to the realities of today and possibilities for the future.

Rather than complaining that "we don't have time to think," let's make *thinking* a part of our everyday business and engage a network of groups in the process.

■ Developing a Plan, Living Strategy, Strategic Vision

Despite some glib comments to the contrary, every education system, any organization for that matter, needs to regularly engage in visionary short-term and long-term planning. Those plans need to be based on informed discussions and decisions.

Plans can no longer be relegated to the top shelf. They need to be squarely in the center of our desks, and they need to be flexible. As we've made clear throughout this book, the pace of change has become intense. Daily, even hourly, we are confronted with problems and opportunities that may have, even yesterday, been beyond our imaginations. We need to be true to our values and our heritage, but also nimble enough to quickly adjust our plan. Freeze the plan, and the world will surge past us, leaving us as an island, disconnected from those we are pledged to serve.

If that sounds disconcerting, it isn't. It's a new way of thinking. The constant process of creating the future we need, rather than simply defending what we currently have, breathes life into an organization.

Let's consider how *Sixteen Trends . . . Their Profound Impact on Our Future* can become an essential part of the planning process. It is designed to provoke discussion, raise important questions, focus on far-reaching trends, provide essential data and ideas, and stimulate thinking about what our education institutions and other organizations should be like and look like in the future. This book is a bit like an "intelligence report" designed to connect us with forces that should affect our decisions and will have an impact on our future. The impact of these trends is already widespread, even global.

Consider the following as you inform your planning process and turn your plan into a living strategy or strategic vision.[380]

■ Forming a Context[381]

- **Appoint a council or councils.** Consider who might serve on a system-wide Futures Council, a diverse group from a span of interests and backgrounds and representative of the community. Staff should also be involved in the process. In fact, you might want to appoint a network of these councils, with rotating memberships, that meet once or twice a year.

- **Inform the discussion.** Ask members of the councils to study trends and issues, using resources such as *Sixteen Trends . . . Their Profound Impact on Our Future*, NASSP's *Breaking Ranks*, AASA's *Preparing Schools and School Systems for the 21st Century*, and a wealth of information available from sources such as Educational Research Service (ERS) and Association for Supervision and Curriculum Development (ASCD). Consider additional readings suggested in this book. Provide copies of *Sixteen Trends* and other materials to the Council, and distribute them to all board members and administrators, as well as staff, community leaders, and members of the media.

- **Clarify the advisory role.** Make clear that the Council is not making decisions but is instead advising on the possible implications of these trends and even on ideas for dealing with them. Let it be known immediately that the Council's thinking will be seriously considered but not always accepted by the system as it plans for the future. Decisions might be a hybrid of several points of view. In many cases, ideas will be offered.

- **Consider multiple types of councils.** Think about holding these types of sessions with teachers, professors, administrators, board members, and various professional associations and groups. For example, math, reading, science, language arts, social studies, early childhood, vocational and career, art, and other teachers and department heads might want to explore implications for their particular disciplines. In some cases, these councils might be formed across disciplines. College presidents, academic directors, planners, elementary and secondary educators, curriculum and instruction directors, human resource professionals, accountability directors and specialists, technology experts, communications professionals, counselors, transportation, facilities, and other groups might want to consider the specific implications of these trends for them and what they do. Broadening the education base, P-16 groups might come together to consider how these trends could or should influence education from pre-school through college. The possibilities don't stop with this list.

- **Broaden the scope.** In considering the scope of the Council's advisory efforts, keep in mind that the effects of these trends are important to every institution in the community. They have direct implications not only for education but also for quality of life and economic growth and development. You'll find businesses, industries, professions, governmental and non-governmental organizations, foundations, even states and nations, will also discover the possible impact of these trends for them. By broadening the context of the discussion, the education system can become the crossroads and central convening point for addressing future needs of the entire community.

■ Holding Council Meetings

- **Leadership, funding, and frequency of meetings.** Meetings of Futures Councils can take many forms. These groups might come together once or twice a year. Their meetings could range in length from two hours to a full day. Consider holding the meeting at a venue that has special significance for the community. Ask a respected and capable member of the community to serve as honorary chair. If you're thinking about keeping in touch with the fast-moving world of the 21st century, you might call these groups Councils of 21.[382] You might even want to consider asking local sponsors to cover the costs of the meetings and follow-up activities, making clear that their sponsorship should not be seen as a way to influence results of the effort.

- **Aim for productive thinking.** Use a highly facilitated process to ensure productive thinking and efficient use of Council members' time. If at all possible, appoint a facilitator who is adept at keeping the meeting moving while bringing out the best, most productive thinking of everyone involved. Ask participants to avoid using "killer" phrases that shut down communication and refrain from insisting that the group limit its discussion to someone's "pet" issue. Facilitated small-group brainstorming sessions followed by sharing with the entire group generally leads to productive thinking, releases ingenuity, and creates a great deal of energy and excitement.

- **Use generative thinking and brainstorming.** As part of the agenda, explain the idea of generative thinking and the process you'll use for brainstorming. Arrange for a presentation on trends and issues, and review background materials you've shared in advance. Ask the group to identify additional trends and issues they believe are emerging. As part of the agenda, include small-group brainstorming sessions (six to eight people to a group) focused on identifying possible implications. Following the small group sessions, have everyone come together to share their ideas.

- **Identify and address operative questions.** If the council is considering education, members of the Council might be asked to respond to driving questions, such as the following: "What are the implications of these trends for our education system?" and " What are the implications of these trends for what students need to know and be able to do to be prepared for the future—their academic knowledge, skills, behaviors, and attitudes." Further questions might include: "What is our education system doing now to deal with each trend?" "What can or should the system be doing to deal with each trend?" (The discrepancy between what the schools are doing now and what they could or should be doing reveals possible gaps and a focus for further planning.) Also consider asking, "What concerns are we seeing in our community that are directly or indirectly related to each of these trends?" "What roles will educators, parents, nonparent taxpayers, public officials, and others need to play to get us from where we are to where we need to be as a community?"

■ Doing the Follow-up

- **Organize results of the meeting(s).** Collate ideas that emerge from the conference, and consider sharing them with a broader cross-section of the community. This sharing can take place through the news media, newsletters, a Web page, speaking engagements, public discussions, and other means.

- **Consider a follow-up questionnaire.** Moving beyond the actual Futures Council(s), compose a brief questionnaire that invites an expanded group of people to consider and comment on the trends and implications that emerge from the meetings. It's an opportunity to increase public engagement and gain further insights about the local impact of these trends from both staff and community. This follow-up questionnaire might be distributed through email or regular mail; serve as a discussion starter at parent, community, or service club meetings; delivered to homes; placed on the agenda for faculty or school family meetings; or be used to stimulate the thinking of key people in many walks of life. In short, trends and their implications can become a program or agenda item wherever people gather. The purpose of the follow-up activity is to elicit the thinking of an expanded group of people in the community, to benefit from the ingenuity that is all around us, and to help us shape the organization for the future. The purpose is *not* to determine the popularity of one issue over another or promote a project or program.

- **Summarize the expanded comments.** Put together a brief summary of comments, including both the ongoing thinking of Futures Councils and responses to questionnaires.

- **Develop suggestions for possible action.** Think about the wisdom of appointing a representative Futures Action Team, made up of staff, to work with a few representatives of the Futures Councils in developing a coherent set of suggestions for addressing the trends. At each step, participants should be reminded to focus their thinking on what the education system will need to do to prepare students for a global knowledge/ information age.

- **Keep the leadership team informed.** Prepare a report for the superintendent, president, or other appropriate organization leader.

- **Update board and community.** The executive leadership team will want to provide regular reports on the activity for board and community. The ongoing flow will be helpful in making even more connected management and policy decisions. However, the purpose is not necessarily to influence immediate decisions but to stimulate even greater interest in the process of thinking about the future.

- **Make adjustments in plans and activities systemwide.** Consider how the ideas might affect the systemwide plan. Use whatever approval process is required to move forward, with adjustments that will help address concerns and make the most of opportunities. In the process, turn the strategic plan into a living strategy.

- **Consider departmental and individual adjustments.** In departments, across departments, and in classrooms, teachers and administrators will be able to consider ingenious ideas that have come from staff and community. Occasionally, they might want to immediately use that expansive thinking to enhance their work.

- **Put the plan in motion.** After adopting or adjusting a plan, develop a theme; set targets; put the plan in motion; and make clear to the community that its support will be crucial. An important part of this effort will be the establishment of a sense of urgency. Expectations should be developed that are mutually shared and somewhat reasonable. If additional resources are needed, the community-wide involvement should increase chances of getting it.

- **Be prepared to address concerns and to energize.** Be ready for the objection that there are no more resources or that resources are scarce. While some of the ideas generated through this process might come with a healthy price tag, many others can simply help us focus or redirect our current energies. Others will provide logic for making further investments that will pay off down the line. If we don't make those investments, we may suffer the cost of neglect. The dividend is a sense of being connected to an organization that is truly making ongoing contributions to people's lives.

- **Set an example.** Remember that this gravity-breaking effort will be seen as an act of leadership and will set an example for others in your community, your state, and possibly even the nation.

■ Making It a Continuous Process

Our responsibility as leaders in society is to *constantly* create the future we need, not just defend what we have. Staying in touch with the environment, getting connected to the world of ideas and possibilities around us, staying on top of issues, and considering the implications of massive trends is an ongoing process.

New trends will emerge. A new mix of generations will populate our planet. Astounding new technologies will burst into our lives and become commonplace. Industries and careers will change. Cultivating human ingenuity will become an increasingly important part of education. New ethical dilemmas will confront us. Peace will need to be won and diseases conquered. All of us, and certainly students in our schools and colleges, must be prepared to coherently deal with problems and opportunities that are beyond our imaginations.

Some will insist on linear goals. They'll want to pretend that the future will just be an extension of the present. In fact, the future will bring us a series of discontinuities. We'll only be able to stay ahead of the curve if we include audacious goals in our vision of the future. Going to the moon and developing a vaccine for polio were audacious goals. This is ours: Creating the education system we need to get students ready for life in a global knowledge/ information age.

While we surely need to tackle today, we simply can't take our eye off the future. We have an opportunity to build an even better world; create what truly are leadership organizations; demonstrate our ability to engage in knowledge creation and breakthrough thinking; and, perhaps selfishly, build our own legacies.

It's time to get the process under way and keep it going. Let's make the most of it.

■ Organizational Renewal, Professional Development, Accreditation, Futures Studies, College and University Courses, and Even More

Let's briefly review a number of other ways we can put the sixteen trends and processes we've discussed in this book to work. Keep in mind that our companion publication, *Future-Focused Leadership: Preparing Schools, Students, and Communities for Tomorrow's Realities*, can also be helpful.

Organizational Renewal. The process we've discussed for developing a plan, living strategy, or strategic vision will work, with some creative modifications, for any type of organization: educational, governmental, non-governmental, business, professional, association, foundation, local, national, international, you name it. The trends are universal in scope, and the processes for dealing with them can apply all the way from single departments of an organization or to entire nations charting their futures.

Professional Development, College and University Courses, Conferences and Seminars. Learning more about identifying and dealing with trends and issues and mastering techniques for thinking about the future can help us stay on the leading edge. This book can serve as a text, subtext, or required reading for a new or existing course. It can stimulate conferences, seminars, and future-oriented themes.

Futures Studies. Books such as *Sixteen Trends . . . Their Profound Impact on Our Future*, *Future-Focused Leadership: Preparing Schools, Students, and Communities for Tomorrow's Realities*, and others noted in the text can help form the basis for futures studies courses at all levels of education. While students are learning about trends and issues, as well as processes for dealing with them, other things are happening. They are enhancing their thinking and reasoning skills, learning across disciplines, engaging in knowledge creation and breakthrough thinking, and finding direct application for what they are learning in other courses. A futures studies course or unit also contributes to active learning. Teachers and professors often use the type of information and activities presented in this book to add energy to nearly any subject.

Accreditation. Environmental scanning—staying close to those we serve—is high on the list for organizational accreditation in education and a number of other fields. In its *NCA Journal of School Improvement*, the North Central Association, a major accrediting organization for schools and colleges, referred to trends covered in the first version of this book as "especially useful to begin[ning] an environmental scan." An NCA editorial note further suggested, "A steering or profile committee might study the issues and trends and report on their potential impact to educators and the community. They could also engage the larger school community in discussion of the trends and seek input on how the school(s) might prepare graduates for a different future."[383]

▪ Questions and Activities

1. Using what you've learned about trends from this publication as well as other readings, discussions, and activities, develop a plan that will further connect you and your organization to the environment.

2. Consider yourself the leader of a school system or college. Use your imagination to develop a basic plan or approach you can legitimately call "a constant process for creating a future."

3. Convene a diverse but knowledgeable group. Together, identify five issues your organization faces. Judge each one based on the probability or likelihood it will become a major issue for you (0 percent low, 100 percent high) and possible impact—high, medium, or low. Consider how you will deal with those issues that are high in probability and high in impact.

4. Engage a diverse and knowledgeable group in studying each of the trends discussed in this book. Then, ask that they work as a group to identify the implications of those trends for the education system or other institution.

5. What steps would you recommend for turning your strategic plan into a living strategy or strategic vision?

6. Follow up with real-life activities suggested in this final chapter of *Sixteen Trends.*

■ Readings

1. Rubenstein, H., & Grundy, T. (1999). *Breakthrough, Inc. . . . High growth strategies for entrepreneurial organizations.* London: Financial Times/Prentice Hall.

2. Marx, G. (2006). *Future-focused leadership: Preparing schools, students, and communities for tomorrow's realities.* Alexandria, VA: Association for Supervision and Curriculum Development.

3. Withrow, F., Long, H., & Marx, G. (1999). *Preparing schools and school systems for the 21st century.* Arlington, VA: American Association of School Administrators.

Appendix

Additional Trends

This book focuses on 16 major trends that are shaping our future. Of course, there are many other trends sweeping across our world, our nations, and our communities. It is our hope that we've stimulated your resolve not only to consider the implications of the trends we've addressed in this publication but also to spot others, and even to become a trendsetter.

Let's take a look at some additional specific trends identified by the advisory council that helped provide insights for both *Sixteen Trends . . . Their Profound Impact on Our Future* and *Future-Focused Leadership: Preparing Schools, Students, and Communities for Tomorrow's Realities.* Then, to further stimulate the thought process, we'll extend our view to some trends revealed by the Education Commission of the States, Denmark's Copenhagen Institute, and both *Red Herring* and *Educational Leadership* magazines.

■ Advisory Council

The Creating a Future Council of Advisors suggested numerous trends. Most had direct implications for the content of this book, and council members are quoted throughout its pages. Many of those comments came in response to a two-round set of emailed questionnaires. To even further reflect the thinking of individual members of that panel, we are including a sampling of some actual trend statements that were submitted and some of the implications that were listed.

Further Advisory Council Trends: A few of the additional specific trends suggested by members of the Council of Advisors included:

- A new time frame for the information age emphasizing getting things done right, even if it takes longer, will rise in importance over getting things done with speed and urgency without regard for due diligence, ethics, and accuracy. **Michael Silver**

- The distractions of highly successful entertainment media threaten to invite youth to live in a penumbra of artifice and surrogacy rather than grapple with personal achievement, rigorous academic work, and meaningful personal relationships. **Gary Rowe**

- Constant changes in the advancement of technology are creating new jobs that many students are not prepared for due to slow changes in the current curriculum of most public high schools. **Betsy Rogers**

- A tendency is growing to ignore, abandon, and blame people in society who are in poverty or who suffer other unfortunate circumstances. **James Rickabaugh**

- There will be tremendous competition for resources among schools, municipalities, and other taxing entities. **Keith Marty**

- The impact and long-term results of universal early childhood education in states that implement it at a quality level will increase the academic and social results for poor and minority students. **Rosa Smith**

- Instability of the family structure directly impacts children and schools. **Betsy Rogers**

- The rapid rate of technological change and the applications of that change for education will be an ongoing challenge. **Douglas Shiok**

- Tomorrow's citizens will be engaged in lifelong learning. **Marvin Cetron**

- Economic incentives will grow to attract top-performing college students into teaching. **Marc Ecker**

Further Advisory Council Implications: After identifying trends, members of the Council each received a cluster of three trends included among the 16 that have been more fully addressed in this book. Members of this distinguished group were asked to comment on what they considered possible implications of those trends. Many of their comments are included in the text. The following are a few of the many additional implications identified by Council members.

- The move to the globalization of the economy would suggest the need for new and innovative partnerships between generations. **Jane Hammond**

- Systems thinking to understand problems and possible solutions should be a core curriculum of teaching K-16. Also included should be a sense of civic duty to help students understand how to bring about change, grades 4-16. **Joseph Coates**

- Critical thinking skills, problem-based approaches, and collaborative learning modalities will be increasingly important. **Frank Method**

- As we move from a majority/minority to a minority/minority society, we will need leaders talented in the language of inclusion, building a larger political tent, and avoiding the politics of opportunism and populism, which seeks to turn various minority groups against each other. **Arnold Fege**

- More kids will need higher levels of education. We need to continue to drive the accepted norms to higher levels, placing a greater percentage of students in what were once considered classes reserved only for top-level students. **Carol Peck**

- Schools will need to revise curriculum tracking and student ability grouping in math and science classes to allow greater numbers of students to proceed to higher levels of learning. **Michael Silver**

- The need for security will require that we have a full appreciation for other cultures and their norms of behavior. The realization that isolationism is no longer possible will lead to a greater desire to share institutions. Could this also include schools shared by all countries on one continent or like-minded countries from all over the world? **Ted Blaesing**

- Communication will be among the most important sets of skills students will need, along with conceptual skills that can be used to solve problems and create solutions. **Jane Hammond**

- Schools will have students demonstrate that they can apply what they have learned, meaning that multiple types of assessments will be used, including rubrics. **George Hollich**

- Students will be given more responsibility to decide the right thing to do. **Rosa Smith**

■ Education Commission of the States Trends, 1999

The following is a list of 21 educational, demographic, technological, economic, political, and social trends identified by the Education Commission of the States and published as we approached the turn of the new millennium under the title, "Future Trends Affecting Education."[384]

- Competition among schools for students, educators, and funds is increasing.

- Calls for education accountability are increasing at all levels.

- More school districts and states are contracting for education services.

- The demand for education professionals is rising.

- Minority students are beginning to form the student majority.

- School segregation is increasing.

- Disproportionate numbers of children and women are filling the ranks of the poor.

- The number of senior citizens is growing.

- Investments in technology infrastructure and equipment for schools are expanding.

- Technology increasingly is being used to change what happens in the classroom or school.

- Wealth is becoming concentrated in a shrinking elite.

- The unemployment rate does not reveal the extent of employment problems.

- The demand for technically skilled workers is high.

- The call for public accountability is increasing as taxpayers question the spending habits and policies of representative government.

- Term limits on governors and state legislators are growing more common.

- Unions are seeking new ways to be effective.

- Distrust of the federal government is rising.

- Consumer behavior is becoming driven by the desire to self-differentiate.

- More Americans are espousing the principles of simplicity and community.

- Nonprofit organizations are playing an increasingly important role in providing social services.

- New social ills are revealing the dark side of progress.

■ Copenhagen Institute for Futures Studies, 10 Tendencies Toward 2010

During 2004, the Copenhagen Institute for Futures Studies revealed a list of tendencies that it expected to affect society as a lead-up to 2010. A few of them include: The Perfect Human Being, The Battle for Values, I Technology, Nation Branding, No Comfort Zones, OFF (shortage of fossil fuels), the Orient is Coming, Climate Changes, Senses and Sensuality, and EU goes East.[385]

■ *Red Herring* Magazine, Top 10 Trends for 2002

The November 2001 issue of *Red Herring* magazine carried a series of articles devoted to 10 trends it considered important for 2002 and beyond. Many of these trends are on their way to becoming commonplace. They include the following:

- Advanced data centers will redirect innovation toward new technologies for truly distributed computing.

- A new military philosophy leads to increased funding for security-related startups.

- Nanotechnology wins over mainstream venture capitalists.

- A new class of wireless company reshapes the industry landscape—and spurs demand for wireless services.

- The value of private-equity-led merger and acquisition deals in the technology sector will skyrocket.

- Europe flexes its regulatory power over the global high-technology industry.

- Renewable energy sources such as wind, solar, and fuel cells become a cost-efficient alternative to oil and coal.

- Biotechnology's focus on neurogenomics will spawn the most successful drugs ever for the treatment of brain disorders.

- Low electronic-component prices spark the emergence of inexpensive, multifunctional, portable computing devices.

- Big business embraces proprietary digital-media networks for highly efficient communications.[386]

■ *Educational Leadership* Magazine

In its December 2003/January 2004 magazine, the Association for Supervision and Curriculum Development presented "A Forecast for Schools," written by Marvin Cetron and Kimberley Cetron, two of our advisors for this book. Those forecasts included the following:

- Funding will become more limited.

- The student population will grow and continue to become more diverse.

- Technology will continue to transform the workplace.

- Tomorrow's citizens will need and expect to engage in lifelong learning.[387]

References/Endnotes

1. Chase, H. (1984). *Issue management . . . Origin of the future*. Stamford, CT: Issue Action Publications, 38.

2. Merriam-Webster, Inc. (1983). *Webster's new collegiate dictionary*. Springfield, MA: Author, 1,258.

3. Gladwell, M. (2002). *The tipping point . . . How little things can make a big difference*. (First Back Bay paperback ed.) Boston: Little, Brown, 7-9.

4. Wilson, E.O. (1998). *Consilience . . . The unity of knowledge*. New York: Borzoi (Alfred A. Knopf), 8-12.

5. Marx, G. (2006). *Future-focused leadership: Preparing schools, students, and communities for tomorrow's realities*. Alexandria, VA: Association for Supervision and Curriculum Development.

6. Bennis, W., & Goldsmith, J. (2003). *Learning to lead*. New York: Basic Books, 8-9.

7. Feynman, R. (2004). Other Feynman quotes. *The Feynman Webring*. Retrieved February 5, 2006, from the Bill Beaty Science Hobbyist Web site, http://www.amasci.com/feynman.html

8. Surowiecki, J. (2004). *The wisdom of crowds*. New York: Doubleday (Random House), 229.

9. Marx, G. (2000). *Ten trends . . . Educating children for a profoundly different future*. Arlington, VA: Educational Research Service.

10. Caption at an exhibit devoted to "The History of the American Office" at the National Building Museum in Washington, DC, opened 2000.

11. Easterbrook, G. (2003). *The progress paradox*. (Trade paperback ed.). New York: Random House, xiii.

12. U.S. Census Bureau. (2004). *National population projections, summary files by age, sex, race, and Hispanic origin, 1998-2100*. (March 4, 2004). Washington, DC: Author. Retrieved from http://census.gov/population

13. Anderson, R.N. (1998). Table 5: United States abridged life tables, 1966. *National Vital Statistics Reports 47*(13). (December 24, 1998). Hyattsville, MD: National Center for Health Statistics, U.S. Centers for Disease Control and Prevention, 17-18. Retrieved February 4, 2006, from http://www.cdc.gov/nchs/data/nvsr/nvsr47/nvs47_13.pdf

14. National Center for Health Statistics. (n.d.). *Life expectancy* (Data for the U.S. in 2001). Washington, DC: Author. Retrieved November 17, 2003, from http://www.cdc.gov/nchs/fastats/lifeexpect.htm

15. Administration on Aging, U.S. Department of Health and Human Services. (1999). A profile of older Americans 1999. *AARP Report*. Washington, DC: American Association of Retired Persons, 1.

16. Reuters News Service. (2005). Expert sees obesity hitting U.S. life expectancy. (February 2, 2005). *Chicago Afterhours.* Retrieved February 2, 2005, from http://www.chicagoafterhours.com/vibe/obesity.php

17. Wallace, P. (1999). *Agequake: Riding the demographic rollercoaster shaking business, finance, and our world.* London: Nicholas Brealey, 6.

18. U.S. Census Bureau. (2002). *National population projections, summary profiles, total population by age, sex, race, and Hispanic origin, middle series, 1999-2100.* (August 2, 2002). Washington, DC: Author.

19. U.S. Census Bureau. (2003). Table 1. No. HS 13. Live births, deaths, infant deaths, and maternal deaths, 1900-2001. *Statistical abstract of the U.S. 2003.* Washington, D.C.: Author. Retrieved March 3, 2004, from http://census.gov/statab/hist/IIS-13.pdf

20. National Center for Health Statistics, U.S. Department of Health and Human Services. (2004). Births and deaths in the U.S. In *World almanac, book of facts, 2004* (p. 73). New York: World Almanac Education Group.

21. *Ibid.*

22. *Ibid,* and Ventura, S.; Martin, J.; Curtin, S.; Matthews, T.J; & Park, M. (2000). Table 1, Births: Final data for 1998. *National Vital Statistics Reports. 48*(3). In Marx, G. (2000). *Ten trends. . . Educating children for a profoundly different future* (p. 1). Arlington, VA: Educational Research Service.

23. National Center for Health Statistics, U.S. Department of Health and Human Services. (2004). Recent trends in vital statistics, and Birth rates; Fertility rates by age of mother, 1950-2000. In *World almanac, book of facts, 2004* (pp. 73-74). New York: World Almanac Education Group.

24. U.S. Census Bureau. (2004). *Sources of population growth.* Retrieved March 4, 2004, from http://www.npg.org/popfacts.htm

25. *Ibid.*

26. U.S. Census Bureau. (1999). *World population profile: 1998—Highlights* (p. 2). (Updated version, March 18, 1999). Retrieved March 3, 2004, from http://www.census.gov/ipc/www/wp98001.html

27. National Center for Health Statistics. (n.d.). *Life expectancy* (Data for the U.S. in 2001). Retrieved November 17, 2003, from http://www.cdc.gov/nchs/fastats/lifeexpect.htm; and Administration on Aging, U.S. Department of Health and Human Services. (1999). *A profile of older Americans 1999.* In *AARP Report.* (p. 1). Washington, DC: American Association of Retired Persons.

28. Aneki.com. (2004.) *Countries with the highest life expectancies in the world.* Retrieved March 3, 2004, from http://www.aneki.com/expectancy.html

29. World Bank. (1999). Sub-Saharan Africa, basic data table: Life expectancy at birth in years, 1998. (Updated version, March 18, 1999). Retrieved March 3, 2004, from http://www.worldbank.org

30. Wallace, P. (1999). *Agequake: Riding the demographic rollercoaster shaking business, finance, and our world.* London: Nicholas Brealey, 6; and U.S. Census Bureau. (2003). *National population projections, summary profiles, total population by age, sex, race, and Hispanic origin, middle series, 1999-2100.* (August 2, 2002). Washington, DC: Author.

31. Wallace, P. (1999) *Agequake: Riding the demographic rollercoaster shaking business, finance, and our world.* London: Nicholas Brealey, 6.

32. National Center for Health Statistics, U.S. Department of Health and Human Services. (2004). Births and deaths in the U.S. In *World almanac, book of facts, 2004* (p. 73). New York: World Almanac Education Group.

33. Aneki.com. (2004). *Countries with the highest birth rates.* Retrieved March 3, 2004, from http://www.aneki.com/birth.html

34. National Center for Health Statistics, U.S. Department of Health and Human Services. (2004). Births and deaths in the U.S. In *World almanac, book of facts, 2004* (p. 73). New York: World Almanac Education Group.

35. *Ibid,* and National Center for Health Statistics (2000), Table 1. In Marx, G. (2000). *Ten trends ... Educating children for a profoundly different future* (p. 1). Arlington, VA: Educational Research Service.

36. Aneki.com. (2004). *Countries with the highest death rates,* and *Countries with the lowest death rates.* Retrieved March 3, 2004, from http://www.aneki.com/death.html and http://www.aneik.com/lowest_death.html

37. U.S. Census Bureau. (2004). *Sources of population growth.* Retrieved March 4, 2004, from http://www.npg.org/popfacts.htm

38. U.S. Census Bureau. (2004). *International database: World population events per time unit.* Retrieved March 2004 from http://www.census.gov/cgi-bin/ipc/pcwe

39. U.S. Census Bureau. (2003). *Total population by age, race, and Hispanic origin, middle series, 1999-2100.* Retrieved March 3, 2004, from http://www.census.gov/population/www/projections/natsum-T3.html

40. U.S. Census Bureau. (2004). *Total midyear population for the world: 1950-2050.* Retrieved February 4, 2006, from http://www.census.gov/ipc/www/worldpop.htm

41. Burtless, G. (1997). Social Security's long-term budget outlook. *National Tax Journal.* (September 1997), *50*(3), 402.

42. U.S. Census Bureau. (2003) *National population projections, projections of the total population by five-year age groups, 2000-2050.* Retrieved March 3, 2004, from http://www.census.gov/population/projections/nation/summary/np-t3-a.txt

43. *Ibid.*

44. U.S. Census Bureau. (2004). International database: Population pyramid summary for the United States—*2000, 2025, 2050.* Retrieved February 4, 2006 from http://www.census.gov/cgi-bin/ipclidpyrs.pl?=us&out=s&ymax=250

45. U.S. Census Bureau. (2004). *Total midyear population for the world: 1950-2050.* Retrieved March 2004 from http://www.census.gov/ipc/www/worldpop.html

46. U.S. Census Bureau. (2004). *International data base: Midyear population by age and sex.* (Data gathered for each individual country). Retrieved March 5, 2004 from http://www census.gov/cgi-bin/ipc/idbagg

47. *Ibid.*

48. National Center for Education Statistics. (2004). *Projections of education statistics to 2012,* Table 1-Enrollment in grades K-8 and 9-12 of elementary and secondary schools, by control of institution, from fall 1987 to fall 2012. Retrieved March 5, 2004, from http://www.nces.gov/pubs2002/proj2012/table_01.asp

49. Yasin, S. (1999). The supply and demand of elementary and secondary school teachers in the United States. *ERIC Digest* (ED436529). (December 1999). Washington, DC: ERIC Clearinghouse on Teaching and Teacher Education, 1.

50. Hussar, W.J. (1999). Predicting the need for newly hired teachers in the United States to 2008-09. *Education Statistics Quarterly.* (Winter 1999), 9.

51. Glass, T.E., Byork, L., & Brunner, C.C. (2000). *The study of the American superintendency 2000.* Arlington, VA: American Association of School Administrators, 21.

52. Marx, G. (2000). *Ten trends . . . Educating children for a profoundly different future.* Arlington, VA: Educational Research Service, 9.

53. National Education Association. (2003). *Attracting and keeping quality teachers.* (Issue Paper.) Retrieved October 6, 2003, from http://www.nea.org/teachershortage

54. Simon, R., & Cannon, A. (2003). American ingenuity . . . The culture of creativity that made a nation great. *U.S. News and World Report.* (Collector's ed.: *Amazing journey.* (Spring 2003), 7-9.

55. Marx, 10-11.

56. Marx, 8.

57. U.S. Census Bureau. (2002). *National population profiles, total population by age, sex, race, and Hispanic origin.* (Rev. ed.). Retrieved August 2, 2002, from http://www.census.gov/population/www/projections/natsum-T3.html

58. U.S. Census Bureau. (2000). *Projections of the resident population by age, sex, race, and Hispanic origin: 1999-2100, NP-D1-A.* Retrieved January 13, 2000, from http://www.census.gov

59. *Ibid.*

60. Richard, A. (2002). Cambridge becomes latest district to integrate by income. *Education Week.* (January 9, 2002), 11.

61. U.S. Census Bureau. (2004). Foreign-born population: Top countries of origin, 1920, 1960, 2000. In *World Almanac* (p. 378). New York: World Almanac Books.

62. U.S. Census Bureau. (2004). *Sources of population growth.* Retrieved March 9, 2004, from http://www.npg.org/popfacts.htm

63. U.S. Census Bureau. (2000). *Components of change for the total resident population, middle series, 1999-2100 (natural increase, births, deaths, net migration, net change).* (January 13, 2000). Retrieved May 4, 2004, from http://www.census.gove/population/projections/nation/summary/np-t6-a.txt

64. Lewis, J. (2000). The civil rights movement past and present. *Buskin lecture proceedings,* Education Writers Association Conference (April 16, 2000, Atlanta, GA), 16.

65. National Center for Health Statistics. (2003). *U.S. birth rate reaches record low.* Retrieved June 25, 2003, from http://www.cdc.gov/ncha/releases

66. Ventura, M.C., et al. (2000). 24 (Table 1) and 30 (Table 6). In Marx, G., *Ten trends . . . Educating children for a profoundly different future* (p. 14). Arlington, VA: Educational Research Service.

67. Kotkin, J. (1992). *Traces . . . How race, religion, and identity determine success in the new global economy.* New York: Random House, 3-4, 255.

68. Booth, W. (1998). The myth of the melting pot, one nation, indivisible: Is it history? *The Washington Post,* (February 22, 1998), A1.

69. Zakariya, S.B. (2004). Bending toward justice: Unfinished legacy of Brown v. Board. *American School Board Journal.* (Special report, April 2004). (pp. 1-3). Retrieved February 2, 2006, from http://www.asbj.com/BrownvBoard/index.html

70. Yang, J. (2003). How to succeed in multicultural marketing. *American Demographics.* (Special supplement), 2-3.

71. Booth, W. (1998). The myth of the melting pot, one nation, indivisible: Is it history? *The Washington Post.* (February 22, 1998), 2. Retrieved from http://www.washsingtonpost.com

72. Huntington, S.P. (2004). The Hispanic challenge. *Foreign Policy.* (March-April 2004), 30.

73. Grow, B. (2004). Hispanic nation. *BusinessWeek.* (March 15, 2004), 62.

74. Edmondson, B. (1999). Projections of minority, Black, Hispanic American, and Asian American populations to the year 2001. *American Demographics.* (Special supplement, *Diversity in America*), 13, 15.

75. Myareaguide.com. (2004). USA CITYLINK: Detroit demographics. Retrieved April 13, 2004, from http://www.detroitmi.usl.myareaguide.com/census.html

76. Hodgkinson, H. (1999). The uneven spread and blurring of student diversity. *The School Administrator.* (December 1999), 13-14.

77. Marx, G. (2000). *Ten trends . . . Educating children for a profoundly different future.* Arlington, VA: Educational Research Service, 16.

78. Helmreich, W.B. (1984). *The things they say behind your back . . . Stereotypes and the myths behind them.* New Brunswick, NJ: Transaction Books, 2-5.

79. Grow, B. (2004). Hispanic nation. *BusinessWeek.* (March 15, 2004), 70.

80. Reid, K. (2001). Prep-school program opens doors for minority teachers. *Education Week.* (August 8, 2001), 6-7.

81. Zehr, M.A. (2001). Schools grew more segregated in 1990s. *Education Week.* (August 8, 2001), 16.

82. Chase, B. (1998). Wanted: Minority teachers. *Bob Chase Column.* (January 11, 1998). Washington, DC: National Education Association. Retrieved April 10, 2000, from http://www.nea.org/society/bc/bc980111.html

83. Glass, T.E., Byork, L., & Brunner, C.C. (2000). *The study of the American superintendency 2000.* Arlington, VA: American Association of School Administrators, 21.

84. James, D.W., Jurich, S., & Estes, S. (2004). *Raising minority academic achievement . . . A compendium of programs and practices.* Washington, DC: American Youth Policy Forum, 5.

85. Orfield, G.; Losen, D.; Wald, J.; & Swanson, C.B. (2004). Losing our future: How minority youth are being left by the graduation rate crisis. (February 1, 2004). Washington, DC: The Urban Institute. Retrieved May 4, 2004, from http://www.urban.org

86. James, Jurich, & Estes.

87. Minority Student Achievement Network. (2003). *What is the relationship between race and achievement in our schools? Minority student achievement network statement of purpose.* (Adopted June 2003). Evanston, IL: Author. Retrieved February 3, 2006, from http://msanetwork.org/pub/relationship.pdf

88. U.S. Census Bureau. (1999). *School enrollment in the United States, social and economic characteristics of students, population characteristics.* (October 1999). Washington, DC: Author, 3-5.

89. Withrow, F., Long, H., & Marx, G. (1999). *Preparing schools and school systems for the 21st century.* Arlington, VA: American Association of School Administrators, 12.

90. Marx, G. (2000). *Ten trends . . . Educating children for a profoundly different future.* Arlington, VA: Educational Research Service, 19.

91. Zehr, M.A. (2004). Close to home: Brown at 50, the promise unfulfilled. *Education Week.* (March 10, 2004), 30-31.

92. Cohn, D., & Witt, A. (2001). Minorities fuel growth in Maryland suburbs. *The Washington Post.* (March 20, 2001), 1, 18.

93. Zehr, M.A. (2001). Schools grew more segregated in 1990s. *Education Week.* (August 8, 2001), 16.

94. Associated Press. (2001). The Latin melting pot. In *Seattle Times.* (May 10, 2001). Retrieved February 2, 2006, from http://archives.seattletimes.nwsource.com/cgi/bin/texis.cgi/web/vortex/display?slug=hispani...

95. Perelman, L. (1997). Leading lights, an interview with Tom Stewart. *Knowledge Inc.* Retrieved March 10, 2004 from http://www.webcom.com/quantera/llistewart.html

96. Stewart, T. (1999). *Intellectual capital . . . The new wealth of organizations.* New York: Currency (Doubleday), 46.

97. Bennis, W. (2002.). Becoming a leader of leaders. In Gibson, R., & Bennis, W. (2002). *Rethinking the future.* (p. 149). London: Nicholas Brealey.

98. Perelman, L. (1997). Leading lights, an interview with Tom Stewart. *Knowledge Inc.* Retrieved March 10, 2004, from http://www.webcom.com/quantera/llistewart.html

99. Bennis.

100. Robert Putnam, addressing a White House conference on the new economy. (April 5, 2000, Washington, DC).

101. Fukuyama, F. (1995). *Trust . . . The social virtues and the creation of prosperity.* New York: Free Press Paperbacks, 10.

102. Gardner, G. (2002). *Invoking the spirit.* Washington, DC: The Worldwatch Institute, 19.

103. Bonner, P. (2003). I can be an entrepreneur. *NCEE Content Standards: 14, EconEdLink.* (October 31, 2003). Washington, DC: National Council on Economic Education. Retrieved April 13, 2004, from http://www.econedlink.org/lessons

104. Bell-Rose, S., & Mariotti, S. (2004). Developing a success orientation. (Commentary). *Education Week,* 37.

105. Thurow, L.C. (1999). *Building wealth . . . The new rules for individuals, companies, and nations in a knowledge-based economy.* New York: HarperCollins, 117.

106. Verity, Inc. (2003). 2003 DM Review 100 ranking and responses. *DM Review.* Retrieved March 10, 2004, from www.dmreview.com/awards/top100/2003

107. Flannery, R. (2004). China embraces franchising. *Forbes.* (February 19, 2004). Retrieved March 10, 2004, from http://www.forbes.com/commerce/2004/02/19

108. Stewart, T.A. (2001). The leading edge, intellectual capital: Ten years later, how far we've come. Anniversaries are a good excuse for taking stock. *Fortune.* (May 28, 2001). Retrieved March 10, 2004, from http://www.fortune.com

109. Thurow, L.C. (1999). *Building wealth . . . The new rules for individuals, companies, and nations in a knowledge-based economy.* New York: HarperCollins, 92.

110. Koo, C. (2000). Drugstore.com falls after buying beauty.com. *The street.com* (*New York Times,* online ed.). (January 12, 2000). Retrieved from http://nytimes.com

111. Emmott, B. (2003). *20:21 vision, twentieth-century lessons for the twenty-first century.* New York: Picador, 245.

112. Kaihla, P. (2004). Boomtowns. *Business 2.0 Magazine.* (March 2004), 96-97.

113. Florida, R. (2004). *The rise of the creative class.* Cambridge, MA: Basic Books (Perseus), xxvii.

114. Kaihla.

115. Harden, B. (2003). Brain-gain cities attract educated young. *The Washington Post.* (November 9, 2003), 1, 14-15.

116. Marx, G. (2000). *Ten trends . . . Educating children for a profoundly different future.* Arlington, VA: Educational Research Service, 23.

117. Former U.S. President William Jefferson Clinton, addressing a White House conference on the new economy (April 5, 2000, Washington, DC).

118. Former World Bank President James Wolfensohn, addressing a White House conference on the new economy (April 5, 2000, Washington, DC).

119. Intellectual Capital Services (ICS). (n.d.). London. Retrieved March 10, 2004, from http://www.intcap.com/value_creation.html

120. Marx, G. (2000). *Ten trends . . . Educating children for a profoundly different future.* Arlington, VA: Educational Research Service, 25.

121. *Ibid.*

122. *Ibid.*

123. Marx, 27.

124. Viadero, D. (2003). Scholars aim to connect studies to schools' needs. *Education Week.* (March 19, 2003), 1, 12.

125. Smith, S. (2005). The blog economy. *EContent*, (January/February 2005), 25-29.

126. The Markle Foundation. (1999). Technology: How technology impacts American life. *Understanding.* Newport, RI: TED Conferences, Inc.

127. Richey, K.W. (1997). *The ENIAC.* Retrieved February 16, 1997, from the Virginia Tech Web site, http://www.ei.cs.vt.edu

128. Winegrad, D., & Akera, A. (2004). *ENIAC . . . A short history of the second American revolution.* Retrieved March 16, 2004, from the University of Pennsylvania Web site, http://www.upenn.edu/almanac/v42/n18/eniac.html

129. Van der Spiegel, J., et al. (2002.) *ENIAC on a chip, team.* First posted June 9, 1995; updated October 14, 2002. Retrieved March 16, 2004, from the University of Pennsylvania Web site, http://www.ee.upenn.edu

130. Carey, J. (2004). Putting the weirdness to work . . . Physicists say quantum materials will be the basis for amazing devices, but when? *BusinessWeek.* (March 15, 2004), 103-105.

131. Webopedia. (2004). *Moore's law.* Retrieved April 2004 from http://www.webopedia.com

132. National Science and Technology Council. (1999). *Nanotechnology . . . Shaping the world atom by atom.* A report of the Committee on Technology, Interagency Working Group on Nanoscience, Engineering, and Technology. (September 1999). Washington, DC: Author, 8.

133. Hilton-Morrow, W. (2003). *McLuhan's wake.* A review of, in *American Communication Journal.* (Summer 2003), *6*(4). Retrieved April 3, 2004, from http://www.acjournal.org

134. Drexler, E. (2004). Why care about nanotechnology? *Foresight Institute Nanotechnology Newsletter.* Retrieved March 31, 2004, from http://www.gmail.foresight.org

135. Britt, R.R. (2005). *Object bigger than Pluto discovered, called 10th planet.* (July 29, 2005). Retrieved from the Space.com Web site, http://www.space.com/scienceastronomy/050729_new_planet.html

136. Achenbach, J. (2004). Distant object sheds light on our universe. *The Washington Post.* (Style Section). (March 17, 2004), C-1.

137. Burton, J., Kinter, M., & Marx, D. (2004). *2005 guide to digital imaging.* Fairfax, VA: Specialty Graphic Imaging Association, and Digital Printing and Imaging Association, 1, 7-9.

138. A band of 20 microwave channels, known as the Instructional Television Fixed Service (ITFS), is licensed by the FCC to credit-granting educational institutions. *About ITFS.* Retrieved September 2, 2005, from http://itfs.org/index/about_ITFS

139. Honawar, V. (2005). Education department tracks growth in distance learning. *Education Week.* (March 9, 2005), 6.

140. Dahms, A.S. (2004). Biotechnology: What it is, what it is not, and the challenges in reaching a national and global consensus. *Biochemistry and Molecular Biology Education, 32*(4), 271-278. Retrieved from http://www.bambed.org/cgi/content/full/32/4/271

141. Keenan, D., Lederer, H., & Vetter, S. (2001). Nanotech and MEMS futures. *World Future Society Conference Program Booklet.* (pp. 46-47). (Conference held July 29-31, 2001, Minneapolis, MN).

142. Ibid.

143. Ibid.

144. Foresight Institute. (2004). *Federal nanotech confusion spreads to California, Michael Crichton mistaken for Richard Feynman.* (January 20, 2004). Retrieved February 4, 2004, from http://www.gmail.foresight.org

145. Cetron, M., & Davies, O. (2003). Trends shaping the future. *The Futurist.* (March-April 2003), 34.

146. Jonietz, E. (2004). Automatic speech translator. *Technology Review.* (February 15, 2004). (p. 1). Retrieved February 4, 2006, from http://www.technologyreview.com/INFOTECH/wtr_13399.294.p2.html

147. BBC News. (2003). *Future flight: The shape of things to come.* (Posted online December 12, 2003, at http://www.news.bbc.co.uk). Published in condensed form in *Future Edition.* (January 7, 2004), *7*(1). Arlington, VA: The Arlington Institute.

148. BBC News. (2003). Epic trip for alternative car. Posted online December 27, 2003, at http://www.news.bbc.co.uk). Published in condensed form in *Future Edition.* (January 7, 2004), *7*(1). Arlington, VA: The Arlington Institute.

149. Cetron, M., & Davies, O. (2003). Trends shaping the future. *The Futurist.* (March-April 2003), 33.

150. Alexander, Col. J.B. (1999). *Future war. . . Non-lethal weapons in twenty first century warfare.* New York: Thomas Dunn Books (St. Martin's), 59-69.

151. Molitor, G.T.T. (1999). Beyond the fourth wave. *Association Management.* (December 1999), 28.

152. Kadaba, L, & Boccella, K. (1999.) Of cribs and PCs: How soon should tots log on? *The Philadelphia Inquirer.* (June 13, 1999), A01.

153. Totty, M. (2003). Ten technologies you need to know about now. *Wall Street Journal.* (March 31, 2003), R-1.

154. Cetron, M., & Cetron, K. (unpublished). *Education is the future.* Paper prepared in 2004 as members of the *Creating a Future* Advisory Council (Falls Church, VA).

155. Marx, G. (2000). *Ten trends . . . Educating children for a profoundly different future.* Arlington, VA: Educational Research Service, 56.

156. Breslau, K., & Chung, J. (2002). Big future in tiny spaces . . . Nanotechnology is moving from labs to businesses. *Newsweek* (Special Report, September 23, 2002), 48.

157. Gibbs, N. (2005). Parents behaving badly. *Time.* (February 21, 2005), 45.

158. Tofts, D., Jonson, A., & Cavallaro, A. (2003). *Prefiguring cyberculture: An intellectual history.* Cambridge, MA: MIT Press.

159. Strauss, V. (2004). Effective assignments, from DNA to Dracula. (Reflections of Peter Petrossian, science teacher at Pyle Middle School, Bethesda, MD.) *The Washington Post.* (January 6, 2004), A-6.

160. Viacom International. (1999). *The future according to kids.* New York: Nickelodeon Books (Roundtable Press), 39.

161. *Ibid*, 16.

162. Strauss, W., & Howe, N. (1999). *Global generations and global aging: A fifty-year outlook.* Presentation at World Future Society 9th General Assembly. (July 1999, Washington, DC)

163. Strauss, W., & Howe, N. (1998). *The fourth turning . . . An American prophesy.* New York: Broadway Books (Bantam Doubleday Dell Publishing Group), 3.

164. Strauss, W., & Howe, N. (1991). *Generations: The history of America's future, 1584-2069.* New York: William Morrow, 36.

165. Brokaw, T. (1998). *The greatest generation.* New York: Random House, xx.

166. *Rolling Stone* (online). (2004). *Frank Sinatra.* Retrieved March 18, 2004, from http://www.rollingstone.com

167. Halberstam, D. (1993). *The fifties.* New York: Fawcett Columbine (Ballantine Books), 456-457.

168. Esswein, P.M., Franklin, M.B., & Rheault, M. (2005). Great places to retire. *Kiplinger's Personal Finance.* (March 2005), 80.

169. Tulgan, B. (1995). *Generation X . . . How to bring out the best in young talent.* Santa Monica, CA: Merritt Publishing, 17.

170. Huntington, S. (1997). *The clash of civilizations and the remaking of the world order.* New York: Touchstone, 28.

171. Weiss, M.J. (2003). The about to be's . . . A new adult generation on the cusp of it all. *American Demographics.* (September 2003), 30.

172. Zollo, P. (2004). *Getting wiser to teens.* New York: New Strategist Publications, 146, 205.

173. Strauss, W., & Howe, N. (2000). *Millennials rising . . . The next great generation.* New York: Vintage Books (Random House), 320.

174. Viacom International. (1999). *The future according to kids.* New York: Nickelodeon Books (Roundtable Press), 131.

175. *Ibid*, front dust cover leaf.

176. *Ibid.*

177. *Ibid*, 50.

178. *Ibid.*

179. Strauss, W., & Howe, N. (2000). *Millennials rising . . . The next great generation.* New York: Vintage Books (Random House), 348.

180. Meredith, G.E., Schewe, C.D., & Karlovich, J. (2002), *Defining markets, defining moments.* New York: Hungry Minds, xvii.

181. Marx, G. (2000). *Ten trends . . . Educating children for a profoundly different future.* Arlington, VA: Educational Research Service, 39-40.

182. Withrow, F., Long, H., & Marx, G. (1999). *Preparing schools and school systems for the 21st century.* Arlington, VA: American Association of School Administrators, 9.

183. Newton, I. (1998). *The Hutchinson encyclopedia of science.* Oxford: Helicon, 520.

184. Hymes, D., Chafin, A., & Gonder, P. (1991). *The changing face of testing and assessment.* Arlington, VA: American Association of School Administrators, 4.

185. Education Writers Association. (2001). High school reform. *Education Reform*, Backgrounder 15. (January 2001). Washington, DC: Author, 1.

186. Hymes, et al, 9-14.

187. National Governors Association. (2005). *A primer on no child left behind.* (Prepared by the NGA Center for Best Practices, Education Policy Studies Division). Washington, DC: Author, 3. Available as of February 2006 from http://www.nga.org

188. Kohn, A. (1999). Confusing harder with better. *Education Week.* (September 15, 1999). Retrieved April 27, 2000, from http://www.edweek.com/ew/1999/02kohn.h19

189. Kohn, A. (2000). *The case against standardized testing . . . Raising the scores, ruining the schools.* Portsmouth, NH: Heinemann, 2.

190. Lewis, A., & Steinberger, E. (1991). *Learning styles: Putting research and common sense into practice.* Arlington, VA: American Association of School Administrators, 10-11.

191. Sweeney, J. (1991). *Tips for improving school climate.* Arlington, VA: American Association of School Administrators, 1.

192. Gardner, H. (1993). *Multiple intelligences, the theory in practice.* New York: BasicBooks (HarperCollins), 15-27.

193. Education Writers Association. (2001). High school reform. *Education Reform*, Backgrounder 15. (January 2001). Washington, DC: Author, 1.

194. The Education Foundation, Charleston (S.C.) Metro Area Chamber of Commerce. (2004). *Smaller learning communities planning grant abstract.* Charleston, SC: Author, 4.

195. Hendrie, C. (2002). N.Y.C. students at Annenberg sites were 'well served,' report finds. *Education Week.* (March 6, 2002), 15.

196. Elling, D.M. (2004). Statewide networks: Shaping the future of after school. *Mott mosaic.* (March 2004). Flint, MI: Charles Stewart Mott Foundation, 1-4.

197. Schaeffer, B. (2004). Virtual savings? *The School Administrator.* (April 2004), 22.

198. Galley, M. (2002). $20 million grant award targets Baltimore high schools. *Education Week.* (March 13, 2002), 9.

199. Council of the Great City Schools. (2004). Urban schools open with achievement focus. *Urban Educator.* (August 2004), *13*(7). Retrieved from http://www.cgcs.org/urbaneducators/ 2004_aug_vol_13_no_7_1.html

200. Kennedy Manzo, K. (2003). Arts, foreign languages getting edged out. *Education Week.* (November 5, 2003), 3.

201. See for example: Fitzhugh, W. (2002). The state of the term paper. *Education Week.* (January 16, 2002), 35. Hoff, D. (2001). Teaching, standards, tests found not aligned. *Education Week.* (October 31, 2001), 6. Kohn, A. (2001). Beware of the standards, not just the tests. *Education Week.* (September 26, 2001), 32. Seymour, L. (2001). SOL tests create new dropouts. *The Washington Post.* (July 17, 2001), 1. Viadero, D. (2004). Study probes enrollment bulge in 9th grade. *Education Week.* (January 28, 2004), 1. Hoff, D. (2001). States spend nearly half-a-billion on testing. *Education Week.* (March 14, 2001), 18.

202. Marx, G. (2000). *Ten trends . . . Educating children for a profoundly different future.* Arlington, VA: Educational Research Service, 31.

203. von Zastro, C. (with Jane, H.). (2004). *Academic atrophy . . . The condition of the liberal arts in America's public schools.* (Special report, March 2004). Washington, DC: Council for Basic Education, 7.

204. Kennedy Manzo, K. (2004). Principals' poll shows erosion of liberal arts curriculum. *Education Week.* (March 17, 2004), 12.

205. Kohn, A. (2000). Standardized testing and its victims, inconvenient facts and inequitable consequences. (Commentary). *Education Week.* (September 27, 2000), 60.

206. Carter, G.R. (2002). Educators bearing witness. The unintended consequences of standards and accountability, advertorial. *Education Week.* (February 13, 2002), 18.

207. Marx, G. (2000). *Ten trends . . . Educating children for a profoundly different future.* Arlington, VA: Educational Research Service, 32.

208. Gelb, M.J. (1998). *How to think like Leonardo da Vinci.* New York: Dell (Random House), 17.

209. Marx, 62.

210. Florida, R. (2002). *The rise of the creative class.* Cambridge, MA: Basic Books (Perseus Books Group), 33.

211. Drucker, P.F. (1980). *Managing in turbulent times.* New York: Harper and Row, 51.

212. Wilber, K. (2000). *A brief history of everything.* Boston: Shambhala, 15-17.

213. Wilson, E.O. (1998). *Consilience . . . The unity of knowledge.* New York: Borzoi (Alfred A. Knopf), 8-9.

214. Gelb, M.J. (1998). *How to think like Leonardo da Vinci.* New York: Dell (Random House), 17.

215. Florida, R. (2002). *The rise of the creative class.* Cambridge, MA: Basic Books (Perseus Books Group), 33.

216. Ayan, J. (1997). *Aha! 10 ways to free your creative spirit and find your great ideas.* New York: Three Rivers Press (Crown), 103.

217. Morris, H.J, et al. (2003). Making music. *U.S. News and World Report.* (Special Collector's Edition: American Ingenuity . . . The Culture of Creativity That Made a Nation Great). (Spring 2003), 32, 39, 40, 47, 48.

218. Amundson, K. (1985). *Performing together . . . The arts and education.* Arlington, VA: John F. Kennedy Center for the Performing Arts, and American Association of School Administrators.

219. Sims, R. (2004). Of satellites and sonatas, searching for the soul of learning. *Education Week.* (January 28, 2004), 33.

220. Gladwell, M. (2005). *Blink . . . The power of thinking without thinking.* New York: Little, Brown, and Co., 69.

221. Henderson, D.W. (1998). *Culture shift.* Grand Rapids, MI: Baker Books (Baker Book House Co.), 119.

222. Wilson, E.O. (1998). *Consilience . . . The unity of knowledge.* New York: Borzoi (Alfred A. Knopf), 113.

223. Daggett, W.R. (1996). The challenge to America's schools: Preparing students for the 21st century. *School Business Affairs.* (April 1996), 10.

224. Ow, A. (2004). The teacher as edupreneur: Exploring new frontiers. (p. 2). In program booklet of a conference sponsored by the Singapore Ministry of Education (June 8-9, 2004, Singapore).

225. Suarez-Orozco, M., & Gardner, H. (2003). Educating Billy Wang for the world of tomorrow. (Commentary). *Education Week.* (October 22, 2003), 44.

226. Attributed to former New York City Mayor Fiorello LaGuardia.

227. Gibson, R. (2002). Rethinking the future. *Rethinking business.* London: Nicholas Brealey, 10-11.

228. Ouchi, W. (1981). *Theory Z . . . How American business can meet the Japanese challenge.* Boston, MA: Addison-Wesley, 5, 14.

229. Peters, T., & Austin, N. (1985). *A passion for excellence . . . The leadership difference.* New York: Random House, 98.

230. Deming, W.E. (1991). *Out of the crisis.* Cambridge, MA: Massachusetts Institute of Technology, Center for Advanced Engineering Study, 23-24.

231. National Institute of Standards and Technology (NIST). (2003). *Malcolm Baldrige national quality award 2002 award recipient, manufacturing category: Motorola, Inc., commercial, government, and industrial solutions sector (CGISS).* (Press release posted online April 1, 2003). Retrieved March 24, 2004, from http://www.nist.gov/public_affairs/releases/cgiss.htm

232. J.D. Power and Associates. (2000). *Lexus dealer service centers regain highest ranking in satisfaction with vehicle service.* (Press release posted online October 16, 2000). Retrieved March 24, 2004, from http://www.jdpa.com/news/releases/pressrelease.asp?ID=2070

233. National Institute of Standards and Technology (NIST). (2003). *Education criteria for performance excellence. Baldrige National Quality Program.* Retrieved March 24, 2004, from NIST, (http//www.quality.nist.gov), and American Society for Quality, (http://www.asq.org).

234. National Institute of Standards and Technology (NIST). (2002). *Malcolm Baldrige national quality award 2001 award recipient, education category: Pearl River School District, New York.* (Press release posted online March 12, 2002. Retrieved from http://www.nist.gov/public_affairs/peralriver.htm

235. Pepson, M. (2002). The Baldrige national quality award: The process for continuous improvement. *Network* (Newsletter, National School Public Relations Association). (April 2002), 1.

236. National Institute of Standards and Technology (NIST). (2002). Malcolm Baldrige national quality award 2001 award recipient, education category: Chugach School District, Alaska. (Press release posted online March 12, 2002). Retrieved March 24, 2004 fromwww.nist.gov/public_affairs/chugach.htm

237. National Institute of Standards and Technology (NIST). (2002). *Malcolm Baldrige national quality award 2001 award recipient, education category: University of Wisconsin-Stout.* (Press release posted online March 12, 2002). Retrieved from http://www.nist.gov/public_affairs/

238. Gewertz, C. (2001). Study estimates 850,000 U.S. children schooled at home. *Education Week.* (August 8, 2001), 12.

239. Marx, G. (2000). *Ten trends Educating children for a profoundly different future.* Arlington, VA: Educational Research Service, 46.

240. Withrow, F., Long, H., & Marx, G. (1999). *Preparing schools and school systems for the 21st century.* Arlington, VA: American Association of School Administrators, 14.

241. Johnson, R. (2000). The zen of quality. *Education Week.* (November 22, 2000), 35.

242. Lacayo, R. & Ripley, A. (2002). Persons of the year: The whistleblowers. *Time.* (December 30, 2002), cover story. Retrieved February 4, 2006, from http://www.time.com/time/subscriber/personoftheyear/2002/poyintro.html

243. Merriam-Webster, Inc. (2003). *Webster's new collegiate dictionary.* New York: Author, 429.

244. Long, R. (2002). Countering corporate arrogance. *The Strategist.* (Spring 2002), 7.

245. Butts, R. F. (1991). *The morality of democratic citizenship.* In Amundson, K. (1991). *Teaching values and ethics.* (pp. 24-25). Arlington, VA: American Association of School Administrators

246. Character Counts. (2004). *Six pillars of character.* Los Angeles: Author. Retrieved March 24, 2004, from http://www.charactercounts.org

247. Task Force on Values Education and Ethical Behavior. (1991). Common core of values, Baltimore County public schools, Maryland. In Amundson, K. (1991). *Teaching values and ethics.* (p. 27). Arlington, VA: American Association of School Administrators.

248. Uchida, D., Cetron, M., & McKenzie, F. (1996). *Preparing students for the 21st century.* Arlington, VA: American Association of School Administrators, 20.

249. Metropolis Magazine. (2004). Best and worst case scenarios for the future. (Interview with Morley Safer, *60 Minutes* correspondent, CBS News). (January 2, 2004). Retrieved March 31, 2004, from http://www.metropolismag.com/html/content_0104/bestworst/index.html

250. James Wolfensohn, former president of the World Bank, addressing a White House conference on the new economy. (April 5, 2000, Washington, DC).

251. Tang, M.Y. (2003). Human rights education in Taiwan: The experience of the workshops for schoolteachers. Retrieved March 25, 2004, from the Hurights Osaka Web site (http://www.hurights.org.jp/hreas/2/24.htm).

252. Lukaszewski, J.E. (2002). The ethical practitioner, dilemmas and moral questions: The heart of ethical decision making. *Tactics*. (February 2002), 22.

253. Vedantam, S. (2005). Report on global ecosystems calls for radical changes. *The Washington Post*. (March 30, 2005), A2.

254. See for example: Huitt, W.G. (2004). *Maslow's hierarchy of needs*. Retrieved March 25, 2004, from the Educational Psychology Interactive Web site (http://www.chiron.valdosta.edu/whuitt/col/regsys/maslow.html), and Simons, J.A., Irwin, D.B., & Drinnien, B.A. (1987). *Maslow's hierarchy of needs*. New York: West Publishing Co. Retrieved March 25, 2004, from the University of Hawaii Honolulu Community College Web site (http://www.honolulu.hawaii.edu).

255. Fuller, R.B. (1969). *Operating manual for spaceship Earth*. New York: Simon and Schuster, 59.

256. Wilber, K. (2000). *A brief history of everything*. Boston: Shambhala, 29.

257. Facts on File News Services. (2004). *Issues and controversies: Asia's economic crisis*. New York: World Almanac Education Group. Retrieved March 25, 2004, from http://www.facts.com/icof/i00063.htm

258. From "The future of planetary defense," a speech by Martin Schwab of the Homeland Defense Institute, delivered during a World Future Society presentation at Capital Science 2004 (March 20, 2004, Arlington, VA).

259. Sawin, J.L. (2003). Severe weather events on the rise. In *Vital Signs 2003*. (p. 92). Washington, DC: The Worldwatch Institute.

260. See for example the following sections in the report *Vital Signs 2003* (Washington, DC: The Worldwatch Institute): Poverty and inequality block progress (Renner, M., & Sheeham, M.O. , p. 18); Rich-poor divide growing (Sarin, R., p. 88); and Harvesting of illegal drugs remains high (Halweil, B., p. 98). Also see *World development report 2000/2001*. (New York: World Bank and Oxford University Press), 51.

261. Human Rights Watch. (2004). *Refugees and displaced persons*. Retrieved April 13, 2004, from http://www.hrw.org

262. See for example the following sections in the report *Vital Signs 2003* (Washington, DC: The Worldwatch Institute): Poverty and inequality block progress (Renner, M., & Sheeham, M.O., p. 20); and, Number of refugees drops (Dhar, A., p. 102).

263. Sheeham, M.O. (2003). Carbon emissions and temperature climb. In *Vital Signs 2003*. (p. 40). Washington, DC: The Worldwatch Institute.

264. Renner, M., & Sheeham, M.O. (2003). Poverty and inequality block progress: Diseases of poverty and wealth. In *Vital Signs 2003*. (p. 19). Washington, DC: The Worldwatch Institute.

265. Renner, M. (2003). Military expenditures on the rise. In *Vital Signs 2003*. (p. 118). Washington, DC: The Worldwatch Institute.

266. Halweil, B. (2003). Harvesting of illegal drugs remains high. In *Vital Signs 2003*. (p. 98). Washington, DC: The Worldwatch Institute.

267. Laszlo, E. (2003). *You can change the world*. New York: Select Books. In *Welcome to the club of Budapest*. (Home page of the Club of Budapest International Web site). Retrieved April 2004 from the http://clubofbudapest.org

268. National Archives and Records Administration. (1995). *Meeting the challenges of global threats, a national security strategy of engagement and enlargement*. (The Clinton administration). Retrieved March 25, 2004, from http://www.clinton4.nara.gov/WH/EOP/OSTP/nssts/html/chapt4.html

269. Goodstein, D. (2004). *Out of gas, the end of the age of oil.* New York: W.W. Norton, 123-126.

270. Lavelle, M., & Kurlantzick, J. (2004). Water, tapped out, the coming water crisis. *U.S. News and World Report* (Special Edition, The Future of Earth). (Summer 2004), 38, 57, 58, 61.

271. Lavelle, & Kurlantzick, 58.

272. Hayden, T. (2004). Trashing the seas. *U.S. News and World Report.* (Special ed., *The future of Earth*). (Summer 2004), 48.

273. Markels, A. (2004). The war over water. *U.S. News and World Report* (Special ed., *The future of Earth*). (Summer 2004), 64-65.

274. *Ibid.*

275. Hirsch, Jr., E.D., Kett, J.F., & Trefil, J. (1988). *The dictionary of cultural literacy . . . What every American needs to know.* Boston: Houghton Mifflin, 300.

276. Cleveland, H. (2002). *Nobody in charge . . . Essays on the future of leadership.* San Francisco: Jossey-Bass, 161.

277. Madison, J., Hamilton, A., & and Jay, J. (1976). *The Federalist . . . A commentary on The Constitution of the United States.* (Bicentennial ed.). Washington, DC: Robert B. Luce, 54-55.

278. Bloom, A. (1987). *The closing of the American mind.* New York: Touchstone (Simon and Schuster), 37.

279. Ward, B. (1966). *Spaceship Earth.* New York: Columbia University Press, 15.

280. Hirsch, Jr., E.D., Kett, J.F., & Trefil, J. (1988). *The dictionary of cultural literacy . . . What every American needs to know.* Boston: Houghton Mifflin, 460.

281. Kotkin, J. (2004). Red, blue and . . . . so 17th century. *The Washington Post* (Outlook Section). (March 28, 2004), B-1.

282. Huntington, S.P. (1997). *The clash of civilizations, and the remaking of the world order.* New York: Touchstone (Simon and Schuster), 14.

283. Annan, K. (2004). *Clear consensus needed on global threats, challenges, says secretary general of the United Nations.* (U.N. press release on Secretary General Kofi Annan's February 3, 2004, speech to The Brookings Institution board). New York: United Nations.

284. Luers, W.H. (2004). A message from UNA-USA's president, looking forward. (Email letter posted to UNA-USA members November 10, 2004). New York: United Nations Association of the United States of America.

285. Diplo Foundation. (1999). *Methodology-teaching diplomacy (1999-2005).* (Updated version, February 27, 1999). Malta: Author. Retrieved March 7, 2005, from http://www.diplomacy.edu/Edu/Methodology/teaching.asp

286. Sheeham, M.O. (2003). Foreign debt declines. In *Vital Signs 2003.* (p. 46). Washington, DC: The Worldwatch Institute; and, Sachs, J., et al. (1999). *Implementing debt relief for the HIPCs.* (August 1999). Cambridge, MA: Harvard University Center for International Development.

287. A.T. Kearney, Inc., & The Carnegie Endowment for International Peace. (2004). Measuring globalization, economic reversals, forward momentum. (A study conducted by the publishers). In *Foreign Policy.* (March-April 2004), 54-60.

288. Mead, W.R. (2004). America's sticky power. *Foreign Policy.* (March-April 2004), 46, 51.

289. Hamilton, L. (2005). Better public diplomacy. *From the desk of Lee Hamilton* (an emailed newsletter from The Center on Congress at Indiana University). Retrieved March 23, 2005, from http://www.congress.indiana.edu.

290. United Nations. (1948). *Universal declaration of human rights.* (Adopted by the U.N. General Assembly as Resolutions 217 A(III) of December 10, 1948). New York: Author. Retrieved March 7, 2005, from http://www.un.org/Overview/rights/html

291. Cover headline, *Kiplinger's Personal Finance.* (August 2001).

292. Cover headlines, *Fortune* (July 16, 2001), and *Kiplinger's Personal Finance* (August 2001).

293. Davis, K., & Franklin, M.B. (2001). Simplify. *Kiplinger's Personal Finance.* (August 2001), 66.

294. Gunther, M. (2001). God & business. *Fortune.* (July 16, 2001), 59.

295. Hill, P. (2002). New dream job: Less money, more family time. *The Washington Times.* (June 24, 2002), 1, 14.

296. *Ibid.*

297. Lorenzo, G. (2000). Spirituality is alive and well on the web. *Access.* (December 23, 2000). Retrieved January 3, 2001, from http://www.accessmagazine.com

298. Comedian George Carlin's "A Wonderful Message," from a 2001 email message, "Irony of the New Century."

299. Easterbrook, G. (2004). *The progress paradox.* (Trade paperback ed.). New York: Random House, 187.

300. Global Futures Forum Pulse Expert Panel 2005 survey results, responses to item stating, "Due to better models of work-life balancing, women more often rise to top management, beyond the glass ceiling." Nearly 64 percent ranked the scenario as likely or highly likely, and 62.3 percent indicated that it would have "some" or "great impact." (March 2005).

301. Bradshaw. T. (1998). *Survey of public participation in the arts, summary report, 1997.* (Research Division Report Number 39, December 1998, in conjunction with Jack Faucett Assoc.). Washington, DC: National Endowment for the Arts.

302. Allen, F. (1954). *Treadmill to oblivion.* Boston: Atlantic-Little Brown Books, 239-240.

303. Gardner, G. (2002). *Invoking the spirit.* Washington, DC: The Worldwatch Institute, 11.

304. EQ At Work. (2004). *What's EQ?* (Updated ver.) Retrieved March 27, 2004. from http://www.eqatwork.com/what_eq.htm

305. Gardner, J. (n.d.) *Quotations about poverty.* Retrieved December 5, 2005, from http://www.quotegarden.com/poverty.html

306. James Wolfensohn, former president of the World Bank, addressing a White House conference on the new economy. (April 5, 2000,Washington, DC).

307. Merriam-Webster, Inc. (2003). Poverty (definition of). *Webster's new collegiate dictionary.* Springfield, MA: Author, 973.

308. Shipler, D.K. (2004). *The working poor . . . Invisible in America.* New York: Borzoi (Alfred A. Knopf), 3-5.

309. Ansell, S. (2004). Achievement gap. *Education Week* Issue Paper. (March 18, 2004). Retrieved May 6, 2004, from http://www.edweek.org

310. U.S. Department of Education, Office of Educational Research and Information. (1994). What do student grades mean? Differences across schools. *OERI research report.* (January 1994). Retrieved May 6, 2004, from http://www.ed.gov/pubs/OR/ResearchRpts/grades.html

311. Wisconsin Education Association Council (WEAC). (2004). Variables affecting student achievement. *Teaching and learning.* Retrieved May 6, 2004 from www.weac.org/resource/primer/variable.htm

312. Hoff, D.J. (1997). Chapter 1 study documents impact of poverty. *Education Week.* (April 16, 1997), 3-4. Retrieved May 6, 2004, from http://www.edweek.org/ew/vol-16/29title.h16

313. Thevenot, B. (2004). Fights pull chief to troubled school, Amato plunges in to define problems. *New Orleans Times-Picayune.* (March 31, 2004). Retrieved March 31, 2004, from http://www.nola.com/search/index.ssf?/base/news-2/1080728760123450.xml?nola

314. National Council of Welfare, Canada. (2002). The cost of poverty. *Canadian Policy Studies.* (February 5, 2002). Retrieved March 28, 2004, from http://www.childcare.canada.org/policy/polstudies/can/ncwpovcost.html

315. OYEZ. (2004). *Plessy v. Ferguson,* 163 U.S. 537 (1896), docket number: 210. (Abstract, U.S. Supreme Court Multimedia). (April 2004). Retrieved April 9, 2004, from http://www.oyez/oyez/resource/case/307

316. Loungani, P. (2003). The global war on poverty, back to basics. *Finance & Development.* (December 2003), 38.

317. *Ibid.*

318. Former U.S. President Ronald Reagan, quoted in a review by Steven S. Berizzi of the book *America's Struggle Against Poverty in the Twentieth Century* by James T. Patterson. (December 21, 2000). Retrieved April 17, 2004, from http://www.amazon.com

319. Lemann, N. (1989). The unfinished war. *The Atlantic Online.* (January 1989). Retrieved March 29, 2004, from http://www.theatlantic.com/politics/poverty/lemunf2.htm

320. Figures compiled from *Social Security Bulletin, Annual Statistical Supplement* (U.S. Social Security Administration, 2002), using the following tables: Weighted Average Poverty Thresholds for Nonfarm Families of Specified Sizes, 1959-2001 (p. 141); Number and Percentage of Poor Persons, by Age, at End of Selected Years 1959-2000 (p. 147); and Shares of Money Income from Earnings and Other Sources for Aged and Nonaged Families (p. 143).

321. Gardner, G., Assadourian, E., & Sarin, R. (2004). The state of consumption today. *State of the world 2004.* Washington, DC: The Worldwatch Institute, 6.

322. Gardner, et al., 8.

323. Food Research and Action Center (FRAC). (2004). *Child nutrition fact sheet.* (National School Lunch Program). (April 2004). Washington, DC: Author.

324. U.S. Committee for Refugees. (2003). The world's refugees, 2002. *World refugee survey, 2003.* In *World almanac and book of facts, 2004.* New York: World Almanac Education Group, 857.

325. Various informational and promotional materials from Global Campaign for Education. Retrieved April 9, 2004, from http://www.campaignforeducationusa.org

326. Aneki.com. (2004). *Richest countries in the world.* Retrieved March 3, 2004, from http://www.aneki.com/richest.html; and, Poorest countries in the world. Retrieved same date from http://aneki.com/poorest.html

327. *A Chorus Line*, Broadway musical. (Music by Marvin Hamlisch, lyrics by Edward Kleban; based on the book by James Kirkwood and Nicholas Dante). Retrieved April 10, 2004, from http://www.imagi-nation.com

328. "16 Tons," song written by Merle Travis and made popular by Tennessee Ernie Ford in 1955. Retrieved May 20, 2002, from http://www.ichimusai.org/artiklar/16tons.html

329. Popcorn, F., & Hanft, A. (2001). *Dictionary of the future.* New York: Hyperion, 299.

330. Pennsylvania Department of Education. (2004). *Pennsylvania's career clusters, focusing education on the future.* Available online as of March 2006 from http://www.careerclusters.org and www.pde.state.pa.us/bcte

331. Stone, B. (2001). Jobs of the future, wanted: Hot industry seeks supergeeks. *Newsweek.* (April 30, 2001), 54-56.

332. Kaihla, P. (2004). Boom towns. *Business 2.0.* (March 2004), 95-98.

333. "The Future of Self Driving Automobiles," a presentation by John F. Meagher, INTERCET, Ltd., at Capital Science 2004. (Session sponsored by World Future Society, March 20, 2004, Arlington, VA).

334. Observations drawn from David Goodstein's *Out of Gas* (W. W. Norton and Co., New York, 2004).

335. Moses, B. (2000). *The good news about careers . . . How you'll be working in the next decade.* New York: Jossey-Bass, xviii.

336. Weiss, R. (2005). Nanotech is booming biggest in U.S., report says. *The Washington Post.* (March 28, 2005), A6.

337. Breslau, K., & Chung, J. (2002). Big future in tiny spaces. *Newsweek.* (September 23, 2002), 48.

338. From two articles in *Monthly Labor Review* (U.S. Department of Labor, Bureau of Labor Statistics, February 2004): Fastest growing occupations, 2002-2012 (retrieved April 3, 2004, from http://www.bls.gov/emp/emptab3.htm), and Occupations with the largest job declines, 2002-2012 (retrieved March 30, 2004, from http://www.bls.gov/emp/emptab5.htm).

339. Popcorn, F., & Hanft, A. (2001). *Dictionary of the future.* New York: Hyperion, 300, 307.

340. Breslau, K., & Chung, J. (2002). Big future in tiny spaces. *Newsweek.* (September 23, 2002), 56.

341. Popcorn & Hanft, 306.

342. Cetron, M. (2001). Forecasting international: Trends now changing the world. *Futurist.* (January/February 2001). Bethesda, MD: World Future Society, 30-43.

343. Breslau, K, & Chung, J. (2002). Big future in tiny spaces. *Newsweek.* (September 23, 2002), 56.

344. Spinrad, L., & Spinrad, T. (1979). *Speaker's lifetime library.* New York: Parker Publishing, 84.

345. Recruiting New Teachers, Inc. (RNT). (n.d.). *Teacher shortage areas, silent crisis.* Retrieved March 31, 2004, from http://www.rnt.org. Also see RNT 2000 study "The Urban Teacher Challenge: Teacher Demand and Supply in the Great City Schools." (Available on the RNT Web site as of March 2004).

346. Schouten, F. (2002). Education secretary calls teacher shortage contrived. *Gannett News Service.* In *Detroit News.* (September 17, 2002), 3A.

347. U.S. Department of Labor. (2004). *Occupation report, average annual job openings, 2002-2012.* Retrieved March 30, 2004, from http://www.bls.gov

348. Cable News Network (CNN). (Online). (2002). *U.N.: Global education gulf deepening.* Retrieved November 14, 2002, from http://www.cnn.com

349. U.S. Department of Labor, Bureau of Labor Statistics. (2004). *Occupation report, average annual job openings, 2002-2012, education administrators, elementary and secondary schools.* Retrieved March 30, 2004, from http://www.bls.gov

350. Fordham University School of Education's Bruce Cooper, a co-author of *Career Crisis in the Superintendency*, quoted in "Superintendents See Shortage of Applicants for Top Spots as a Serious Crisis," *Leadership News.* Retrieved January 27, 2000, from the American Association of School Administrators (AASA) Web site (http://www.aasa.org).

351. Results of an Educational Research Service study quoted by the author in *Ten trends ... Educating children for a profoundly different future.* (Educational Research Service, Arlington, VA, 2000), 77.

352. American Association for Employment in Education. (2001). *Educator supply and demand in the United States, 2000 research report.* Columbus, OH: Author, 7.

353. An estimate of the percentage increase in teaching positions based on BLS figures for 2002 and 2012 considering the six categories of teachers included in the report *Occupation Report, Annual Job Openings, 2002-2012.* Retrieved March 30,2004, from http://www.bls.gov

354. Education Week. (2000). Who should teach? The states decide. (Quality Counts 2000). *Education Week.* (Online ed.). Retrieved February 4, 2006, from http://counts.edweek.org/reports/qc00/templates/article.dfm?slug=execsum.htm

355. American Association for Employment in Education. (2001). *Educator supply and demand in the United States, 2000 research report.* Columbus, OH: Author , 7.

356. Bradley, A. (1998). New teachers are hot commodity. *Education Week.* (Online ed.). Retrieved September 9, 1998, from http://www.edweek.org

357. National Center for Educational Statistics (NCES). (2000). *Projections of education statistics to 2012, enrollments in grades K-8 and 9-12 of elementary and secondary schools.* (Covers fall 1987 to fall 2012). Washington, DC: Author. Retrieved March 5, 2004, from http://www.nces.ed.gov

358. National Center for Education Statistics (NCES). (n.d.) *Figure J: Pupil/teacher ratios, projections of education statistics to 2013.* Washington, DC: Author. Retrieved March 31, 2004 from www.nces.gov

359. Recruiting New Teachers, Inc. (1999). *Urban teacher shortages most severe in areas critical to raising performance.* (News release, January 19, 1999).Retrieved March 31, 2004, from http://www.rnt.org/channels/clearinghouseaudie...lg17_media_pressurbanteachershortage.ht

360. U.S. Department of Labor, Bureau of Labor Statistics. (2003). *Education pays.* Retrieved August 7, 2003, from http://www.bls.gov/emp/emptab7.htm

361. A quote from Lee Shulman, president, Carnegie Foundation for the Advancement of Teaching. In "Teachers Wanted," by Barbara Kantrowitz and Pat Wingert. (*Newsweek*, October 2, 2000, p. 39).

362. Explanatory material from the Teach for America Web site: *Who we are*, and *What we're looking for.* Retrieved in 2005 from http://www.teachforamerica.org

363. Recruiting New Teachers, Inc. (1999). *Urban teacher shortages most severe in areas critical to raising performance.* (News release, January 19, 1999). Washington, DC: Author.

364. National Education Association. (2004). *Attracting and keeping quality teachers.* (Issue Paper, updated April 29, 2004). Retrieved March 21, 2005, from http://www.nea.org/teachershortage

365. Rebora, A. (2003). Importance of school culture. (Web chat on recruitment highlights, *Teacher Recruiter*). In *Education Week* (online ed.) (December 2003). Retrieved March 30, 2004, from http://www.agentk-12.edweek.org/tchrcrt_article.cfm?slug=12chat_tr.03&sec=employers

366. National Education Association.

367. Rebora, A.

368. *Ibid.*

369. Recruiting New Teachers, Inc. (1999). *Urban teacher shortages most severe in areas critical to raising performance.* (News release, January 19, 1999). Retrieved March 31, 2004 from http://www.rnt.org/channels/clearinghouse/audie…/lg17_media_pressurbanteachershortage.ht

370. U.S. Bureau of Labor Statistics. (2004). *Monthly labor review.* (February 2004). In *Nursing shortage fact sheet* (American Association of Colleges of Nursing, Washington, DC). Retrieved May 6, 2004, from http://www.aacn.nche.edu

371. Carter, G.R. (2002). Content knowledge without pedagogy shortchanges students. *Is it good for the kids?* (Issue paper, August 2002). Alexandria, VA: Association for Supervision and Curriculum Development.

372. Voke, H. (2002). Understanding and responding to the teacher shortage. *Infobrief.* (May 2002). Alexandria, VA: Association for Supervision and Curriculum Development, 2.

373. Hendrie, C. (2004). Philadelphia teacher assignments questioned in complaint. *Education Week.* (March 17, 2004), 4.

374. See: *Hutchinson Encyclopedia of Science.* "Archimedes." (Helicon Publishing, Oxford, U.K., 1998, p. 49), and *World Book Encyclopedia,* "Archimedes," (Field Enterprises Educational Corp., Chicago, IL, 1971, Vol. A, pp. 564-565).

375. "Wiser Futures," a presentation by Clem Bezold, Marsha Rhea, and Bill Rowley, of the Institute for Alternative Futures. (Preconference program, World Future Society Annual Conference, San Francisco, July 18, 2003).

376. Drawn from comments by Herb Rubenstein, CEO, Growth Strategies, Inc., and co-author with Tony Grundy, of *Breakthrough, Inc.-High Growth Strategies for Entrepreneurial Organizations.* In Strategic planning for futurists. *Futures Research Quarterly* (World Future Society). (pp. 7-8). (Fall 2000).

377. RAND. (n.d.) Scenarios. *RAND Europe.* Retrieved February 27, 2004, from http://www.rand.org/randeurope/fields/scenarios.html

378. Marx, G. (2006). *Future-focused leadership: Preparing schools, students, and communities for tomorrow's realities.* Alexandria, VA: Association for Supervision and Curriculum Development.

379. Smyre, R. (unpublished). *Core skills for transformational learning.* (Paper, written in 2004).

380. Borawski, P., & Ward, A. (2004). Living strategy: Guiding your association through the rugged landscape ahead. *Journal of Association Leadership.* (Winter 2004), 6-9, 12-13.

381. Three sections on engaging people in planning based in part on Marx, G., *Ten trends … Educating children for a profoundly different future.* (Educational Research Service, Arlington, VA, 2000), 81.

382. Withrow, F., Long, H., & Marx, G. (1999). *Preparing schools and school systems for the 21st century.* Arlington, VA: American Association of School Administrators, 100-101.

383. Marx, G. (2002). Ten trends: Educating children for tomorrow's world. *NCA Journal of School Improvement*. (Spring 2002), *3*(1), 18.

384. Information on education trends is available as of March 2006 from the Education Commission of the States (ECS) Web site: http://www.ecs.org/clearinghouse/13/27/1327.htm

385. Copenhagen Institute for Futures Studies. (2004). *Members' report 2003/4: 10 tendencies toward 2010*. Retrieved March 31, 2004, from http://www.cifs.dk

386. Drawn from trends discussed by Blaise Zerega in Ten trends for what's ahead. (*Red Herring*, November 2001, pp. 47-66).

387. Drawn from writings of Marvin Cetron and Kimberly Cetron in A forecast for schools. (*Educational Leadership*, December 2003/January 2004, pp. 22-29).

About the Author

Gary Marx, CAE, APR, is president of the Center for Public Outreach (CPO), in Vienna, Va., an organization he founded in 1998. CPO provides counsel on future-oriented leadership, communication, education, community, and democracy.

As an international speaker, workshop leader, and consultant, Marx has worked with education, community, business, association, and government leaders at all levels on four continents and in all 50 of the United States. He has been called an "intellectual entrepreneur, who is constantly pursuing ideas," and a "deep generalist."

As a futurist, Marx has directed studies such as *Preparing Students for the 21st Century* (1996), *Preparing Schools and School Systems for the 21st Century* (1999), *Ten Trends . . . Educating Children for a Profoundly Different Future* (2000), *Future-Focused Leadership: Preparing Schools, Students, and Communities for Tomorrow's Realities* (2006), and the current *Sixteen Trends . . . Their Profound Impact on Our Future*. He is also author or co-author of numerous other books and articles, such as: *Excellence in Our Schools . . . Making It Happen, Building Public Confidence in Our Schools, Public Relations for Administrators*, and *Working With the News Media*. During his career, Marx has been a source for local, national, and international news media on issues affecting education and society.

Prior to launching the Center for Public Outreach, Marx served for nearly 20 years as a senior executive for the American Association of School Administrators (AASA) and as executive editor of more than 150 education leadership publications. He provided communications leadership as an administrator for the 10,000-student Westside Community Schools in Omaha, Neb., and the 82,000-student Jefferson County Public Schools in Colorado. His numerous contributions have included: the Steering Committee of CIVITAS International, the PBS Education Advisory Board, NBC's "The More You Know" Advisory Board, the Emmy Awards Selection Committee (for children's television), and planning and executive committees for education for both the restoration of the Statue of Liberty and Ellis Island and the Bicentennial of the U.S. Constitution. He has served on the boards of both the Education Writers Association and Horace Mann League. He has also taught courses at a number of universities. Marx was a television and radio broadcaster and station owner before moving into education. He has narrated many soundtracks and programs, including events such as the Presidential Scholars program at both the John F. Kennedy Center for the Performing Arts and Constitution Hall.

Marx was presented the coveted President's Award by the National School Public Relations Association (NSPRA) in 1999 and the Distinguished Service Award by the American Association of School Administrators (AASA) in 2000. He is accredited by the National School Public Relations Association (NSPRA), the Public Relations Society of America (PRSA), and the American Society of Association Executives (ASAE), and is a professional member of the World Future Society.

Gary Marx resides in the Washington, D.C., area and can be reached by phone, (703) 938-8725, or email, gmarxcpo@aol.com.

Acknowledgments

Sixteen Trends is based on the premise that people can come together to create and constantly re-create an even better future for our schools, education systems, and for the whole of society. In that spirit, dozens of thoughtful professionals in numerous fields became part of the team that resulted in this publication.

First, our thanks to the Creating a Future Council of Advisors. The Council of 34 listing follows these acknowledgments. They responded to either one or two questionnaires, helping us identify, sort, and expand on issues and trends. On top of that, they provided insights on the leader's role as connected generalist.

Second, we are grateful to Educational Research Service, which worked with us to make this publication possible. The foresight, wise counsel, and support of ERS President and Director of Research John Forsyth have been essential in our pursuit of this project. Director of Special Research Projects Nancy Protheroe, Manager of Editorial Services Jeanne Chircop, and Senior Director of Marketing and Member Services Katherine Behrens are just a few of the organization's staff who made a significant contribution to this effort.

Third, we appreciate the thinking and inspiration of numerous World Future Society colleagues who are constantly stretching our thinking; people like Edward Cornish, Tim Mack, Jeff Cornish, Susan Echard, Graham T.T. Molitor, Joseph Coates, Marvin Cetron, David Pearce Snyder, James Morrison, Edie Weiner, Herb Rubenstein, Rick Smyre, John Meagher, John Petersen, Kenneth Hunter, Mika Mannermaa, Ted Gordon, Bill Halel, Clem Bezold,

Marsha Rhea, and Bill Rowley, to name just a few. Some served as members of the advisory council.

Virtually dozens of thoughtful leaders provided information and ideas through their writings and research. We're especially grateful for the many professionals who work each day with the U.S. Census Bureau, the Social Security Administration, and the Bureau of Labor Statistics.

As a speaker and workshop leader in many parts of the nation and world, I have gained inspiration and ideas from legions of thoughtful people in many walks of life, including education. Their wisdom helped to guide us. I am also grateful to my family. They have long supported my quest to seek, develop, explain, and encourage the thoughtful consideration of ideas for creating an even brighter future.

While preparing *Sixteen Trends,* we also researched and wrote a companion book, *Future-Focused Leadership: Preparing Schools, Students, and Communities for Tomorrow's Realities,* for the Association for Supervision and Curriculum Development (ASCD). ASCD's Scott Willis and Ernesto Yermoli have been particularly helpful.

Finally, thanks to you, our readers. You are the ones who will lift words and ideas from the page and turn them into actions that will help us create the education system of the future. As we noted in our companion book, we want you to read this book, use it as a reference, and get copies for others to stimulate their thinking about the future. Most of all, we'd like to have *Sixteen Trends . . . Their Profound Impact on Our Future* serve as a launching pad, not a resting place. Your assignment, if you accept it, is "to run with it."

Gary Marx

The Creating a Future Council of Advisors

Early in 2004, members of the Creating a Future Council of Advisors responded to either one or two rounds of questionnaires. In the first, advisors were asked to identify significant trends and issues that might affect education and society in the early part of the 21st century. In the second, they were asked to share what they considered the implications of a cluster of three trends and to comment on the importance of leaders capable of making connections in a complex, fast-moving world.

The Council's views helped shape this book, *Sixteen Trends ... Their Profound Impact on Our Future,* published by the Educational Research Service, as well as *Future-Focused Leadership: Preparing Schools, Students, and Communities for Tomorrow's Realities,* published by the Association for Supervision and Curriculum Development. Views expressed in these publications do not necessarily reflect the beliefs or opinions of any member of the Council or the Council as a whole, nor do they reflect the official views of ERS.

Members of the Council of Advisors included: **Drew Allbritten,** former executive director, Council for Exceptional Children, Arlington, Va.; **Kenneth Bird,** superintendent, The Westside Community Schools in Omaha, Neb.; **Ted Blaesing,** superintendent, White Bear Lake Area Schools in White Bear Lake, Minn.; **Carol Brown,** 2003-04 president, National School Boards Association, Alexandria, Va.; **Kimberley Cetron,** a teacher in the Fairfax

County, Va., Public Schools; **Marvin Cetron,** president, Forecasting International, Ltd., Falls Church, Va.; **Joseph F. Coates,** president, Consulting Futurist, Inc., Washington, D.C.; **Kenneth Dragseth,** superintendent of schools, Edina, Minn., and 2003 National Superintendent of the Year; **Marc Ecker,** former president, National Middle School Association, and superintendent of schools, Fountain Valley, Calif.; **Arnold Fege,** president, Public Advocacy for Kids, Annandale, Va.; **Douglas Greenberg,** president and CEO, Survivors of the Shoah Visual History Foundation in Los Angeles, Calif.; **Elizabeth L. Hale,** president, the Institute for Educational Leadership, Washington, D.C.; **Jane Hammond,** superintendent in residence, Stupski Foundation, Mill Valley, Calif.; **Linda Hodge,** 2003-05 president, the National PTA, Chicago, Ill.; **George Hollich,** (retired) director of curriculum and summer programs, Milton Hershey School, Hershey, Pa.; **David Hornbeck,** president, Children's Defense Fund, Washington, D.C., and former president and CEO, International Youth Foundation, Baltimore, Md.; **John Hoyle,** professor of educational administration, Texas A&M University, College Station, Texas; **Ryan Hunter,** a middle school student, Long Island, N.Y.; **Rick Kaufman,** former executive director, public engagement and communication, Jefferson County (Colo.) Public Schools, and 2003-04 president, the National School Public Relations Association; **Keith Marty,** superintendent, School District of Menomonee Falls, Wis.; **Radwan Masmoudi,** founder and president, Center for the Study of Islam and Democracy, Washington, D.C.; **Frank Method,** director, education policy, Research Triangle Institute, International, Washington, D.C.; **Graham T.T. Molitor,** president, Public Policy Forecasting, Potomac, Md., and vice president and legal counsel, the World Future Society, Bethesda, Md.; **Bob Mooneyham,** executive director, National Rural Education Association, Norman, Okla.; **Carol G. Peck,** president and CEO, Rodel Charitable Foundation, Scottsdale, Ariz.; **James Rickabaugh,** superintendent, Whitefish Bay School District, Whitefish Bay, Wis.; **Betsy Rogers,** teacher, Jefferson County School System, Birmingham, Ala., and 2003 National Teacher of the Year; **Gary**

Rowe, president, Rowe Inc., Lawrenceville, Ga.; **Douglas Shiok,** superintendent, Orange North Supervisory Union (school district), Williamstown, Vt.; **Michael Silver,** veteran superintendent, and assistant professor of education administration, Seattle University; **Rosa Smith,** president, Schott Foundation for Public Education and Schott Center, Cambridge, Mass.; **David Pearce Snyder,** consulting futurist, The Snyder Family Enterprise, Bethesda, Md.; **Ted Stilwill,** eduation counsel, Iowa Environmental Project, and former director, Iowa Department of Education, Des Moines, Iowa; and **V. Wayne Young,** executive director, the Kentucky Association of School Administrators, Frankfort, Ky.

List of Figures

Index

A

B

D

E

O

P

T

ERS

ORDER FORM

Quantity	Title and Item Number	Price Per Item			Total Price
		Base Price	ERS Individual Subscriber Price	ERS School District Subscriber Price	
	An Overview of Sixteen Trends... Their Profound Impact on Our Future (#0633)	$14	$10.50	$7	
	Sixteen Trends... Their Profound Impact on Our Future (#0630)	$30	$22.50	$15	

** Please double for international orders.

Postage and Handling ** (Add the greater of $4.50 or 10% of purchase price.):	
Express Delivery ** (Add $20 for second-business-day service.):	
TOTAL DUE:	

SATISFACTION GUARANTEED!
If you are not satisfied with an ERS resource, return it in its original condition within 30 days of receipt, and we will give you a full refund.

Method of payment:

☐ Check enclosed (payable to Educational Research Service).

☐ Purchase order enclosed (P.O.#_____).

Bill my: ☐ VISA ☐ MasterCard ☐ American Express

Visit us online at www.ers.org for a complete listing of resources!

Name on Card (print) _____

Account Number _____ Expiration Date _____

Signature _____ Date _____

Shipping address:

☐ Dr. ☐ Mr. ☐ Mrs. ☐ Ms. Name _____

Position _____ ERS Subscriber ID# _____

School District or Agency _____

Street Address _____

City _____ State _____ Zip _____

Phone _____ Fax _____ Email _____

Return completed order form to: Educational Research Service
1001 North Fairfax Street, Suite 500, Alexandria, VA 22314-1587
Phone: 800-791-9308 • Fax: 800-791-9309 • Email: ers@ers.org • Web site: www.ers.org